The History of Civilization in Europe

François-Pierre-Guillaume Guizot

THE
HISTORY OF
CIVILIZATION
IN EUROPE

François Guizot

TRANSLATED BY WILLIAM HAZLITT

EDITED AND WITH AN INTRODUCTION BY
LARRY SIEDENTOP

LIBERTY FUND
Indianapolis

William Hazlitt's translation of *The History of Civilization in Europe* was first published in 1846. Larry Siedentop's edited version was first published by Penguin Books in 1997.

Revised translation, introduction, and editorial matter © 1997 by Larry Siedentop. Reprinted by permission.

Cover image: *Maison Carrée, the Arenas and the Tour Magne in Nîmes.* Oil on canvas. By Hubert Robert (1733–1808). © RMN-Grand Palais/Art Resource, N.Y.

Frontispiece: Portrait of François-Pierre-Guillaume Guizot after a painting by Paul de Laroche. © Michael Nicholson/Corbis.

C   10   9   8   7   6   5   4   3   2   1
P   10   9   8   7   6   5   4   3   2   1

Library of Congress Cataloging-in-Publication Data
Guizot, François, 1787–1874.
[Histoire de la civilisation en Europe. English]
The history of civilization in Europe / François Guizot; translated by William Hazlitt; edited and with an introduction by Larry Siedentop.
pages   cm
Translation of: Histoire de la civilisation en Europe.
Originally published: London; New York, N.Y.: Penguin Books, 1997.
Includes bibliographical references and index.
ISBN 978-0-86597-836-2 (hardcover: alk. paper)—
ISBN 978-0-86597-837-9 (pbk.: alk. paper)
1. Europe—Civilization.   I. Hazlitt, William, 1811–1893, translator.
II. Siedentop, Larry, editor.   III. Title.
CB71 .G8413 2013
940—dc23   2012043007

LIBERTY FUND, INC.
8335 Allison Pointe Trail, Suite 300
Indianapolis, Indiana 46250-1684

Contents

Introduction

Sometimes it is better *not* to be moderate when making a claim. François Guizot's *History of Civilization in Europe* (1828) is one such occasion. For it is, in my opinion, the most intelligent general history of Europe ever written. It is not, to be sure, a narrative history. It is rather an analytical or sociological history—belonging to a genre with roots in the eighteenth century, what Guizot himself calls "philosophical history." By that he means history understood as the search for the underlying causes and effects of particular events, the identification of "general facts" and the moral reflections they suggest. In that genre Guizot has had no peer.

The claim just made would not have caused much surprise in intellectual circles in Paris or London in the 1830s. For Guizot's reputation as an utterly remarkable historian was then well established. Not only had his 1828 lectures, on the History of Civilization in Europe, caused something of a sensation in Paris, becoming a rallying point for liberal youth and intelligentsia after the downfall of the ultra-royalist government of Villèle in 1827. That liberal enthusiasm also guaranteed Guizot a large, attentive audience for two more years of lectures on the History of Civilization in France, a lecturing career brought to a close only by the July Revolution of 1830. By that time Guizot's lectures, quickly published as books, were causing comment and excitement outside France as well. In London especially, John Stuart Mill was to write appreciative reviews of Guizot's work, using them to argue that historical writing had entered a new era—an era which had not yet dawned in the English-speaking world. For Mill, Guizot's analysis of the development of European institutions opened up new vistas for social and political thought. Nor was he alone in thinking so. For the two greatest social and political thinkers of the nineteenth century, Alexis de

Tocqueville and Karl Marx, were also decisively influenced by Guizot at this period. It is hardly too much to say that Guizot's *Histories* thus helped to shape the major contours of nineteenth-century European thought.

Yet by the end of the nineteenth century, despite his earlier reputation and influence, Guizot's historical work had almost dropped out of sight. What had happened? Why had his fame as an historian been eclipsed by writers such as Michelet and Macaulay—writers who, however eloquent and imaginative, could not really match Guizot's analytical acumen? Why did Guizot's ideas survive only indirectly, in arguments put forward by J. S. Mill, Tocqueville and Marx?

One thing more than any other contributed to the eclipse of Guizot's reputation as an historical thinker. That was his subsequent career as a politician. The July Revolution of 1830—which, as we have seen, ended his lecturing career—led to Guizot becoming a deputy and minister in the new regime, soon to be dubbed the July Monarchy. During the 1830s Guizot's work on the reform of public education rapidly brought him into prominence. By 1840 his formidable ability led to his becoming the Dominant minister and remaining so until the 1848 Revolution put an end to the regime. Guizot's association with the manipulative "bourgeois" monarchy— parodied in his famous reply to critics of the regime who called for a lower property qualification for voting, that they should "get richer"—led to his being crucified with the regime itself. By 1848 the policy pursued by King Louis-Philippe and Guizot was perceived as serving narrowly middle-class interests at the expense of other social classes, whether the peasantry, the new industrial working class or the old *noblesse*. Guizot's period in power came to epitomize a self-interested bourgeois settlement, in which French national interests were reduced to those of bankers, merchants and shop- keepers—what the aristocratic Tocqueville dismissed contemptuously as a bourgeois casserole.

The Revolutionary insurrection in Paris in February 1848 forced Guizot to take refuge in England. When he returned to France the following year, both political circumstances and personal choice led him to withdraw from the public scene. He spent increasingly long parts of the year at his Norman château, Val Richer, where he resumed a life of study and writing. Like many former parliamentarians, he considered Louis Napoleon's *coup d'état* (1851) and the proclamation of the Second Empire (1852) disasters for France—comparing his compatriots to dissolute sons who neglect their inheritance and leave its management to others. Guizot continued to write occasionally about public issues, with pamphlets on *Democracy in Europe* and *Meditations on the Christian Religion*. But his chief work became once again historical, with studies of the English Revolution, a *History of France as told to my grandchildren,* as well as his own *Memoirs.* In fact Guizot survived long enough to see the fall of the Second Empire in 1870 and the establishment of the Third Republic. By this time he was a venerable figure, and his only public role was that of *de facto* leader of French Protestantism. He died in 1874, eighty-six years old.

It is, however, the younger Guizot, the Guizot of the 1820s, who must occupy us, a Guizot as yet untainted by the July Monarchy and the 1848 Revolution. So it is important to put to one side the much caricatured politician of the 1840s and try to recapture the intellectual who had perhaps the most trenchant historical mind of the nineteenth century.

One day in 1806 a pale young man with deep-set eyes and an extraordinarily fine, prominent forehead arrived in Paris by coach from Geneva. He was called François Pierre Guillaume Guizot. He had come to Paris to complete his education and make his way in the world. He had almost no money, but nonetheless he already had marked advantages—a disciplined will, strong religious beliefs and an education beyond the common run. For an attentive observer, the nature of his education and the austerity of his manner might have suggested something about his origins. For Guizot, though born in Nîmes, had spent some of his youth in Geneva and was a Protestant. The reason for his being educated in Geneva rather than Nîmes and the fact that he was Protestant shaped his later career and help to account for what was to be a widespread reaction to Guizot in France—that there was something about him not quite French, and that perhaps he did not always understand the French.

François Guizot had been born in 1787 to a Protestant family, in a country which did not yet confer full civil rights on Protestants and had only just allowed them to marry legally. Doubtless, that background would have created some detachment in any case. But when he was only seven, Guizot lived through events which put him on his guard and removed any naïvety about social relations. Spreading from Paris, the Reign of Terror had, as one of its consequences in Nîmes, the arrest of Guizot's father, a leading advocate, who was condemned to die on the scaffold in 1794. It is hardly surprising that Guizot's mother, a staunch Calvinist, later took her two small children away from Nîmes to the city of Geneva, where she sought shelter with relations and fellow Protestants. That experience of civil war and its consequences—Guizot would never forget the day that Robespierre fell—doubtless contributed to the analytical frame of mind for which Guizot the historian later became famous.

Civil war and the death of his father created in the young man a passionate need to understand events, their causes and effects. The Academy of Geneva, where he was soon enrolled, gave him an unusual opportunity to satisfy that desire. "Geneva was my intellectual cradle." Swiss education had not suffered to anything like the extent of French education from the disorders of Revolution. Besides, the Protestant culture of Geneva had always favoured education, witnessed by the way the young Guizot learned not only Greek and Latin, but several modern European languages, especially those of the important Protestant states, German and English. Guizot's classical studies at Geneva also enabled him eventually to combine two disciplines, history and philosophy, which have since been separated almost completely by the division of intellectual labour. It is tempting to see his passion for philosophy, though contained within the essentially historical cast of his mind, as an important source of the distinctive form of historical argument he developed—a form which involved laying down premises and arguing from them in order to get behind the surface of events to their causes. History, for Guizot, always involved comparison and argument, which in turn required making assumptions and testing them against the narrative of events.

But that historical sophistication lay in the future when Guizot arrived in Paris in order to study law. He found that the older law schools had disappeared with the Revolution and, perhaps because of the cost involved, he did not enrol in one of the new private schools. Instead he pursued legal studies on his own. It has been remarked that his first years in Paris saw Guizot isolated and lonely, and indeed it must have been so. But for a twenty year old, deeply immersed in books and ideas, that had its compensations. The study of law was also to serve him well in later years, helping to give his historical writing a profoundly sociological cast. For Guizot's approach to analysing European or French society at any period was to relate the conditions of persons to the condition of properties—in his view, property relations and class structure provided indispensable keys to understanding social change.

Hardly a year after his arrival in Paris, Guizot took up a post of tutor to the children of the Swiss Envoy in Paris, M. Stapfer—no doubt arranged through his Genevan contacts. This post proved surprisingly important for Guizot's career. Through Stapfer he was introduced to leading literary and intellectual figures in Paris, including Suard, who held a much frequented salon. There Guizot encountered the remnants of a brilliant pre-Revolutionary society, whose openness to new ideas and delight in conversation impressed him and began to give his fervent Calvinism a more worldly flavour. It was through Stapfer and Suard that, in 1810, Guizot met the most original French philosopher of the day, Maine de Biran. Biran was the centre of a philosophical circle which met fortnightly and which Guizot began to attend. There he was exposed to Biran's critique of eighteenth-century empiricist philosophy—an attack which focused on the inadequacy of its conception of the mind as a mere passive receptacle, a bundle of sensations. Biran argued for the essential activity of the mind or will against the passive model of eighteenth-century sensationalism. That insistence on the activity of the self or will and the need for a concept of causation which allowed explanation to account for the "two facts" or types of experience, active and passive, was to shape Guizot's method of writing history.

It was also through Stapfer and Suard that the young Guizot met his future wife. The episode has often been described. But it retains great charm, and throws a sharp light on Guizot's character. Pauline de Meulan came from an aristocratic family (throughout his life Guizot took pleasure in aristocratic company) which had been reduced to near poverty by the Revolution. She supported her relations by writing, and, in particular, editing a journal. However, one day she fell seriously ill, and had to discontinue her writing. Faced with ruin, she received an anonymous letter from someone who enclosed an article written in her own style and announced that he would supply such articles regularly until she recovered her health. And so it happened, with Pauline de Meulan only discovering the identity of her benefactor after her recovery. She had, in print, repeatedly begged the benefactor to reveal himself. Finally the young Guizot came forward as the author. In fact, they had already met at the Suard salon. In 1812 they married, despite Pauline being fourteen years older than Guizot. Their mutual involvement had taken time, for Guizot's rather austere Calvinism stood in sharp contrast to Pauline's cosmopolitan culture, which had been shaped by eighteenth-century salons. Each changed the other. In a note written many years later, Guizot observed: "Our perfect harmony came only after a long and reciprocal influence. I raised and enlarged the sphere of her concerns; she greatly contributed to my . . . being open to the truth."

Guizot had begun to make his mark as a writer. He drew on his command of German to introduce the French public to the remarkable developments in later eighteenth-century German philosophy and literature. He also translated and provided elaborate notes for an edition of Gibbon's *Decline and Fall of the Roman Empire*. But the real breakthrough came in 1812 through the patronage of the Academician Fontanes. Guizot was appointed an Assistant Professor of History in the University, and, remarkably soon afterwards, received the Chair of Modern History at the Sorbonne. Only twenty-five years old, his historical erudition was still largely to come. But his character emerged immediately. He refused to include the conventional encomium to the Emperor Napoleon in his Inaugural Lecture.

This new appointment brought Guizot into contact with another professor, who was to have a great influence on his future by introducing him to the world of politics. Pierre Royer-Collard, Professor of Philosophy at the Sorbonne, had long been discreetly active on behalf of the exiled Bourbons. After Napoleon's fall in 1814 and the Restoration of the Bourbon Monarchy, Royer-Collard's patronage led to Guizot's appointment as Secretary General of the Ministry of the Interior. Napoleon's return during the Hundred Days obliged Guizot to return to his University post, but only momentarily. For he soon became the envoy of royalists who wished Louis XVIII, on his return from Ghent after Waterloo, to strengthen his commitment to the Constitutional Charter issued in 1814 and resist the pressure from ultra-royalists bent on restoring the *ancien régime.* Thus, at the Second Restoration in 1815 Guizot found himself at the very centre of a political struggle between the constitutional royalists sustained by Louis XVIII and the ultra-royalists who had a majority in what was called the "Unthinkable Chamber" (*Chambre introuvable),* a majority more royalist than the King himself. The issue that emerged and continued to dominate Restoration politics was that of representative government itself. Was the King obliged to accept a ministry supported by a majority of the Chamber or were ministers responsible instead to the Crown? Awkwardly, the moderate royalist defenders of representative government had at first to ignore the principle which defined their own position, because of the ultra-royalist majority!

To rescue the moderate party, Louis XVIII dissolved the Unthinkable Chamber in 1815, and new elections resulted in a shift to the centre and the emergence of a series of moderate ministries. Indeed, the next five years saw French government dominated by a group of cautious liberal intellectuals led by Royer-Collard, which included Prosper de Barante and Camille Jordan as well as Guizot. Because of their erudition and interest in ideas, they became known as the Doctrinaires—though the term is misleading if taken to mean inflexibility. For the Doctrinaires were pragmatic, to say the least, in their attempt to steer a middle course between the forces of reaction and residually Revolutionary or Jacobin groups. During these years, as Secretary-General of the Ministry of Justice and as Director of Communes and Departments in the Ministry of the Interior, Guizot drew on his legal background and acquired a considerable experience of the workings of French government, experience which contributed to his later political convictions.

In 1820, the assassination of the heir to the throne, the Duc de Berri, put an end to the Doctrinaires' ascendancy. Expelled from office, they took up the cudgels against the reactionary policies of the new ultra-royalist government in different ways. While Royer-Collard became the leader of the liberal opposition in the Chamber of Deputies, arguing trenchantly against measures to restrict freedom of the press and curtail the suffrage, Guizot, still too young to be a deputy, returned to his University professorship. He began to lecture on topics in French history and, in particular, on the history of representative government in Europe—topics which provided him with a scarcely veiled means of attacking the ultra-royalist government which, by 1822, was dominated by a Girondin lawyer, Villèle.

From 1822 to 1827 the Villèle government embarked on an ambitious legislative programme which the liberal opposition saw as nothing less than an attempt to recreate an aristocratic society and government in France. The Villèle government appeared to be subverting the principle of civil equality on which French society had rested since 1789, substituting a regime of privilege instead. Among the bills it put forward were those to restrict the suffrage to large landholders, to censor the press and abolish University lectures, to restore primogeniture and entail in order to reconstruct a landed aristocracy in France, to strengthen the role of the clergy in the state and restrict certain careers, particularly in the military, to sons of the nobility. It was even rumoured that the Villèle government might restrict the mobility of labour and the freedom of contracts. Guizot quickly became the leading intellectual inspiration of the liberal opposition to the ultra-royalist government. But it was not long before the government hit back by suspending University lectures.

Guizot now had to rely on income from writing to keep himself. But he was not content to do only that. He threw himself into active opposition by helping to organize two liberal pressure groups, the Society for Christian Morality and Aide-toi, le ciel t'aidera. These liberal groups arranged public meetings, and encouraged publications about a wide range of liberal causes such as the emancipation of slaves in the French colonies and the new penitentiary system. But underlying all these particular causes was a larger theme, the need to defend free institutions or representative government in France—to avert the threat that the reactionary Charles X, who succeeded his more tolerant brother in 1824, might conspire with the ultra-royalists and dispense with the Constitutional Charter which had established France's new liberties in 1814. The essential liberalism of "young France," when civil liberty and representative government were called into doubt, was revealed by public anxieties over the coronation of Charles X, when the King dramatically prostrated himself before the Archbishop of Paris. For perhaps the most worrying feature of ultra-royalist government was the favour it showed the Church and the influence over public policy which the higher clergy had allegedly regained, to the point, it seemed, of threatening the very distinction between Church and State. The result was a resurgent anticlericalism in France, excited especially by the processions of expiation for "the sins of the Revolution" organized by the government and the higher clergy throughout the country. This virulent anticlericalism co-existed, strangely, with a taste for the medieval which had become all the rage in the 1820s.

By 1827 French public opinion had turned decisively against the ultra-royalists and Villèle. Elections in that year returned a majority hostile to the government, and Villèle's resignation paved the way for a moderate government under Martignac. But how would Charles X react? His opinions were known to be hostile to the system of representative government with which his older brother had endowed France, with the *de facto* responsibility of ministers to a majority in the Chamber, even when the strict letter of the Charter of 1814 had left ambiguous the question of whether ministers were responsible finally to the King or a majority in Chamber. The issue looming large by 1827, therefore, was whether Charles X would acquiesce in representative government. Or, would he attempt to defy the Chamber, replacing the new ministry with men favourable to his own views? For that reason the Martignac Ministry carried with it the hopes of liberal France.

One of the first acts of the Martignac Ministry was to lift the ban on University lectures. Guizot seized the opportunity offered. He announced that he would give a course of lectures on the "History of Civilization in Europe." It was clear that his lectures—along with others given by Victor Cousin on philosophy and Villemain on eighteenth-century French literature—would become a major event, an event not just intellectual but political in character. For they coincided with the mounting crisis about the future of representative government in France. He had already acquired a reputation as the most formidable of the younger Doctrinaires, a reputation which even gave him a certain ascendancy over his seniors such as Royer-Collard and Barante. Doubtless he wanted to confirm and extend that reputation by means of his lectures—for he would soon reach the age at which he could qualify for election to the Chamber and launch a political career.

It was, to say the least, a dramatic moment. The lecture hall at the Old Sorbonne where Guizot began his lectures on a spring day in 1828 was teeming with an excited crowd, young and committed. But just what were they committed to? They were committed to "free" institutions, to a representative form of government which would, they believed, put France, along with England, at the forefront of European civilization. They were excited because of the threat to those institutions. That threat had, for the moment, abated. But it might soon return. Hence they looked to Guizot for instruction about the direction of social and political change in France. Nor were they to be disappointed.

Guizot was now far better prepared by the historical studies he had undertaken during his years in the wilderness after 1820. His collections of documents on French and English history, his study of the development of representative government in Europe as well as lectures on medieval French history and a subsequent book on the English Civil War, had enabled him to examine the development of European institutions at crucial junctures. At the same time his administrative experience, especially when charged with overseeing the administration of communes and departments in 1819–20, and his participation in the political debate against the ultra-royalist government after 1820—the "Great Debate"—had reinforced both his analytical skills and his political convictions.

Just how did the Great Debate of the 1820s contribute to Guizot's *History of Civilization in Europe*? During the debate the Doctrinaires had been obliged to use history as evidence in order to demonstrate how French institutions had been transformed long before 1789, as part of their argument that the ultra-royalist project of recreating an aristocratic society in France was not only unjust but impossible. "The destruction of aristocracy" in France had become the Doctrinaires' leading theme in the 1820s, a destruction they traced back into the middle ages. They became adept at showing how the corporate character of an "aristocratic" society of fixed ranks had—through the growth of towns, the development of a market economy and an increasing social division of labour—steadily been eroded, and prepared the way for a "democratic" society, organized on the basis of civil equality and individual rights. They traced the gradual collapse of the original castes of feudal society, the nobles and the serfs, into a new intermediate social condition, that of the middle classes or bourgeoisie. It was this transformation of the structure of society which Guizot was to call the "rise of the middle classes."

But if Guizot and the other Doctrinaires could congratulate themselves on a social transformation which conformed to their intuitions of justice, they had serious reservations about the political changes which had accompanied this social transformation in France. For the destruction of aristocracy or "atomization" of society—as Royer-Collard called it in a famous speech to the Chamber in 1822—had been accomplished through the "centralization" of government, that is, through the concentration of power in the French Crown and creation of a bureaucratic form of the state. That, Royer-Collard observed sadly, was how the French had become "an administered people."

Guizot had largely shaped this argument, drawing on his experience in the Ministry of the Interior and fully aware of the extent to which local autonomy in France had been destroyed, with the communes reduced simply to the passive agents of central government. Barante, with whom he worked closely, had made the argument central to his book *Aristocracy and the Communes* (1822). Barante argued that, in contrast to England, France in the middle ages had witnessed an alliance develop between the communes, seeking enfranchisement from the tyranny of powerful local lords, and an originally weak Crown. Both royalty and the communes had benefited from this alliance directed against the feudal aristocracy. But the unfortunate result was that the communes acquiesced in the transfer of political rights to the Crown until the latter successfully claimed, by the seventeenth century, a monopoly of "sovereign" authority and power. Guizot deepened the contrast between England and France in this respect in his *Essays on the History of France,* also published in 1822—arguing that a centralized form of feudalism in England, where a powerful Crown was needed after the Norman Conquest to keep a hostile population under control, led the English aristocracy by the thirteenth century to resist royal encroachments and form an alliance with leaders of the Commons. That alliance in due course forced the English Crown to share "sovereign" power with parliament and created an open or "natural" aristocracy based on wealth and education as well as birth. Thus, the Doctrinaires identified a crucial difference between the structure of society and government in France and England. In England a powerful "natural aristocracy" protected local autonomy, whereas in France the destruction of local autonomy had been an unintended consequence of the destruction of aristocracy.

In the same year (1822), then, all the leading Doctrinaires deployed the same argument to account for the social and political condition of France after the Revolution—the collapse of the original castes of feudal society into a new middle-class condition (atomization) had been accompanied by an excessive concentration of power at the centre (centralization), in a bureaucratic form of the state. Guizot, in particular, emphasized that France had developed a bureaucratic despotism which Europe had not seen since the heyday of the Roman Empire, when the municipal system was subject to a similar strait-jacket imposed from the centre. Since 1818 he had argued for the introduction of the elective principle and the responsibility of local agents to local councils within their sphere of interests. His experience, in 1819–20, as Director of Local Government had reinforced his belief in decentralization, and after being dismissed from government in 1820, he had argued in his *Origins of Representative Government in Europe* (1822) that France had moved from excessive decentralization to excessive centralization and that the time was ripe to reject the latter.

By 1828, Guizot's message was even more emphatic. It was the task of the new generation of the 1820s to undo the excessive centralization of French government—originally the work of Richelieu and Louis XIV but restored by Napoleon—and find a new balance between central power and local autonomy. Like Barante, he believed that representative government could only succeed with free local as well as national institutions, both contributing to the formation of a natural aristocracy or open political elite which could bring classes together locally and draw back power from central government. Guizot introduces this agenda in an early lecture of 1828 by analysing the decomposition of the Roman Empire in the West—attributing it to an administrative despotism which had destroyed local autonomy, impoverished the cities, undermined local elites and left the population unable to defend themselves against the Germanic invaders. Roman unity had been imposed from above rather than developing from below. And so, once the Imperial administrative machine was shattered, everything became local again, despite vain attempts by a late emperor to introduce something like representative government. It was too late. Yet Guizot does not only open the *History of Civilization in Europe* with an analysis of the consequences of Roman despotism. He returns to the theme in his final lecture, when he considers the consequences for eighteenth-century France of the administrative despotism constructed by Richelieu and Louis XIV in the seventeenth century. He implies that it was the primary cause of the failure to reform French institutions in the eighteenth century and thus of violent revolution in 1789. In that way he is able to identify the chief virtue of representative institutions as that of providing a peaceful means of adjusting civil law and government to changes in the structure of society.

If Guizot had a political agenda firmly in mind, he was also anxious that liberal enthusiasm unleashed by the fall of the ultra-royalist government in 1827 should not get out of control, that it should remain constructive. And it was that motive which prevailed when he laid out his larger historical argument in the second lecture, before revealing his political agenda. Guizot seeks to distinguish European from other civilizations, and his argument illustrates the way the political context of 1827–8 contributed to the richness of his lectures. For, mindful of the class conflicts raging in France as well as rampant anticlericalism, Guizot goes out of his way to do justice to the different values and institutions which, after the fall of the Roman Empire, contributed to the amalgam which became "Europe." His theme is that of pluralism. What distinguishes European from other civilizations is that no *one* value or institution has ever won complete supremacy or been able to drive the others underground. In setting out this argument about pluralism Guizot identifies three chief components of European civilization at its outset: Roman, Christian and Germanic. In each case he identifies both values or principles and institutions which gradually helped to constitute European society. From Rome, he argues, Europe has received on the one hand the institution of the municipality or commune, with the value of self-government or local liberty; and, on the other hand, the idea of a sovereign power and uniform civil legislation—the idea of a state— carried by the memory of the Emperor. The second constituent Guizot explores is the Christian Church and its moral beliefs—on the one hand, the insistence that there is a moral law superior to all human legislation and which ought to serve as a criterion for it; on the other, an ecclesiastical government which, in protecting itself from secular encroachments after the fall of the Roman Empire in the West, laid the foundation for liberty of conscience by defending the separation of spiritual and temporal power.

The third constituent was Germanic—the bond between warriors and their leaders which, voluntary at the outset, became the germ of feudal or aristocratic organization centuries later; and the sentiment of individual independence and the relish for it, which helped to introduce an idea of liberty very different from that associated with the city-states of antiquity.

The competition of these values or principles and institutions becomes, in Guizot's hands, the key to the development of European civilization. Firstly, it helps to account for a very long period of gestation, the five or six hundred years after the fall of Rome before Europe really achieved coherence and self-consciousness. Secondly, it helps to account for the almost unlimited potential retained by European civilization—for the diversity and competition of its elements means that it had not exhausted itself in an initial flowering in the fashion of ancient Greece, or become merely stationary like ancient Egypt or modern China. "While in other civilizations, the exclusive, or, at least, the excessively preponderating dominion of a single principle, of a single form, has been the cause of tyranny, in modern Europe the diversity of elements which constitute the social order, the impossibility under which they have been placed of excluding each other, have given birth to the freedom which prevails in the present day."

Clearly, Guizot's insistence on the pluralism of European civilization in contrast to the unity of other civilizations was designed to assuage class conflict in France in his own day—to lead the nobility, clergy and the bourgeoisie to understand their respective contributions to European development. But that didactic intent did not make the insight any less profound or true. Nor did it prevent Guizot from attributing a creative role to class conflict in Europe later in the lectures. Altogether, the second lecture gives the reader an immediate taste of what becomes the dominant flavour of the 1828 lectures—the sheer quality and intensity of thought compressed into relatively few pages, the extraordinary general ideas which Guizot deploys to penetrate below the surface of events to reveal the changing structure of European society. Ironically, the short time he had to prepare his text after the Martignac government lifted the ban on University lectures helped to concentrate Guizot's mind, helping him to make the most of the analytical potential of the ideas of atomization and centralization which had played such a part in the Great Debate of the 1820s. With only a few months at his disposal, he needed to rely on general ideas. But that need also perfectly suited what had become the warp of his mind.

During the Great Debate, the Doctrinaires had deployed abstract models to develop their case about the direction of social change, as their argument about the "irresistible" movement from "aristocracy" to "democracy" in France since the eleventh century reveals. For that argument depends upon a distinction between social structure and political institutions, which Guizot had put forward in his *History of France* in 1822:

> It is by the study of political institutions that most writers . . . have sought to understand the state of a society, the degree or type of its civilization. It would have been wiser to study first the society itself in order to understand its political institutions. Before becoming a cause, political institutions are an effect; a society produces them before being modified by them. Thus, instead of looking to the system or forms of government in order to understand the state of the people, it is the state of the people that must be examined first in order to know what must have been, what could have been its government . . . Society, its composition, the manner of life of individuals according to their social position, the relations of the different classes, the condition [*l'état*] of persons especially—that is the first question which demands attention from . . . the inquirer who seeks to understand how a people are governed.
>
> The study of the condition of lands must thus precede that of the condition of persons. In order to understand the political institutions, it is necessary to understand the different social conditions (classes) and their relations. In order to understand the different social conditions, it is necessary to understand the nature and relations of properties.

Relying on this model of argument Guizot and other Doctrinaires had been able to demonstrate how the destruction of feudal property relations in favour of individual property rights (the atomization of society) had contributed to the centralization of government.

But Guizot's use of models went far beyond that of the other Doctrinaires. They became absolutely central to his historical method, giving it a sociological character which was highly original. Thus, whenever Guizot confronts some new historical development—say, the development of the Christian Church as a form of ecclesiastical government, the transformation of the Roman municipal system or the effects of landed property rights on German customs with the end of a wandering life and the beginnings of a sedentary life west of the Rhine—he relies upon a model which identifies the different forms such an institution can take in order to locate this particular development. For example, the government of the Church can take a democratic, aristocratic or monarchical form, while the relations between Church and State can vary between fusion, complete separation, intermingling, etc. Guizot prefers to identify different possible forms— e.g., family types such as the patriarchal, clannish or nuclear—before using one of them to elucidate changes undergone by the family under the impact of feudal institutions.

By proceeding in this way, Guizot drew on eighteenth-century ideas which had given an extraordinary fillip to sociological understanding. Pioneered by Montesquieu in his *De l'esprit des lois* (1748), probably the most ambitious example of this new form of explanation was the "four stages" theory developed by Scottish Enlightenment thinkers such as Adam Smith and Adam Ferguson. Their theory laid emphasis on the "mode of subsistence" as the crucial factor shaping social development. Social development was traced through four stages according to the mode of subsistence—(a) hunting and gathering, (b) nomadic or pastoral, (c) agricultural and (d) commercial—while other institutions such as property rights, class structure, type of family, government and even religion, were related to the mode of subsistence as the dominant variable. The results held great potential for a more analytical form of historical writing, and Scottish writers such as Ferguson, Robertson and John Miller soon began to get behind narrative history in order to understand causes and effects with the help of such models. However, the kind of model building which thus entered historical explanation with the Scottish Enlightenment was somewhat reductionist. It was constrained by Hume's notion of causation as observable regularities of behaviour, a notion which—inspired by the physical sciences—excluded beliefs or reasons as causes.

Guizot's Genevan education and Protestantism had brought him into early contact with the Scottish Enlightenment and its achievements—for Geneva retained close ties with Britain even in the face of the blockade of Napoleon's continental Empire. But after arriving in Paris he also came into contact with a growing philosophical reaction against the reductionism of the causal model of explanation which had dominated eighteenth-century epistemology. This reaction took different forms in Germany, Scotland and France. Probably all of them influenced the young Guizot. Yet the most important influence was, as we have seen, the philosophical work of Maine de Biran, whose circle in Paris Guizot joined. Reacting against the sensationalist model of the mind associated with Locke and Condillac, Biran argued that the self or will is essentially "active" and that voluntary experience differs intrinsically from externally caused or "passive" experience. Intentional action, experience of ourselves as causes, is just as fundamental as externally caused or passive experience. Neither can be reduced to the other. These "two facts" of experience require different modes of explanation. Biran's epistemology thus gives beliefs or reasons, as the sources of intentions, a status co-equal with that of causes in Hume's sense of observable regularities of behaviour.

These new philosophical convictions shaped Guizot's discussion of the meaning of civilization in the very first chapter of the *History of Civilization in Europe.* He argues that civilization is a complex or "general" fact with a "dual" character. For the idea of civilization is not exhausted by developments in social relations or the division of labour, improvements in the production and distribution of wealth or power in society. Rather, the idea embraces another, internal factor, the development of "man himself, of his faculties, his sentiments, his ideas." Guizot's account of general facts entails that historical explanation must account for the role of ideas as well as institutions, beliefs as well as social practices. For the common sense of mankind testifies to the intimate relationship between the two, to the way that improvements in social relations in due course affect the inner man, while developments in the inner man in turn eventually shape social relations. "The inward is reformed by the outward, as the outward by the inward," Guizot insists. "We shall find that all the great developments of the internal man have turned to the profit of society; all the great developments of the social state to the profit of individual man." Thus, Guizot transformed Maine de Biran's voluntarism into a new form of philosophical history which freed itself from the reductionist bias of the eighteenth-century genre, by exploring intellectual change as well as social change without attributing an exclusive causal role to either. ". . . These two histories of civilization are closely connected with each other; they are the reflection, the image of each other."

Guizot's pluralist account of the development of European civilization is shaped by this dual method. He carries forward both principles or values and the institutional forms corresponding to them—whether theocratic, aristocratic, monarchical or democratic—and shows how each of these social elements in turn sought to predominate, before at last establishing mutual relations of respect and order. France becomes the centre-piece of the story because in France each of these different social elements for a time took almost complete possession of society and developed its full consequences. But Guizot emphasizes that England provides a different model, in which these social elements learned to limit their claims and develop side by side earlier than elsewhere in Europe, creating the system of representative government which became England's great contribution to European civilization.

From the fifth to the tenth century each of the social elements surviving the fall of the Roman Empire sought to impose itself exclusively on what became Europe, but none succeeded. In Italy and the south of France, vestiges of the Roman municipal system survived and, up to a point, revived. In Spain, the Church took a dominant role in the Visigothic kingdom. In France, in the ninth century, Charlemagne sought to recreate something like the Roman Empire. Guizot insists that Charlemagne's project was bound to fail because social relations and ideas were too limited and local, existences too circumscribed, to make possible the enterprise of centralization that Charlemagne embarked upon. Inspired by the memory of the Roman Empire, he sought to create a regular state and to reconstruct, at least in part, the system of despotic administration which had characterized the Empire. But social conditions did not permit it. Everything was now local, and there was no stability in either social relations or ideas— nothing to provide the supports of a great centralized state. With the disappearance of Charlemagne and his vision, the Empire he had tried to build began to disintegrate.

Localism triumphed. In the tenth century feudalism emerged as that form of localism, a localism with a social organization derived from the

Germanic warrior band, with the reciprocal obligations of leader and followers transmuted into those of lord and vassals, through the granting of fiefs. Thus, the first attempt at a general organization of European society after the Germanic invasions belonged, not surprisingly, to the invaders and reflected their customs. Feudalism, Guizot argues, made an extraordinary difference to the distribution of population in Europe. It replaced the essentially urban character of ancient civilization with a society in which rural areas predominated, so that the thin spread of population over the whole national territory which we take for granted, and which was not at all the case in antiquity, really owes its origins to feudalism. For in antiquity, by contrast, the owners of land inhabited the cities. Their beliefs and practices were formed by being members of a city-state. For them, the countryside was associated with work and servility, the cities with social superiority and leisure. One of the important consequences of feudalism was to reverse those assumptions.

Rather than just telling a story, Guizot analyses feudalism by exploring the different social positions created by feudal property relations: the lord or possessor of the fief; the serfs or colonists on his domain; and the priest. He seeks to discover what was distinctive about the condition of each. In the case of the feudal lord, it was the extraordinary importance which the possessor of the fief had, both in his own eyes and in the eyes of those around him. This was an importance without precedent in antiquity. Aristocratic positions of the ancient world such as the Roman patrician had, like the feudal lord, involved being head of the family and magistrate. But as a religious magistrate the patrician's importance came to him from his role as interpreter of a public religious cult, while as a political magistrate his importance derived from his membership of the Senate, a corporation which governed. The ancient patrician was therefore always in the presence of his peers. Not so the feudal lord, who lived an isolated life and derived his rights entirely from himself, rather than from membership of a corporation. The moral result was inordinate pride, an unbounded confidence and energy.

Above himself there was no superior of whom he was the representative or interpreter; there was no equal near him; no powerful and general law which weighed upon him; no external rule which influenced his will; he knew no curb but the limits of his strength and the

presence of danger. Such was the necessary moral result of this situation upon the character of man.

If that was the effect of feudalism on the self-image of the possessor of the
fief, it had a no less important effect on the structure of his family.

In earlier types of family, patriarchal or clannish, not only was the family
very numerous, all its members shared traditions and affections as well as
the same name. The result was a kind of rough equality between members
of such family types, at least between male members (even though in a
clan its head no longer led the same life as others and was raised somewhat
above them in status). But the feudal lord's family was utterly different. It
did not share a name or family traditions with the population surrounding
the castle. It was small and lived apart. Such an isolated situation gave a
quite new importance to domestic life, to the intimacy of the family. That,
in turn, gradually had a profound consequence, an increase in the importance of women and an improvement in their circumstances. The new
importance of domestic life also contributed to the identification of the
"nuclear" feudal family with the fief itself and created a powerful hereditary
spirit.

Turning from the possessor of the fief to the surrounding population,
Guizot finds another striking effect of feudalism. Whereas, in theocratic
or monarchical systems, power is exercised in the name of shared beliefs
or a common public interest, in feudalism power was exercised merely in
the name of the lord himself, as an aspect of his "personal and capricious"
will. In consequence it could establish no real moral tie or society between
the possessor of the fief and the serfs who were merely his property. That
is why, Guizot argues, feudalism aroused such prodigious hatred and could
not establish itself as a stable or enduring social system. The arbitrary will
of the lord never provided a sufficient condition of legitimacy. It provided
no guarantees for those living under its sway. Feudalism aroused antipathy because "whenever, in his master, he beholds a mere man, from the
moment that the will which oppresses him appears a merely human and
individual will like his own, [man] becomes indignant and supports the
yoke wrathfully." Nor could the Church do much to restrain this unjust relationship. Usually a serf himself by origin, the priest could at best nurture

some sort of moral life among the subordinate population. He could not oppose lordly arrogance.

Guizot's analysis of the different social conditions under feudalism meant that there was no extended or general society except for the possessors of fiefs and priests. They alone had social relations at a distance. For the inferior class of serfs everything was local. They had no extended social relations, no ideas which would correspond to our ideas of a country or people. Indeed, there were not any shared names by virtue of which they could identify themselves as belonging to a wider nation. Still another consequence was that feudalism could not create durable political institutions. For the panoply of feudal institutions, from the *seigneur*'s court, through the local assemblies of his peers, to the suzerain's court, lacked any real substance. They did not create the kind of guarantee which is necessary for a political society. Only two forms of such a guarantee, Guizot argues, are possible: "the despotism of one or of a body, or free government." The former could not develop under feudalism, for though the King was formally suzerain, he was not in a position to impose his will or enforce obedience. In feudal monarchies, "all the permanent means of power and action were wanting; there were no permanent troops, no permanent taxes, no permanent tribunals. Social powers and institutions had, after a fashion, to recommence and recreate themselves anew every time they were required." At the same time the dispersed strongholds of the feudal nobility offered them plentiful means of resistance. Thus, despite an apparent hierarchy of feudal jurisdictions, the only real guarantee of rights was violence or brute force.

If feudalism dispersed power in a way that made a despotic central government impossible, it could not provide the conditions for a representative government founded on consent either. The idea of a public or "sovereign" power, the idea of the state—enjoying the sovereign rights to impose law, tax and punish—was utterly foreign to the ideas and habits of feudal society. The rights which have since come to be identified with a public power or state were understood by the possessors of fiefs merely as part of their private domain or property. "What are at present public rights were then private rights; what is now public power was then private power." Such ideas did not prepare feudal lords to acknowledge a higher or public claim, to bow before the public weal. Thus, without any notion of a superior and general jurisdiction or state, feudal lords saw only others like themselves "acting in the name of their personal will." If they disagreed with any decision, it was natural for them to appeal to force rather than submit.

What feudalism on the surface established was a kind of federalism. But it was an unreal, premature federalism. For the dispersal of authority and power required by a federal system presupposes moral and intellectual conditions which did not obtain in early medieval Europe. Unruly passions, the absence of education or even literacy, combined with the habitual resort to force, ruled out any systematic dispersal of authority, any balance between central power and local autonomy. Hence, Guizot argues, the apparent dispersal of authority under feudalism which might seem to resemble American federalism was entirely illusory. It was an argument which, as we shall see, lodged in the mind of at least one of his audience, Alexis de Tocqueville.

How, then, was feudalism undermined? Guizot's argument proceeds at two levels. The larger argument appears in the first lecture. It is an argument about the moral revolution accomplished by Christianity, with its belief in the underlying or "natural" equality of all humans, and the more than thousand years' process by which the intuitions of justice, fostered by Christian moral beliefs, gradually transformed social institutions, culminating in the proclamation of civil equality in 1789.

> How many centuries, what infinite events passed away before the regeneration of the moral man by Christianity exercised upon the regeneration of the social state its great and legitimate influence. Yet who will deny that it any the less succeeded?

The implication was that the new democratic society formalized in 1789 represented the logical extension of Christian morality into social practices by founding them on the principle of equal liberty. In effect, feudalism could not perpetuate itself because it was radically unjust. But Guizot accompanies that larger argument with an analysis which pays equal attention to economic factors, to the distribution of population, property rights and class structure. Guizot demonstrates how the revival of commerce involved the growth of urban centres, which became the foyer of property rights utterly different to and ultimately subversive of feudal property relations. Then, in the course of what Guizot does not hesitate to call the "insurrection" of the communes in the twelfth century, the feudal class was obliged to concede the right of burghers to move about freely, to buy and sell. The seeds of a new social class were thus planted, the seeds of what became the bourgeoisie, a class resting on individual property rights.

By the thirteenth century Europe consisted of a number of different social elements, each of which was a self-contained society in its own right. The Church, the feudal nobility and the newly enfranchised boroughs ". . . had a situation, laws and manners, all entirely different; they were so many societies which governed themselves, each upon its own account, and by its own rules and power." While they ". . . came into contact, there was no true union; they did not form, properly speaking, a nation, a state." The distinctive development of modern times, Guizot contends, has been the fusion of these different social elements into one society under one government. "The former social elements have been reduced to two, the government and the people."

This great work of centralization and atomization did not occur, however, without earlier attempts to organize Europe differently. From the thirteenth to the fifteenth century there were two other kinds of attempt. One consisted of efforts by the clergy, feudal nobility and the boroughs to organize society exclusively on their own terms—to construct a theocratic Europe under the Papacy, to extend the republican system (especially in Italy) or to destroy the independence of the boroughs through coalitions of the larger feudatories. When all of these had failed, there appeared another sort of enterprise, the attempt to unite the various social elements in a single state, while respecting their "diversity and independence." That attempt at a "mixed" or corporate organization of Europe took the form of assemblies representing the different estates or orders of the realm, the States-General in France, the Cortes in Spain and Portugal, the Diets in Germany and the English Parliament. These assemblies sought to make it possible for different social elements to "live and act together." Yet only in England did this attempt have any success, with Parliament becoming a permanent means of government.

On the continent the failure of endeavours to organize a Europe of estates or orders paved the way, after the fifteenth century, for the centralization of both social relations and ideas. Local special interests and ideas were gradually replaced by "universal" interests and ideas, through a process both economic and political. On the one hand, market forces led to greater interdependence and a more complex social division of labour. On the other, national monarchies developed financial, military and administrative structures which by the late sixteenth century meant that feudalism was really over and the modern era had begun. There emerged "what had hitherto never existed on a large scale, nations and governments"—and with them a new structure of society. For the expansion of the bourgeoisie from the fifteenth to the eighteenth century meant that the original castes of feudal society were increasingly assimilated to a new "middle class" condition. In order to compete with the growing wealth of the bourgeoisie the feudal aristocracy itself sought to elude feudal property constraints such as entail, while the resulting parcelling out of property meant that many serfs became landowners.

Laying the foundation of this new type of society had involved the creation of a new form of government, the sovereign state. Unfortunately, on the continent, and especially in France, that state took a bureaucratic form. For the inhabitants of the communes had turned to the kings in their struggle against local feudal lords, and that alliance had led the communes to acquiesce in the transfer of political rights to the Crown, until the whole of France was governed by royal agents in the time of Richelieu and Louis XIV. Thus, a social revolution which was essentially just, had been accompanied by the emergence of a tyrannical form of the state. It was that combination which led Guizot, like other Doctrinaires in the 1820s, to identify for his audience an unfinished political agenda in France. The adoption of representative government, properly understood, required the rebuilding of local autonomy.

To illustrate the transformation of the structure both of French society and of government from the twelfth to the eighteenth century, Guizot invites his readers to perform a mental experiment. He invites them to compare the reactions of a bourgeois of the twelfth and one of the eighteenth century, when each is taken into the other's world. What would be the reaction of a twelfth-century burgher, coming from a commune

which had recently won its own liberty, to the social circumstances of
the eighteenth-century French bourgeoisie? On the one hand, he would
be astonished by the high claims made for the role and rights of the
bourgeoisie in French national life. The boldness and pride behind such
claims would, Guizot suggests, have terrified a twelfth-century burgher,
who was used to a submissive demeanour when dealing with the dominant orders in feudal society. The language of the eighteenth-century
bourgeois would have struck him as presumptuous and dangerous. For
his ideas and experience were merely local. He did not see himself as
belonging to a great national social class. But if the twelfth-century burgher were then taken to visit an eighteenth-century city such as Laon,
his astonishment would increase to the point of incredulity. For there he
would discover that the same bourgeoisie who made such claims for the
importance of their class, lived in cities without walls or fortifications,
had no urban militia or effective means of self-government—indeed, that
they were ruled by agents of a remote central power and that their rights
were defined not by their own efforts at resistance, but by the decrees of
that remote power. Suddenly, the proud claims of the eighteenth-century
bourgeoisie would have struck him as founded on quicksand, on local
powerlessness.

Next Guizot reverses the experiment. How would an eighteenth-century
bourgeois react to the social conditions of a newly enfranchised commune
of the twelfth century? His reaction would also be two-fold. On the one
hand, he would be astonished by the timidity and embarrassment of the
burghers in their dealings with the nobility, clergy or monarchy, with their
utter lack of confidence. On the other hand, when he looked into the interior of a commune, he would be equally astonished by the vigour and
self-reliance of the populace, by the way they formed their own militia
and defended themselves, making their own laws and taxes, declaring
war and judging law-suits—exercising, in fact, what by the eighteenth century were called sovereign rights, the rights of the state.

The political moral suggested by these contrasts is clear enough. Guizot
draws it out especially in his last lecture, devoted to France in the eighteenth century. But it is the political moral which permeates the whole of
the *History of Civilization in Europe*—as it had dominated an earlier book

on which Guizot had collaborated, his friend Barante's *On Aristocracy and the Communes.* The moral is about the social and political consequences of destroying local liberty. Guizot, like Barante, argues that the centralization of power under Richelieu and Louis XIV had contributed not only to the terrible political impotence of France in the next century but to its frivolity and cynicism as well. Guizot leaves it to his audience to draw the appropriate conclusion: the excessive concentration of power at the centre of any society is, in the long run, its own undoing.

At the beginning of this Introduction I made a strong claim about the intellectual quality of Guizot's *History of Civilization in Europe.* That quality made it a work of decisive importance in the development of some of the most gifted and influential social and political thinkers of the nineteenth century. Indeed, when one looks more closely at the influence of Guizot's writings on Tocqueville, Marx and J. S. Mill, a fascinating set of interactions becomes clear, and a pattern begins to emerge. It is a pattern of influence which throws quite a new light on the development of nineteenth-century thought. In a sense Guizot's *History of Civilization in Europe* provides the missing link, the key to an epoch which has not previously been fully understood and an opening up of relationships not previously suspected.

Alexis de Tocqueville was only twenty-three when he came under Guizot's influence. A junior magistrate at Versailles, Tocqueville began to make a weekly journey into Paris in 1828, in order to attend the lectures which gave rise to this book. He continued to attend Guizot's lectures for two more years. His enthusiasm for them knew no bounds. For he recognized that Guizot was providing not just an ordinary historical account but a subtle course in social and political thought. "The analytical mind" at work in Guizot's *Histories* overwhelmed him. "It is prodigious in its analysis of ideas and choice of words, truly prodigious," Tocqueville wrote excitedly to his friend Gustave de Beaumont in 1829. He and Beaumont began to use Guizot's ideas to organize their joint studies, relying on the Doctrinaires' categories of atomization and centralization when trying to understand the transition from aristocracy to democracy in Europe. From Guizot, Tocqueville also learned to contrast the development of English and French institutions. He took on board the argument that the destruction of local autonomy in France had been an unintended consequence of the struggle to destroy aristocratic power, while in England a more powerful crown led the feudal aristocracy to organize and ally itself with leaders of the Commons, calling them to Parliament and supporting their claims. "Once Parliament had been created, the Lords nearly always sought out the Commons and supported them on all occasions, which served slowly to unite the two orders which were such irreconcilable enemies elsewhere in Europe," Tocqueville wrote to Beaumont in 1828, echoing Guizot.

The result was a decentralized state in England, where a "natural" or open aristocracy had kept local affairs in its own hands and had not handed local power to agents of the Crown. England thus avoided the bureaucratic state which had emerged in France by the later seventeenth century. It was that analysis which prompted Tocqueville to move beyond Guizot, however. For Tocqueville concluded that Guizot's analysis cast grave doubt on the usual liberal prescription for "ending" the French Revolution and reforming the French state. If the local autonomy which existed alongside parliamentary sovereignty in England depended on a powerful natural aristocracy—parliamentary sovereignty itself offering no intrinsic obstacle to centralization—then France could not rely on the adoption of English parliamentary institutions to produce the same result. The destruction of aristocracy in France meant that the social conditions which supported local autonomy in England were missing. Evidently that conclusion forced itself on Tocqueville's mind and began to draw his attention to the United States. Might American federalism provide a more useful model for reforming the French state?

Guizot's analysis of the difficulties of striking a balance between central power and local autonomy had made a deep impression on Tocqueville. In 1828, shortly after he began to attend Guizot's lectures, Tocqueville wrote to Beaumont:

> There are two great disadvantages to be avoided in the organization of a people: either all social power is united at one point or it is dispersed among the regions. Each of these has its advantages and disadvantages. When everything is joined on a single bundle, once

the bundle is broken, everything falls apart and a people disappears. When power is disseminated, action is evidently circumscribed, but resistance is everywhere. I don't know if a balance between these two extremes can be found.

The contrast Guizot drew in 1828 between feudalism as premature federalism and the exacting moral and social preconditions for "true" federalism such as that of the United States may well have started Tocqueville thinking along the lines which led him to visit the United States in 1831–2. If so, Guizot can be said to have pointed the way to fame for Tocqueville—an ironical fact, in view of Tocqueville's later hostility to the Guizot government of the 1840s. In Tocqueville's eyes, Guizot then betrayed the decentralizing programme which he had originally inspired Tocqueville to pursue, using the bureaucratic structure of the French state to manipulate elections and subvert representative government.

There was still another way in which Guizot formed Tocqueville's mind, a way of which Tocqueville himself was perhaps less aware. Guizot's emphasis on the "two kinds of facts" which historical analysis must run side by side, external and internal facts, the development of social relations and the development of mind, had permeated Tocqueville's thinking in his formative years, the late 1820s and early 1830s. Guizot's assumption that the two kinds of fact are necessarily joined, and that each is the image of the other, became Tocqueville's working assumption, and helped him to develop a sociological approach largely free of the reductionism which often plagued nineteenth-century thinkers aspiring to create a "science of society" modelled on the physical sciences. Indeed, Guizot's method of moving between "active" and "passive" experience led Tocqueville, in *Democracy in America,* to create a form of social explanation which was to have an important future. Tocqueville began to explore the differences between two types of society by using the device of typical agents ("aristocratic man" and "democratic man") in order to explore the meanings available to such agents in the beliefs and practices of each society. Nor was it only in *Democracy in America* that Tocqueville made use of this device. When he returned to writing in the 1850s, after Louis Napoleon's Second Empire had destroyed political liberty in France, he fell back on this habit of examining the interaction of states of society and states of mind in order to explore the roots of the French Revolution, in *The Ancien Régime and the Revolution* (1856).

The case of Karl Marx is rather different. Marx fell under Guizot's spell only in 1843–4, when he began to read what he called the "bourgeois French historians" during the year before he left the Rhineland for Paris. He was thus considerably older than Tocqueville had been when he first encountered Guizot's writings. But the result was hardly less decisive. For reading Guizot's sociological history enabled Marx to break away from the German metaphysical tradition which had previously shaped his mind, both in its idealist Hegelian form and in the form elaborated by the young Hegelians in opposition to their master. Marx was enormously impressed by the way Guizot used property relations and class structure to get beneath the surface of political events and analyse the dynamics of social change.

Marx adopted Guizot's dictum that class conflict was the key to European history—"Modern Europe was born from the struggle of the various classes in society"—and gave it even greater scope than his mentor. No doubt other French writers such as Thierry had brought the same point home to Marx. For the theme of class conflict was suggested almost irresistibly by the conflicts of Restoration politics, conflicts in which parties were the ill-disguised agents of social classes. Failure to understand the class analysis put forward by the bourgeois historians always made Marx impatient with his critics. He wrote, for instance, to Joseph Weydemeyer in 1852:

> . . . they would do better first to acquaint themselves with bourgeois literature before they presume to yap at the opponents of it. For instance, these gentlemen should study the historical works of Thierry, Guizot, John Wade, and others in order to enlighten themselves as to the past "history of classes."

Yet arguably it was in the form that Guizot presented the history of class conflict—in particular, Guizot's analysis of the rise of a "middling" or bourgeois social condition antagonistic to feudalism and resting on a different form of property rights—which left the deepest imprint on Marx's thought.

It is hardly too much to say that Marx turned Guizot's account of the transition from feudalism to capitalism into a paradigm of all such major historical transitions. He did this by fixing on the way that feudal property relations increasingly became "fetters" on the development of bourgeois property rights and, *a fortiori,* on the development of a new type of economy and society—what Guizot called a "democratic" society, but what Marx was to dub "capitalist" society. Similarly, Marx's analysis of the role of the state in a capitalist society had roots in Guizot's argument that the transfer of political rights to the French Crown, an unintended consequence of the "destruction of aristocracy" justified by Roman lawyers appealing to the concept of sovereignty, had been a necessary condition of the destruction of feudal property relations. In effect, Marx interpreted Guizot as arguing that the Crown and its lawyers had been the "vanguard" of the bourgeoisie—to borrow a term Marx employs in postulating the next major historical transition, when bourgeois property rights would be overthrown by a militant, class-conscious proletariat who would use their control of the state machine ("the dictatorship of the proletariat") to destroy those bourgeois property rights which that state had originally created.

> Long before me bourgeois historians had described the historical development of this class struggle. What I did that was new was to demonstrate: 1) that the existence of classes is merely linked to particular historical phases in the development of production, 2) that class struggle necessarily leads to the dictatorship of the proletariat, 3) that this dictatorship itself only constitutes the transition to the abolition of all classes and to a classless society.

What Marx did, in effect, was to extend the use of Guizot's concept of centralization, applying it to the supposed next stage of historical development, and showing how capitalist concentration and centralization prepared the way for the overthrow of the bourgeoisie and the advent of socialism.

Nor was that all. Marx was struck by Guizot's analysis of another difference between the feudal aristocracy and clergy on the one hand, and the serfs on the other. Guizot insists that while the former belonged to general classes, by virtue of the relations they had at a distance with others in the same condition, the latter—or what is sometimes called "the people"— were not really a social class in the same sense. Why not? They were not conscious of themselves as a class.

> Every time that, in order to designate the population of the country at this period, we make use of a general word, which seems to imply one and the same society, the word *people* for example, we do not convey the truth. There was for this population no general society; its existence was purely local. Beyond the territory which they inhabited, the serfs had no connection with any thing or person. For them there was no common destiny, no common country; they did not form a people.

There is a striking parallel here with the way Marx later characterized the peasantry as an unhistorical class, whose isolated, merely local existence prevented them developing any consciousness of their own interests as a class. Hence they did not play any significant part in the process which shaped the development of European institutions, class conflict. This was in striking contrast to the way the bourgeoisie became conscious of sharing interests as a class, through struggling against local feudal lords.

This facet of Guizot's argument fascinated Marx. It probably shaped his predictions about the way the proletariat would become conscious of itself as a class through struggling against the capitalist order. On Guizot's analysis, the crucial development had been the "insurrection" of the communes from the eleventh to the thirteenth century, an insurrection at first local and uncoordinated, but which slowly led to the creation of a new and general class, the bourgeoisie. For the similarity of the conditions and interests of the burghers did not fail gradually to establish a "bond and unity" among them, by which Guizot clearly means a consciousness of their own existence as a class. The alliance between kings and burghers, directed against the feudal class, developed the consciousness of the bourgeoisie as such. Although the bourgeoisie did not at first contain much more than merchants, artisans and small property-holders, by the seventeenth century it had come to include magistrates, physicians and lawyers, "learned men of all sorts." It thus became a formidable social force. But, of course, for Marx the triumph of the bourgeoisie in 1789 was not final. In the nineteenth century the contest of classes would resume until the bourgeoisie was in turn subdued, with the victory of the proletariat paving the way for a classless society—the "end of history." In that sense Marx simply carried the story of class conflict one step further.

The case of John Stuart Mill is different again. Mill did not only review Guizot's *Histories* with deep appreciation. He also wrote enthusiastically about Tocqueville's *Democracy in America,* becoming, indeed, something of a protégé of Tocqueville for a time. Thus, Guizot's influence on Mill can be said to have been both direct and indirect. Like Tocqueville, Mill became acquainted with the problem of centralization and the threat of bureaucratic tyranny through his reading of Guizot—*both* the sense in which the state, through its creation of a structure of individual rights, was central to the erosion of feudalism and development of a democratic society; *and* the danger that destroying a corporate or aristocratic society could, as in France, result in a bureaucratic form of the state which destroyed local autonomy. But, of course, Mill lived in an England where administrative centralization was only just beginning in the 1830s. That probably made this political threat seem far less urgent to him.

It was a different argument in Guizot's *History of Civilization in Europe* that left an indelible mark on J. S. Mill's mind. That was Guizot's analysis of what set European civilization apart from other civilizations and made it progressive rather than stationary. Guizot, it will be recalled, argues that the failure of any one institution or value to impose itself to the exclusion of others has been the crucial fact about European history—making that history tempestuous and even tragic, but fecund and liberating. The competition between classes, between values and life-styles, has prevented European society ever falling into a stagnant condition in which differences of status are no longer questioned, values no longer have to defend themselves against others, and the life of the mind becomes contained within a fixed set of assumptions. That is the sense in which Guizot portrays European history as the story of liberty.

It is abundantly clear from Mill's review of Guizot's *Histories* that he assimilated this argument of Guizot. The argument re-emerges in a rather different form in Mill's most famous work, *On Liberty,* published in 1859.

Mill's idiom is, to be sure, very different from Guizot's. Shaped by the utilitarianism of Bentham and his father James Mill, J. S. Mill tended to think in an individualist and essentially unhistorical way. He did not put forward anything like a systematic theory of social change. So when he introduces Guizot's argument in *On Liberty* it is in a markedly different idiom, an individualist idiom. Mill opens the essay by laying down his famous principle of non-interference—the principle that government or society is justified in interfering with an individual's actions only to prevent harm to others. But, as if aware that this principle might be a disguised Natural Rights principle and inconsistent with his professed standard of general happiness or utility, Mill soon offers a different justification for individual liberty. It is, he argues, necessary as a condition of social progress. For only "experiments with living" can introduce the competition which makes possible a gradual "accumulation of truth"—which for Mill, by analogy with the natural sciences, was the grand object of society. Thus, Mill translated Guizot's sociological argument into the unhistorical language of nineteenth-century English moral philosophy. But the continuity with Guizot is nonetheless obvious. In *On Liberty,* instead of competing institutions and the principles underlying them—theocracy, aristocracy, monarchy and democracy—we have individuals choosing to pursue different values, and, without necessarily intending to contribute to the process whereby truth is sifted from falsehood, in fact doing so. For both Guizot and Mill, then, a competition of values or principles is necessary to prevent the sort of moral stagnation which nineteenth-century European intellectuals conventionally associated with China and India.

Is Guizot's pluralist account of European history and the creative role of class conflict any less important now than it seemed in the 1830s? Guizot helped both Tocqueville and J. S. Mill to identify a danger facing Europeans as they moved along the road from aristocracy to democracy. Aristocratic societies formerly gave a corporate basis to different values such as the patriotism and love of display of a military aristocracy, the prudence of the bourgeoisie, the stoicism of the peasantry, the otherworldliness of the clergy (at their best). These values or attitudes were, so to speak, permanently held up to society, and provided an inherent pluralism. But the destruction of a corporate society means that these values have lost their institutional foundation. Instead, their espousal has become a matter of individual choice. But as social conditions become more equal, will the springs of diversity, innovation and moral dissent be weakened? Will market pressures and a bourgeois ethic turn mass consumerism into a new form of tyranny? Or will individuals learn to stand up against the force of public opinion?

The questions remain. It was Guizot's genius in the *History of Civilization in Europe* to show that the pluralism which created Europe and which formerly had an institutional foundation can now rely only on individual freedoms or rights for its sustenance.

Larry Siedentop
Keble College, Oxford

A Short Bibliography

Artz, F. B., *France Under the Restoration.* New York, 1963.

Bardoux, M. A., *Guizot.* Paris, 1894.

Collingham, H. A. C., *The July Monarchy, 1830–1848.* London, 1988.

Furet, F., "French Historians and the Reconstruction of the Republican Tradition, 1800–1848," in B. Fontana (ed.), *The Invention of the Modern Republic.* Cambridge, 1994.

Hudson, N., *Ultra-Royalism and the French Restoration.* Cambridge, 1936.

Jardin, A., *Histoire du Liberalisme Politique.* Paris, 1985.

Jardin, A., and A. J. Tudseq, *Restoration and Reaction, 1815–1848.* Cambridge, 1984.

Johnson, D., *Guizot, Aspects of French History (1787–1874).* London, 1963.

Kelly, G. A., *The Humane Comedy: Constant, Tocqueville & French Liberalism.* Cambridge, 1992.

Lucas-Dubreton, J., *The Restoration and the July Monarchy.* London, 1929.

Mellon, S., *The Political Uses of History: A Study of Historians in the French Restoration.* Stanford, 1958.

Mill, J. S., "On Guizot's Essays and Lectures on History," in *Dissertations and Discussions* (reprinted from the Edinburgh and Westminster Reviews), vol. II, pp. 218–82. London, 1875.

O'Connor, M., *The Historical Thought of François Guizot.* Washington, 1955.

Pouthas, C., *La Jeunesse de Guizot (1787–1814).* Paris, 1936.

———, *Guizot pendant la Restauration.* Paris, 1923.

Rosanvallon, P., *Le Moment Guizot.* Paris, 1985.

Siedentop, L. A., *Tocqueville.* Oxford, 1994.

———, "Two Liberal Traditions," in *The Idea of Freedom* (ed. Alan Ryan). Oxford, 1979.

A Note on the Text

This edition reproduces the first English translation of François Guizot's *History of Civilization in Europe* (1828), originally given as lectures in Paris at the Old Sorbonne. Hazlitt's three volumes, published in 1846, also included Guizot's *History of Civilization in France.* I have found it necessary to make only occasional changes to the original translation.

THE

HISTORY OF CIVILIZATION,

FROM THE FALL OF THE ROMAN EMPIRE

TO THE FRENCH REVOLUTION.

BY F. GUIZOT,

AUTHOR OF

"HISTORY OF THE ENGLISH REVOLUTION OF 1640."

TRANSLATED BY WILLIAM HAZLITT, ESQ.

OF THE MIDDLE TEMPLE, BARRISTER-AT-LAW.

VOL. I.

LONDON:

H. G. BOHN, YORK STREET, COVENT GARDEN.

MDCCCLVI.

Contents

3

THIRD LECTURE

*Object of the lecture—All the various systems pretend to be
legitimate—What is political legitimacy?—Co-existence of all
systems of government in the fifth century—Instability in the
condition of persons, properties, and institutions—There were two
causes of this, one material, the continuation of the invasion; the
other moral, the selfish sentiment of individuality peculiar to the
barbarians—The germs of civilization have been the necessity for
order, the recollections of the Roman empire, the Christian church,
and the barbarians—Attempts at organization by the barbarians,
by the towns, by the church of Spain, by Charlemagne, and Alfred
—The German and Arabian invasions cease—The feudal*

FOURTH LECTURE

*Object of the lecture—Necessary alliance between facts and
doctrines—Preponderance of the country over the towns—
Organization of a small feudal society—Influence of feudalism
upon the character of the possessor of the fief, and upon the spirit of
family—Hatred of the people towards the feudal system—The priest
could do little for the serfs—Impossibility of regularly organizing
feudalism: 1. No powerful authority; 2. No public power; 3. Difficulty
of the federative system—The idea of the right of resistance inherent
in feudalism—Influence of feudalism favourable to the development
of the individual, unfavourable to social order.*

FIFTH LECTURE

*Object of the lecture—Religion is a principle of association—
Constraint is not of the essence of government—Conditions of the
legitimacy of government: 1. The power must be in the hands of the
most worthy; 2. The liberty of the governed must be respected—The
church being a corporation, and not a caste, fulfilled the first of these
conditions—Of the various methods of nomination and election*

SIXTH LECTURE

SEVENTH LECTURE

EIGHTH LECTURE

NINTH LECTURE

TENTH LECTURE

FOURTEENTH LECTURE

LECTURE THE FIRST

Object of the course—History of European civilization—Part taken by France in the civilization of Europe—Civilization a fit subject for narrative—It is the most general fact in history—The ordinary and popular meaning of the word civilization—*Two leading facts constitute civilization: 1. The development of society; 2. The development of the individual—Demonstration—These two facts are necessarily connected the one with the other, and, sooner or later, produce the one with the other—Is the destiny of man limited wholly within his actual social condition?—The history of civilization may be exhibited and considered under two points of view—Remarks on the plan of the course—The present state of men's minds, and the prospects of civilization.*

Gentlemen,

I AM DEEPLY AFFECTED by the reception you give me, and which, you will permit me to say, I accept as a pledge of the sympathy which has not ceased to exist between us, notwithstanding so long a separation— Alas! I speak as though you, whom I see around me, were the same who, seven years ago, used to assemble within these walls, to participate in my then labours; because I myself am here again, it seems as if all my former hearers should be here also; whereas, since that period, a change, a mighty change, has come over all things.[1] Seven years ago we repaired hither depressed with anxious doubts and fears, weighed down with sad thoughts

---

1. Guizot refers to the large student audience he had enjoyed in 1821, when, forced from government like the other Doctrinaires after the assassination of the heir to the throne in 1820, he had resumed his University lecturing. But that lecturing career was short-lived. As the political reaction prompted by the assassination gained strength and led to the emergence of an ultra-royalist government under Villèle by 1822, University lectures—which Guizot had undoubtedly, if discreetly, used as a political platform—were suspended.

and anticipations; we saw ourselves surrounded with difficulty and danger; we felt ourselves dragged on towards an evil which we essayed to avert by calm, grave, cautious reserve, but in vain. Now, we meet together, full of confidence and hope, the heart at peace, thought free. There is but one way in which we can worthily manifest our gratitude for this happy change; it is by bringing to our present meetings, our new studies, the same calm tranquillity of mind, the same firm purpose, which guided our conduct when, seven years ago, we looked, from day to day, to have our studies placed under rigorous supervision, or, indeed, to be arbitrarily suspended. Good fortune is delicate, frail, uncertain; we must keep measures with hope as with fear; convalescence requires well nigh the same care, the same caution, as the approaches of illness. This care, this caution, this moderation, I am sure you will exhibit. The same sympathy, the same intimate conformity of opinions, of sentiments, of ideas, which united us in times of difficulty and danger, and which at least saved us from grave faults, will equally unite us in more auspicious days, and enable us to gather all their fruits. I rely with confidence upon your co-operation, and I need nothing more.

The time between this our first meeting and the close of the year is very limited; that which I myself have had, wherein to meditate upon the lectures I am about to deliver, has been infinitely more limited still. One great point, therefore, was the selection of a subject, the consideration of which might best be brought within the bounds of the few months which remain to us of this year, within that of the few days I have had for preparation; and it appeared to me, that a general review of the modern history of Europe, considered with reference to the development of civilization—a general sketch, in fact, of the history of European civilization, of its origin, its progress, its aim, its character, might suitably occupy the time at our disposal. This, accordingly, is the subject of which I propose to treat.

I have used the term European civilization, because it is evident that there is an European civilization; that a certain unity pervades the civilization of the various European states; that, notwithstanding infinite diversities of time, place, and circumstance, this civilization takes its first rise in facts almost wholly similar, proceeds everywhere upon the same principles, and tends to produce well nigh everywhere analogous results. There is, then, an European civilization, and it is to the subject of this aggregate civilization that I will request your attention.

Again, it is evident that this civilization cannot be traced back, that its history cannot be derived from the history of any single European state. If, on the one hand, it is manifestly characterized by brevity, on the other, its variety is no less prodigious; it has not developed itself with completeness, in any one particular country. The features of its physiognomy are widespread; we must seek the elements of its history, now in France, now in England, now in Germany, now in Spain.

We of France occupy a favourable position for pursuing the study of European civilization. Flattery of individuals, even of our country, should be at all times avoided: it is without vanity, I think, we may say that France has been the centre, the focus of European civilization. I do not pretend, it were monstrous to do so, that she has always, and in every direction, marched at the head of nations. At different epochs, Italy has taken the lead of her, in the arts; England, in political institutions; and there may be other respects under which, at particular periods, other European nations have manifested a superiority to her; but it is impossible to deny, that whenever France has seen herself thus outstripped in the career of civilization, she has called up fresh vigour, has sprung forward with a new impulse, and has soon found herself abreast with, or in advance of, all the rest. And not only has this been the peculiar fortune of France, but we have seen that when the civilizing ideas and institutions which have taken their rise in other lands, have sought to extend their sphere, to become fertile and general, to operate for the common benefit of European civilization, they have been necessitated to undergo, to a certain extent, a new preparation in France; and it has been from France, as from a second native country, that they have gone forth to the conquest of Europe. There is scarcely any great idea, any great principle of civilization, which, prior to its diffusion, has not passed in this way through France.

And for this reason: there is in the French character something sociable, something sympathetic, something which makes its way with greater facility and effect than does the national genius of any other people; whether from our language, whether from the turn of our mind, of our manners, certain it is that our ideas are more popular than those of other people, present themselves more clearly and intelligibly to the masses, and penetrate among them more readily; in a word, perspicuity, sociability, sympathy, are the peculiar characteristics of France, of her civilization, and it is these qualities which rendered her eminently fit to march at the very head of European civilization.

In entering, therefore, upon the study of this great fact, it is no arbitrary or conventional choice to take France as the centre of this study; we must needs do so if we would place ourselves, as it were, in the very heart of civilization, in the very heart of the fact we are about to consider.

I use the term *fact*, and I do so purposely; civilization is a fact like any other—a fact susceptible, like any other, of being studied, described, narrated.

For some time past, there has been much talk of the necessity of limiting history to the narration of facts: nothing can be more just; but we must always bear in mind that there are far more facts to narrate, and that the facts themselves are far more various in their nature, than people are at first disposed to believe; there are material, visible facts, such as wars, battles, the official acts of governments; there are moral facts, nonetheless real that they do not appear on the surface; there are individual facts which have denominations of their own; there are general facts, without any particular designation, to which it is impossible to assign any precise date, which it is impossible to bring within strict limits, but which are yet no less facts than the rest, historical facts, facts which we cannot exclude from history without mutilating history.

The very portion of history which we are accustomed to call its philosophy, the relation of events to each other, the connexion which unites them, their causes and their effects—these are all facts, these are all history, just as much as the narratives of battles, and of other material and visible events. Facts of this class it is doubtless more difficult to disentangle and explain; we are more liable to error in giving an account of them, and it is no easy thing to give them life and animation, to exhibit them in clear and vivid colours; but this difficulty in no degree changes their nature; they are nonetheless an essential element of history.

Civilization is one of these facts; a general, hidden, complex fact; very difficult, I allow, to describe, to relate, but which nonetheless for that exists, which, nonetheless for that, has a right to be described and related. We may raise as to this fact a great number of questions; we may ask, it has been asked, whether it is a good or an evil? Some bitterly deplore it; others rejoice at it. We may ask, whether it is an universal fact, whether there is an universal civilization of the human species, a destiny of humanity; whether the nations have handed down from age to age, something which has never been lost, which must increase, form a larger and larger mass, and thus pass on to the end of time? For my own part, I am convinced that there is, in reality, a general destiny of humanity, a transmission of the aggregate of civilization; and, consequently, an universal history of civilization to be written. But without raising questions so great, so difficult to solve, if we restrict ourselves to a definite limit of time and space, if we confine our-selves to the history of a certain number of centuries, of a certain people, it is evident that within these bounds, civilization is a fact which can be described, related—which is history. I will at once add, that this history is the greatest of all, that it includes all.

And, indeed, does it not seem to yourselves that the fact civilization is the fact *par excellence*—the general and definitive fact, in which all the others terminate, into which they all resolve themselves? Take all the facts which compose the history of a nation, and which we are accustomed to regard as the elements of its life; take its institutions, its commerce, its in-dustry, its wars, all the details of its government: when we would consider these facts in their aggregate, in their connexion, when we would estimate them, judge them, we ask in what they have contributed to the civilization of that nation, what part they have taken in it, what influence they have exercised over it. It is in this way that we not only form a complete idea of them, but measure and appreciate their true value; they are, as it were, rivers, of which we ask what quantity of water it is they contribute to the ocean? For civilization is a sort of ocean, constituting the wealth of a peo-ple, and on whose bosom all the elements of the life of that people, all the powers supporting its existence, assemble and unite. This is so true, that even facts, which from their nature are odious, pernicious, which weigh painfully upon nations, despotism, for example, and anarchy, if they have contributed in some way to civilization, if they have enabled it to make an onward stride, up to a certain point we pardon them, we overlook their wrongs, their evil nature; in a word, wherever we recognize civilization, whatever the facts which have created it, we are tempted to forget the price it has cost.

There are, moreover, facts which, properly speaking, we cannot call social; individual facts, which seem to interest the human soul rather than the public life: such are religious creeds and philosophical ideas, sciences, letters, arts. These facts appear to address themselves to man with a view to his moral perfection, his intellectual gratification; to have for their object his internal amelioration, his mental pleasure, rather than his social condition. But, here again, it is with reference to civilization that these very facts are often considered, and claim to be considered.

At all times, in all countries, religion has assumed the glory of having civilized the people; sciences, letters, arts, all the intellectual and moral pleasures, have claimed a share in this glory; and we have deemed it a praise and an honour to them, when we have recognized this claim on their part. Thus, facts the most important and sublime in themselves, independently of all external result, and simply in their relations with the soul of man, increase in importance, rise in sublimity from their affinity with civilization. Such is the value of this general fact, that it gives value to everything it touches. And not only does it give value; there are even occasions when the facts of which we speak, religious creeds, philosophical ideas, letters, arts, are especially considered and judged of with reference to their influence upon civilization; an influence which becomes, up to a certain point and during a certain time, the conclusive measure of their merit, of their value.

What, then, I will ask, before undertaking its history, what, considered only in itself, what is this so grave, so vast, so precious fact, which seems the sum, the expression of the whole life of nations?

I shall take care here not to fall into pure philosophy; not to lay down some ratiocinative principle, and then deduce from it the nature of civilization as a result; there would be many chances of error in this method. And here, again, we have a fact to verify and describe.

For a long period, and in many countries, the word *civilization* has been in use; people have attached to the word ideas more or less clear, more or less comprehensive; but there it is in use, and those who use it, attach some meaning or other to it. It is the general, human, popular meaning of this word that we must study. There is almost always in the usual acceptation of the most general terms, more accuracy than in the definitions, apparently more strict, more precise, of science. It is commonsense which gives to words their ordinary signification, and commonsense is the characteristic of humanity. The ordinary signification of a word is formed by gradual progress, and in the constant presence of facts; so that when a fact presents itself which seems to come within the meaning of a known term, it is received into it, as it were, naturally; the signification of the term extends itself, expands, and by degrees, the various facts, the various ideas which from the nature of the things themselves men should include under this word, are included.

When the meaning of a word, on the other hand, is determined by science, this determination, the work of one individual, or of a small number of individuals, takes place under the influence of some particular fact which has struck upon the mind. Thus scientific definitions are, in general, much more narrow, and, hence, much less accurate, much less true, at bottom, than the popular meanings of the terms. In studying as a fact the meaning of the word civilization, in investigating all the ideas which are comprised within it, according to the commonsense of mankind, we shall make a much greater progress towards a knowledge of the fact itself, than by attempting to give it ourselves a scientific definition, however more clear and precise the latter might appear at first.

I will commence this investigation by endeavouring to place before you some hypotheses: I will describe a certain number of states of society, and we will then inquire whether general instinct would recognize in them the condition of a people civilizing itself; whether we recognize in them the meaning which mankind attaches to the word civilization?

First, suppose a people whose external life is easy, is full of physical comfort; they pay few taxes, they are free from suffering; justice is well administered in their private relations—in a word, material existence is for them altogether happy, and happily regulated. But at the same time, the intellectual and moral existence of this people is studiously kept in a state of torpor and inactivity; of, I will not say, oppression, for they do not understand the feeling, but of compression. We are not without instances of this state of things. There has been a great number of small aristocratic republics in which the people have been thus treated like flocks of sheep, well kept and materially happy, but without moral and intellectual activity. Is this civilization? Is this a people civilizing itself?

Another hypothesis: here is a people whose material existence is less easy, less comfortable, but still supportable. On the other hand, moral and intellectual wants have not been neglected, a certain amount of mental pasture has been served out to them; elevated, pure sentiments are cultivated in them; their religious and moral views have attained a certain degree of development; but great care is taken to stifle in them the principle of liberty; the intellectual and moral wants, as in the former case the material wants, are satisfied; each man has meted out to him his portion of truth; no one is permitted to seek it for himself. Immobility is the characteristic of moral life; it is the state into which have fallen most of the populations of Asia; wherever theocratic dominations keep humanity in check; it is the state of the Hindoos, for example. I ask the same question here as before; is this a people civilizing itself?

I change altogether the nature of the hypothesis: here is a people among whom is a great display of individual liberties, but where disorder and inequality are excessive: it is the empire of force and of chance; every man, if he is not strong, is oppressed, suffers, perishes; violence is the predominant feature of the social state. No one is ignorant that Europe has passed through this state. Is this a civilized state? It may, doubtless, contain principles of civilization which will develop themselves by successive degrees; but the fact which dominates in such a society is, assuredly, not that which the common sense of mankind calls civilization.

I take a fourth and last hypothesis: the liberty of each individual is very great, inequality amongst them is rare, and at all events, very transient. Every man does very nearly just what he pleases, and differs little in power from his neighbour; but there are very few general interests, very few public ideas, very little society—in a word, the faculties and existence of individuals appear and then pass away, wholly apart and without acting upon each other, or leaving any trace behind them; the successive generations leave society at the same point at which they found it: this is the state of savage tribes; liberty and equality are there, but assuredly not civilization.

I might multiply these hypotheses, but I think we have before us enough to explain what is the popular and natural meaning of the word civilization.

It is clear that none of the states I have sketched corresponds, according to the natural good sense of mankind, to this term. Why? It appears to me that the first fact comprised in the word civilization (and this results from the different examples I have rapidly placed before you), is the fact of progress, of development; it presents at once the idea of a people marching onwards, not to change its place, but to change its condition; of a people whose culture is conditioning itself, and ameliorating itself. The idea of progress, of development, appears to me the fundamental idea contained in the word civilization. What is this progress? what this development? Herein is the greatest difficulty of all.

The etymology of the word would seem to answer in a clear and satisfactory manner: it says that it is the perfecting of civil life, the development of society, properly so called, of the relations of men among themselves.

Such is, in fact, the first idea which presents itself to the understanding when the word civilization is pronounced; we at once figure forth to ourselves the extension, the greatest activity, the best organization of the social relations: on the one hand, an increasing production of the means of giving strength and happiness to society; on the other a more equitable distribution, amongst individuals, of the strength and happiness produced.

Is this all? Have we here exhausted all the natural, ordinary meaning of the word civilization? Does the fact contain nothing more than this?

It is almost as if we asked: is the human species after all a mere ant-hill, a society in which all that is required is order and physical happiness, in which the greater the amount of labour, and the more equitable the division of the fruits of labour, the more surely is the object attained, the progress accomplished.

Our instinct at once feels repugnant to so narrow a definition of human destiny. It feels at the first glance, that the word civilization comprehends something more extensive, more complex, something superior to the simple perfection of the social relations, of social power and happiness.

Fact, public opinion, the generally received meaning of the term, are in accordance with this instinct.

Take Rome in the palmy days of the republic, after the second Punic war, at the time of its greatest virtues, when it was marching to the empire of the world, when its social state was evidently in progress. Then take Rome under Augustus, at the epoch when her decline began, when, at all events, the progressive movement of society was arrested, when evil principles were on the eve of prevailing: yet there is no one who does not think and say that the Rome of Augustus was more civilized than the Rome of Fabricius or of Cincinnatus.

Let us transport ourselves beyond the Alps: let us take the France of the seventeenth and eighteenth centuries: it is evident that, in a social point of view, considering the actual amount and distribution of happiness amongst individuals, the France of the seventeenth and eighteenth centuries was inferior to some other countries of Europe, to Holland and to England, for example. I believe that in Holland and in England the social activity was greater, was increasing more rapidly, distributing its fruit more fully, than in France, yet ask general good sense, and it will say that the France of the seventeenth and eighteenth centuries was the most civilized country in Europe. Europe has not hesitated in her affirmative reply to the question: traces of this public opinion, as to France, are found in all the monuments of European literature.

We might point out many other states in which the prosperity is greater, is of more rapid growth, is better distributed amongst individuals than elsewhere, and in which, nevertheless, by the spontaneous instinct, the general good sense of men, the civilization is judged inferior to that of countries not so well portioned out in a purely social sense.

What does this mean? what advantages do these latter countries possess? What is it gives them, in the character of civilized countries, this privilege? what so largely compensates in the opinion of mankind for what they so lack in other respects?

A development other than that of social life has been gloriously manifested by them; the development of the individual, internal life, the development of man himself, of his faculties, his sentiments, his ideas. If society with them be less perfect than elsewhere, humanity stands forth in more grandeur and power. There remain, no doubt, many social conquests to be made; but immense intellectual and moral conquests are accomplished;

worldly goods, social rights, are wanting to many men; but many great men live and shine in the eyes of the world. Letters, sciences, the arts, display all their splendour. Wherever mankind beholds these great signs, these signs glorified by human nature, wherever it sees created these treasures of sublime enjoyment, it there recognizes and names civilization.

Two facts, then, are comprehended in this great fact; it subsists on two conditions, and manifests itself by two symptoms: the development of social activity, and that of individual activity; the progress of society and the progress of humanity. Wherever the external condition of man extends itself, vivifies, ameliorates itself; wherever the internal nature of man displays itself with lustre, with grandeur; at these two signs, and often despite the profound imperfection of the social state, mankind with loud applause proclaims civilization.[2]

Such, if I do not deceive myself, is the result of simple and purely commonsense examination, of the general opinion of mankind. If we interrogate history, properly so-called, if we examine what is the nature of the great crises of civilization, of those facts which, by universal consent, have propelled it onward, we shall constantly recognize one or other of the two elements I have just described. They are always crises of individual or social development, facts which have changed the internal man, his creed, his manners, or his external condition, his position in his relation with his fellows. Christianity, for example, not merely on its first appearance, but during the first stages of its existence, Christianity in no degree addressed itself to the social state; it announced aloud, that it would not meddle with the social state; it ordered the slave to obey his master; it attacked none of the great evils, the great wrongs of the society of that period. Yet who will deny that Christianity was a great crisis of civilization? Why was it so? Because

---

2. Here we can see the impact of Maine de Biran's epistemology on Guizot's conception of historical explanation. Biran's insistence on the radical difference between volition or "active" experience and sensation or "passive" experience enabled Guizot to argue that two sorts of explanation must be run side by side—explanation in terms of reasons for acting on the one hand, and explanation in terms of causes (in Hume's sense) on the other. He stakes out this philosophical ground through an analysis of the two different kinds of fact included in the concept of civilization.

it changed the internal man, creeds, sentiments; because it regenerated the moral man, the intellectual man.[3]

We have seen a crisis of another nature, a crisis which addressed itself, not to the internal man, but to his external condition; one which changed and regenerated society. This also was assuredly one of the decisive crises of civilization. Look through all history; you will find everywhere the same result; you will meet with no important fact instrumental in the development of civilization, which has not exercised one or other of the two sorts of influence I have spoken of.

Such, if I mistake not, is the natural and popular meaning of the term; you have here the fact, I will not say defined, but described, verified almost completely, or, at all events, in its general features. We have before us the two elements of civilization. Now comes the question, would one of these two suffice to constitute it; would the development of the social state, the development of the individual man, separately presented, be civilization? Would the human race recognize it as such? or have the two facts so intimate and necessary a relation between them, that if they are not simultaneously produced, they are notwithstanding inseparable, and sooner or later one brings on the other.

We might, as it appears to me, approach this question on three several sides. We might examine the nature itself of the two elements of civilization, and ask ourselves whether by that alone, they are or are not closely

---

3. It is no accident that Guizot introduces the role of Christianity at this early point in the 1828 lectures. He was part of a Protestant group which had dominated Restoration liberalism intellectually, a group which included Madame de Staël, Benjamin Constant and (as a Jansenist fellow-traveller) Royer-Collard. These Protestant liberals were at pains to distance themselves from the materialism and atheism of eighteenth-century proto-liberalism, as well as from the virulent anti-clericalism of the *philosophes*. Rejecting the ultra-royalist view that the movement towards democracy was a consequence of the rejection of Christianity, Protestant liberals under the Restoration began to argue the contrary view—namely, that the democratic social revolution, the movement from a society founded on privilege ("aristocracy") to a society founded on civil equality ("democracy"), reflected the cumulative impact of Christian moral beliefs since the early middle ages. Guizot, in particular, propagated that view in his *Society for Christian Morality*. There was a widespread belief among Protestant intellectuals in Paris after 1815 that irreligion had taken such a toll among Catholic intellectuals in France that the defence of Christianity, philosophically and historically, now fell to Protestants instead.

united with, and necessary to each other. We might inquire of history whether they had manifested themselves isolately, apart the one from the other, or whether they had invariably produced the one the other. We may, lastly, consult upon this question the common opinion of mankind—commonsense. I will address myself first to commonsense.

When a great change is accomplished in the state of a country, when there is operated in it a large development of wealth and power, a revolution in the distribution of the social means, this new fact encounters adversaries, undergoes opposition; this is inevitable. What is the general cry of the adversaries of the change? They say that this progress of the social state does not ameliorate, does not regenerate, in like manner, in a like degree, the moral, the internal state of man; that it is a false, delusive progress, the result of which is detrimental to morality, to man. The friends of social development energetically repel this attack; they maintain, on the contrary, that the progress of society necessarily involves and carries with it the progress of morality; that when the external life is better regulated, the internal life is refined and purified. Thus stands the question between the adversaries and partisans of the new state.

Reverse the hypothesis: suppose the moral development in progress: what do the labourers in this progress generally promise? What, in the origin of societies, have promised the religious rulers, the sages, the poets, who have laboured to soften and to regulate men's manners? They have promised the amelioration of the social condition, the more equitable distribution of the social means. What, then, I ask you, is involved in these disputes, these promises? What do they mean? What do they imply?

They imply that in the spontaneous, instinctive conviction of mankind, the two elements of civilization, the social development and the moral development, are closely connected together; that at sight of the one, man at once looks forward to the other. It is to this natural instinctive conviction that those who are maintaining or combating one or other of the two developments address themselves, when they affirm or deny their union. It is well understood, that if we can persuade mankind that the amelioration of the social state will be adverse to the internal progress of individuals, we shall have succeeded in decrying and enfeebling the revolution in operation throughout society. On the other hand, when we promise mankind the amelioration of society by means of the amelioration of the individual, it is well understood that the tendency is to place faith in these promises, and it is accordingly made use of with success. It is evidently, therefore, the instinctive belief of humanity, that the movements of civilization are connected the one with the other, and reciprocally produce the one the other.

If we address ourselves to the history of the world, we shall receive the same answer. We shall find that all the great developments of the internal man have turned to the profit of society; all the great developments of the social state to the profit of individual man. We find the one or other of the two facts predominating, manifesting itself with striking effect, and impressing upon the movement in progress a distinctive character. It is, sometimes, only after a very long interval of time, after a thousand obstacles, a thousand transformations, that the second fact, developing itself, comes to complete the civilization which the first had commenced. But if you examine them closely, you will soon perceive the bond which unites them. The march of Providence is not restricted to narrow limits; it is not bound, and it does not trouble itself, to follow out to-day the consequences of the principle which it laid down yesterday. The consequences will come in due course, when the hour for them has arrived, perhaps not till hundreds of years have passed away; though its reasoning may appear to us slow, its logic is nonetheless true and sound. To Providence, time is as nothing; it strides through time as the gods of Homer through space: it makes but one step, and ages have vanished behind it. How many centuries, what infinite events passed away before the regeneration of the moral man by Christianity exercised upon the regeneration of the social state its great and legitimate influence. Yet who will deny that it any the less succeeded?

If from history we extend our inquiries to the nature itself of the two facts which constitute civilization, we are infallibly led to the same result. There is no one who has not experienced this in his own case. When a moral change is operated in man, when he acquires an idea, or a virtue, or a faculty, more than he had before—in a word, when he develops himself individually, what is the desire, what the want, which at the same moment takes possession of him? It is the desire, the want, to communicate the new sentiment to the world about him, to give realization to his thoughts externally. As soon as a man acquires anything, as soon as his being takes in his own conviction a new development, assumes an additional value, forthwith he attaches to this new development, this fresh value, the idea of possession; he feels himself impelled, compelled, by his instinct, by an inward voice, to extend to others the change, the amelioration, which has been accomplished in his own person. We owe the great reformers solely to this cause; the mighty men who have changed the face of the world, after having changed themselves, were urged onward, were guided on their course, by no other want than this. So much for the alteration which is operated in the internal man; now to the other. A revolution is accomplished in the state of society; it is better regulated, rights and property are more equitably distributed among its members—that is to say, the aspect of the world becomes purer and more beautiful, the action of government, the conduct of men in their mutual relations, more just, more benevolent. Do you suppose that this improved aspect of the world, this amelioration of external facts, does not re-act upon the interior of man, upon humanity? All that is said as to the authority of examples, of customs, of noble models, is founded upon this only: that an external fact, good, well-regulated, leads sooner or later, more or less completely, to an internal fact of the same nature, the same merit; that a world better regulated, a world more just, renders man himself more just; that the inward is reformed by the outward, as the outward by the inward; that the two elements of civilization are closely connected the one with the other; that centuries, that obstacles of all sorts, may interpose between them; that it is possible they may have to undergo a thousand transformations, in order to regain each other; but sooner or later they will rejoin each other: this is the law of their nature, the general fact of history, the instinctive faith of the human race.

I think I have thus—not exhausted the subject, very far from it—but, exhibited in a well-nigh complete, though cursory manner, the fact of civilization; I think I have described it, settled its limits, and stated the principal, the fundamental questions to which it gives rise. I might stop here; but I cannot help touching upon a question which meets me at this point; one of those questions which are not historical questions, properly so called; which are questions, I will not call them hypothetical, but conjectural; questions of which man holds but one end, the other end being permanently beyond his reach; questions of which he cannot make the circuit, nor view on more than one side; and yet questions not the less real, not the less calling upon him for thought; for they present themselves before him, despite himself, at every moment.

Of those two developments of which we have spoken, and which constitute the fact of civilization, the development of society on the one hand and of humanity on the other, which is the end, which is the means? Is it to perfect his social condition, to ameliorate his existence on earth, that man develops himself, his faculties, sentiments, ideas, his whole being?— or rather, is not the amelioration of the social condition, the progress of society, society itself, the theatre, the occasion, the *mobile,* of the development of the individual, in a word, is society made to serve the individual, or the individual to serve society? On the answer to this question inevitably depends that whether the destiny of man is purely social; whether society drains up and exhausts the whole man; or whether he bears within him something extrinsic—something superior to his existence on earth.

A man, whom I am proud to call my friend, a man who has passed through meetings like our own to assume the first place in assemblies less peaceable and more powerful; a man, all of whose words are engraven on the hearts of those who hear them, M. Royer-Collard, has solved this question, according to his own conviction at least, in his speech on the Sacrilege Bill.[4] I find in that speech these two sentences: "Human societies are born, live, and die, on the earth; it is there their destinies are accomplished. . . . But they contain not the whole man. After he has engaged himself to society, there remains to him the noblest part of himself, those high faculties by which he elevates himself to God, to a future life, to unknown felicity in an invisible world. . . . We, persons individual and identical, veritable beings endowed with immortality, we have a different destiny from that of states."*

---

* *Opinion de M. Royer-Collard sur le Projet de Loi relatif au Sacrilège,* pp. 7, 17.

4. Royer-Collard, a very powerful orator, was the most senior and prominent figure among the Doctrinaires, leading what remained of the liberal party in the Chamber of Deputies after the crisis of 1820. He had already played an important part in Guizot's earlier career, securing his appointment as Secretary General of the Interior Ministry at the extraordinarily early age of twenty-seven. The two men had first met and become friends when Guizot arrived as an assistant professor of history at the Sorbonne in 1812.

I will add nothing to this; I will not undertake to treat the question itself; I content myself with stating it. It is met with at the history of civilization: when the history of civilization is completed, when there is nothing more to say as to our present existence, man inevitably asks himself whether all is exhausted, whether he has reached the end of all things? This, then, is the last, the highest of all those problems to which the history of civilization can lead. It is sufficient for me to have indicated its position and its grandeur.

From all I have said, it is evident that the history of civilization might be treated in two methods, drawn from two sources, considered under two different aspects. The historian might place himself in the heart of the human mind for a given period, a series of ages, or among a determinate people; he might study, describe, relate, all the events, all the transformations, all the revolutions, which had been accomplished in the internal man; and when he should arrive at the end, he would have a history of civilization amongst the people, and in the period he had selected. He may proceed in another manner: instead of penetrating the internal man, he may take his stand—he may place himself in the midst of the world; instead of describing the vicissitudes of the ideas, the sentiments, of the individual being, he may describe external facts, the events, the changes of the social state. These two portions, these two histories of civilization, are closely connected with each other; they are the reflection, the image of each other. Yet, they may be separated; perhaps, indeed, they ought to be so, at least at the onset, in order that both the one and the other may be treated in detail, and with perspicuity. For my part, I do not propose to study with you the history of civilization in the interior of the human soul; it is the history of external events, of the visible and social world that I shall occupy myself with. I had wished, indeed, to exhibit to you the whole fact of civilization, such as I can conceive it in all its complexity and extent, to set forth before you all the high questions which may arise from it. At present, I restrict myself; mark out my field of inquiry within narrower limits; it is only the history of the social state that I propose investigating.

We shall begin by seeking all the elements of European civilization in its cradle, at the fall of the Roman empire; we will study with attention

society, such as it was, in the midst of those famous ruins. We will endeavour, not to resuscitate, but to place its elements side by side; and when we
have done so, we will endeavour to make them move, and follow them in
their developments through the fifteen centuries which have elapsed since
that epoch.

I believe that when we have got but a very little way into this study, we
shall acquire the conviction that civilization is as yet very young; that
the world has by no means as yet measured the whole of its career. Assuredly human thought is at this time very far from being all that it is
capable of becoming; we are very far from comprehending the whole
future of humanity: let each of us descend into his own mind, let him
interrogate himself as to the utmost possible good he has formed a conception of and hopes for; let him then compare his idea with what actually exists in the world; he will be convinced that society and civilization
are very young; that notwithstanding the length of the road they have
come, they have incomparably further to go. This will lessen nothing of
the pleasure that we shall take in the contemplation of our actual condition. As I endeavour to place before you the great crises in the history
of civilization in Europe during the last fifteen centuries, you will see to
what a degree, even up to our own days, the condition of man has been
laborious, stormy, not only in the outward and social state, but inwardly,
in the life of the soul. During all those ages, the human mind has had to
suffer as much as the human race; you will see that in modern times, for
the first time, perhaps, the human mind has attained a state, as yet very
imperfect, but still a state in which reigns some peace, some harmony. It
is the same with society; it has evidently made immense progress; the
human condition is easy and just, compared with what it was previously;
we may almost, when thinking of our ancestors, apply to ourselves the
verses of Lucretius:

> Suave mari magno, turbantibus aequora ventis,
> E terrâ magnum alterius spectare laborem.*

---

* "'Tis pleasant, in a great storm, to contemplate, from a safe position on shore, the
perils of some ships tossed about by the furious winds and the stormy ocean."

We may say of ourselves, without too much pride, as Sthenelus in Homer:

*Ηµεῖς τοὶ πατερων µεγ' ἀµείνονες εὐχόµεθ, εἶναι.**

Let us be careful, however, not to give ourselves up too much to the idea of our happiness and amelioration, or we may fall into two grave dangers, pride and indolence; we may conceive an over-confidence in the power and success of the human mind, in our own enlightenment, and, at the same time, suffer ourselves to become enervated by the luxurious ease of our condition. It appears to me that we are constantly fluctuating between a tendency to complain upon light grounds, on the one hand, and to be content without reason, on the other. We have a susceptibility of spirit, a craving, an unlimited ambition in the thought, in our desire, in the movement of the imagination; but when it comes to the practical work of life, when we are called upon to give ourselves any trouble, to make any sacrifices, to use any efforts to attain the object, our arms fall down listlessly by our sides, and we give the matter up in despair, with a facility equalled only by the impatience with which we had previously desired its attainment. We must beware how we allow ourselves to yield to either of these defects. Let us accustom ourselves duly to estimate beforehand the extent of our force, our capacity, our knowledge; and let us aim at nothing which we feel we cannot attain legitimately, justly, regularly, and with unfailing regard to the principles upon which our civilization itself rests. We seem at times tempted to adopt the very principles which, as a general rule, we assail and hold up to scorn—the principles, the right of the strongest of barbarian Europe; the brute force, the violence, the downright lying which were matters of course, of daily occurrence, four or five hundred years ago. But when we yield for a moment to this desire, we find in ourselves neither the perseverance nor the savage energy of the men of that period, who, suffering greatly from their condition, were naturally anxious, and incessantly essaying, to emancipate themselves from it. We, of the present day, are content with our condition; let us not expose it to danger by indulging in vague desires, the time for realizing which has not come. Much has been given to us, much

---

* "Thank Heaven, we are infinitely better than those who went before us."

will be required of us; we must render to posterity a strict account of our conduct; the public, the government, all are now subjected to discussion, examination, responsibility. Let us attach ourselves firmly, faithfully, undeviatingly, to the principles of our civilization—justice, legality, publicity, liberty; and let us never forget, that while we ourselves require, and with reason, that all things shall be open to our inspection and inquiry, we ourselves are under the eye of the world, and shall, in our turn, be discussed, be judged.

SECOND LECTURE

Purpose of the lecture—Unity of ancient civilization—Variety of modern civilization—Its superiority—Condition of Europe at the fall of the Roman empire—Preponderance of the towns—Attempt at political reform by the emperors—Rescript of Honorius and of Theodosius II—Power of the name of the Empire—The Christian church—The various stages through which it had passed at the fifth century—The clergy exercising municipal functions—Good and evil influence of the church—The barbarians—They introduce into the modern world the sentiments of personal independence, and the devotion of man to man—Summary of the different elements of civilization in the beginning of the fifth century.

I N MEDITATING THE PLAN of the course with which I propose to present you, I am fearful lest my lectures should possess the double inconvenience of being very long, by reason of the necessity of condensing much matter into little space, and, at the same time, of being too concise.

I dread yet another difficulty, originating in the same cause: the necessity, namely, of sometimes making affirmations without proving them. This is also the result of the narrow space to which I find myself confined. There will occur ideas and assertions of which the confirmation must be postponed. I hope you will pardon me for sometimes placing you under the necessity of believing me upon my bare word. I come even now to an occasion of imposing upon you this necessity.

I have endeavoured, in the preceding lecture, to explain the fact of civilization in general, without speaking of any particular civilization, without regarding circumstance of time and place, considering the fact in itself, and under a purely philosophical point of view. I come, to-day, to the history of European civilization; but before entering upon the narrative itself, I wish to make you acquainted, in a general manner, with the particular physiognomy of this civilization; I desire to characterize it so clearly to you, that it may appear to you perfectly distinct from all other civilizations which have developed themselves in the world. This I am going to attempt, more than which I dare not say; but I can only affirm it, unless I could succeed in depicting European society with such faithfulness, that you should instantly recognize it as a portrait. But of this I dare not flatter myself.

When we regard the civilizations which have preceded that of modern Europe, whether in Asia or elsewhere, including even Greek and Roman civilization, it is impossible to help being struck with the unity which pervades them. They seem to have emanated from a single fact, from a single idea; one might say that society has attached itself to a solitary dominant principle, which has determined its institutions, its customs, its creeds, in one word, all its developments.

In Egypt, for instance, it was the theocratic principle which pervaded the entire community; it reproduced itself in the customs, in the monuments, and in all that remains to us of Egyptian civilization. In India, you will discover the same fact; there is still the almost exclusive dominion of the theocratic principle. Elsewhere you will meet with another organizing principle—the domination of a victorious caste; the principle of force will here alone possess society, imposing thereupon its laws and its character. Elsewhere, society will be the expression of the democratic principle; it has been thus with the commercial republics which have covered the coasts of Asia Minor and of Syria, in Ionia, in Phenicia. In short, when we contemplate ancient civilizations, we find them stamped with a singular character of unity in their institutions, their ideas, and their manners; a sole, or, at least, a strongly preponderating force governs and determines all.

I do not mean to say that this unity of principle and form in the civilization of these states has always prevailed therein. When we go back to their earlier history, we find that the various powers which may develop themselves in the heart of a society, have often contended for empire. Among the Egyptians, the Etruscans, the Greeks themselves, &c., the order of warriors, for example, has struggled against that of the priests; elsewhere, the spirit of clanship has struggled against that of free association; the aristocratic against the popular system, &c. But it has generally been in ante-historical times that such struggles have occurred; and thus only a vague recollection has remained of them.

The struggle has sometimes reproduced itself in the course of the existence of nations; but, almost invariably, it has soon been terminated; one of the powers that disputed for empire has soon gained it, and taken sole possession of the society. The war has always terminated by the, if not exclusive, at least largely preponderating, domination of some particular principle. The co-existence and the combat of different principles have never, in the history of these peoples, been more than a transitory crisis, an accident.

The result of this has been a remarkable simplicity in the majority of ancient civilizations. This simplicity has produced different consequences. Sometimes, as in Greece, the simplicity of the social principle has led to a wonderfully rapid development; never has any people unfolded itself in so short a period, with such brilliant effect. But after this astonishing flight, Greece seemed suddenly exhausted; its decay, if it was not so rapid as its rise, was nevertheless strangely prompt. It seems that the creative force of the principle of Greek civilization was exhausted; no other has come to renew it.

Elsewhere, in Egypt and in India, for instance, the unity of the principle of civilization has had a different effect; society has fallen into a stationary condition. Simplicity has brought monotony; the country has not been destroyed, society has continued to exist, but motionless, and as if frozen.

It is to the same cause that we must attribute the character of tyranny which appeared in the name of principle and under the most various forms, among all the ancient civilizations. Society belonged to an exclusive power, which would allow of the existence of none other. Every differing tendency was proscribed and hunted down. Never has the ruling principle chosen to admit beside it the manifestation and action of a different principle.

This character of unity of civilization is equally stamped upon literature and the works of the mind. Who is unacquainted with the monuments of Indian literature, which have lately been distributed over Europe? It is impossible not to see that they are all cast in the same mould; they seem all to be the result of the same fact, the expression of the same idea; works of religion or morals, historical traditions, dramatic and epic poetry, everywhere the same character is stamped; the productions of the mind bear the same character of simplicity and of monotony which appears in events and institutions. Even in Greece, in the centre of all the riches of the human intellect, a singular uniformity reigns in literature and in the arts.

It has been wholly otherwise with the civilization of modern Europe. Without entering into details, look upon it, gather together your recollections: it will immediately appear to you varied, confused, stormy; all forms, all principles of social organization co-exist therein; powers spiritual and temporal; elements theocratic, monarchical, aristocratic, democratic; all orders, all social arrangements mingle and press upon one another; there are infinite degrees of liberty, wealth, and influence. These various forces are in a state of continual struggle among themselves, yet no one succeeds in stifling the others, and taking possession of society. In ancient times, at every great epoch, all societies seemed cast in the same mould: it is sometimes pure monarchy, sometimes theocracy or democracy, that prevails; but each, in its turn, prevails completely. Modern Europe presents us with examples of all systems, of all experiments of social organization; pure or mixed monarchies, theocracies, republics, more or less aristocratic, have thus thrived simultaneously, one beside the other; and, notwithstanding their diversity, they have all a certain resemblance, a certain family likeness, which it is impossible to mistake.[1]

In the ideas and sentiments of Europe there is the same variety, the same struggle. The theocratic, monarchic, aristocratic, and popular creeds, cross, combat, limit, and modify each other. Open the boldest writings of the middle ages; never there is an idea followed out to its last consequences. The partisans of absolute power recoil suddenly and unconsciously before the results of their own doctrine; they perceive around them ideas and influences which arrest them, and prevent them from going to extremities. The democrats obey the same law. On neither part exists that imperturbable audacity, that blind determination of logic, which show themselves

1. Guizot uses his contrast between the unity (and therefore tyranny) of most civilizations and the pluralism of European civilization to prepare the ground for his later account of the nature of representative government and its emergence in Europe. He explains it as a result of the need to accommodate different social claims and institutions within a single legal framework or state.

in ancient civilizations. The sentiments offer the same contrasts, the same variety; an energetic love of independence, side by side with a great facility of submission; a singular faithfulness of man to man, and, at the same time, an uncontrollable wish to exert free will, to shake off every yoke, and to live for oneself, without caring for any other. The souls of men are as different, as agitated as society.

The same character discovers itself in modern literatures. We cannot but agree that, as regards artistic form and beauty, they are very much inferior to ancient literature; but, as regards depth of sentiment and of ideas, they are far more rich and vigorous. We see that the human soul has been moved upon a greater number of points, and to a greater depth. Imperfection of form results from this very cause. The richer and more numerous the materials, the more difficult it is to reduce them to a pure and simple form. That which constitutes the beauty of a composition, of that which we call form, in works of art, is clearness, simplicity, and a symbolic unity of workmanship. With the prodigious diversity of the ideas and sentiments of European civilization, it has been much more difficult to arrive at this simplicity, this clearness.

On all sides, then, this predominant character of modern civilization discovers itself. It has, no doubt, had this disadvantage, that, when we consider separately such or such a particular development of the human mind in letters, in the arts, in all directions in which it can advance, we usually find it inferior to the corresponding development in ancient civilizations; but, on the other hand, when we regard it in the aggregate, European civilization shows itself incomparably richer than any other; it has displayed, at one and the same time, many more different developments. Consequently, you find that it has existed fifteen centuries, and yet is still in a state of continuous progression; it has not advanced nearly so rapidly as the Greek civilization, but its progress has never ceased to grow. It catches a glimpse of the vast career which lies before it, and day after day it shoots forward more rapidly, because more and more of freedom attends its movements. Whilst, in other civilizations, the exclusive, or, at least, the excessively preponderating dominion of a single principle, of a single form, has been the cause of tyranny, in modern Europe, the diversity of elements, which constitute the social order, the impossibility under which they have been placed of excluding each other, have given birth to the freedom which prevails in the present day. Not having been able to exterminate each other, it has become necessary that various principles should exist together—that they should make between them a sort of compact. Each has agreed to undertake that portion of the development which may fall to its share; and whilst elsewhere the predominance of a principle produced tyranny, in Europe liberty has been the result of the variety of the elements of civilization, and of the state of struggle in which they have constantly existed.[2]

This constitutes a real and an immense superiority; and if we investigate yet further, if we penetrate beyond external facts into the nature of things, we shall discover that this superiority is legitimate, and acknowledged by reason as well as proclaimed by facts. Forgetting for a moment European civilization, let us turn our attention to the world in general, on the general course of terrestrial things. What character do we find? How goes the world? It moves precisely with this diversity and variety of elements, a prey to this constant struggle which we have remarked in European civilization. Evidently it has not been permitted to any single principle, to any particular organization, to any single idea, or to any special force, that it should possess itself of the world, moulding it once for all, destroying all other influences to reign therein itself exclusively.

Various powers, principles, and systems mingle, limit each other, and struggle without ceasing, in turn predominating, or predominated over, never entirely conquered or conquering. A variety of forms, of ideas, and of principles, then, struggles, their efforts after a certain unity, a certain ideal which perhaps can never be attained, but to which the human race tends by freedom and work; these constitute the general condition of the world. European civilization is, therefore, the faithful image of the world: like the course of things in the world, it is neither narrow, exclusive, nor stationary. For the first time, I believe, the character of specialty has vanished from

2. Here we can see not only how class conflict under the Restoration contributed to Guizot's analysis of European pluralism, but also the way he sought to use this pluralist analysis to reconcile the different classes in France and thereby contribute to the survival of representative government under the Restoration.

civilization; for the first time it is developed as variously, as richly, as laboriously, as the great drama of the universe.[3]

European civilization has entered, if we may so speak, into the eternal truth, into the plan of Providence; it progresses according to the intentions of God. This is the rational account of its superiority.

I am desirous that this fundamental and distinguishing character of European civilization should continue to be present to your minds during the course of our labours. For the moment I can only make the affirmation: the development of facts must furnish the proof. It will, nevertheless, you will agree, be a strong confirmation of my assertion, if we find, even in the cradle of our civilization, the causes and the elements of the character which I have just attributed to it; if, at the moment of its birth, at the moment of the fall of the Roman empire, we recognize in the state of the world, in the facts that, from the earliest times, have concurred to form European civilization, the principle of this agitated but fruitful diversity which distinguishes it. I am about to attempt this investigation. I shall examine the condition of Europe at the fall of the Roman empire, and seek to discover, from institutions, creeds, ideas, and sentiments, what were the elements bequeathed by the ancient to the modern world. If, in these elements, we shall already find impressed the character which I have just described, it will have acquired with you, from this time forth, a high degree of probability.

First of all, we must clearly represent to ourselves the nature of the Roman empire, and how it was formed.

Rome was, in its origin, only a municipality, a corporation. The government of Rome was merely the aggregate of the institutions which were suited to a population confined within the walls of a city: these were municipal institutions—that is their distinguishing character.

This was not the case with Rome only. If we turn our attention to Italy, at this period, we find around Rome nothing but towns. That which was then called a people was simply a confederation of towns. The Latin people were a confederation of Latin towns. The Etruscans, the Samnites, the

---

3. Undoubtedly Guizot introduces this "providential" theme to give European pluralism a moral claim in so far as it reflects human diversity and respects freedom.

Sabines, the people of Graecia Magna, may all be described in the same terms.

There was, at this time, no country—that is to say, the country was wholly unlike that which at present exists; it was cultivated, as was necessary, but it was uninhabited. The proprietors of lands were the inhabitants of the towns. They went forth to superintend their country properties, and often took with them a certain number of slaves; but that which we at present call the country, that thin population—sometimes in isolated habitations, sometimes in villages—which everywhere covers the soil, was a fact almost unknown in ancient Italy.

When Rome extended itself, what did she do? Follow history, and you will see that she conquered or founded towns; it was against towns that she fought, with towns that she contracted alliances; it was also into towns that she sent colonies. The history of the conquest of the world by Rome is the history of the conquest and foundation of a great number of towns. In the East, the extension of Roman dominion does not carry altogether this aspect: the population there was otherwise distributed than in the West—it was much less concentrated in towns. But as we have to do here with the European population, what occurred in the East is of little interest to us.

Confining ourselves to the West, we everywhere discover the fact to which I have directed your attention. In Gaul, in Spain, you meet with nothing but towns. At a distance from the towns, the territory is covered with marshes and forests. Examine the character of the Roman monuments, of the Roman roads. You have great roads, which reach from one city to another; the multiplicity of minor roads, which now cross the country in all directions, was then unknown; you have nothing resembling that countless number of villages, country seats, and churches, which have been scattered over the country since the middle ages. Rome has left us nothing but immense monuments, stamped with the municipal character, and destined for a numerous population collected upon one spot. Under whatever point of view you consider the Roman world, you will find this almost exclusive preponderance of towns, and the social non-existence of the country.

This municipal character of the Roman world evidently rendered unity, the social bond of a great state, extremely difficult to establish and maintain. A municipality like Rome had been able to conquer the world, but it was much less easy to govern and organize it. Thus, when the work appeared completed, when all the West, and a great part of the East, had fallen under Roman dominion, you behold this prodigious number of cities, of little states, made for isolation and independence, disunite, detach themselves, and escape, so to speak, in all directions. This was one of the causes which rendered necessary the Empire, a form of government more concentrated, more capable of holding together elements so slightly coherent. The Empire endeavoured to introduce unity and combination into this scattered society. It succeeded up to a certain point. It was between the reigns of Augustus and Diocletian that, at the same time that civil legislation developed itself, there became established the vast system of administrative despotism which spread over the Roman world a network of functionaries, hierarchically distributed, well linked together, both among themselves and with the imperial court, and solely applied to rendering effective in society the will of power, and in transferring to power the tributes and energies of society.[4]

And not only did this system succeed in rallying and in holding together the elements of the Roman world, but the idea of despotism, of central power, penetrated minds with a singular facility. We are astonished to behold rapidly prevailing throughout this ill-united assemblage of petty republics, this association of municipalities, a reverence for the imperial majesty alone, august and sacred. The necessity of establishing some bond between all these portions of the Roman world must have been very pressing, to ensure so easy an access to the mind for the faith and almost the sentiments of despotism.

It was with these creeds, with this administrative organization, and with the military organization which was combined with it, that the Roman empire struggled against the dissolution at work inwardly, and against the invasion of the barbarians from without. It struggled for a long time, in

4. This is the first appearance of the concept and theme of centralization, which had played such an important role in liberal argument during the Great Debate of the 1820s, beginning with Royer-Collard's famous speech on the freedom of the press in 1822. Guizot applies the concept retrospectively to understand the decline of municipal freedom under the Roman empire, the destruction of local élites and the inability of the empire to defend itself against the Germanic invasions.

a continual state of decay, but always defending itself. At last a moment came in which dissolution prevailed: neither the skill of despotism nor the indifference of servitude sufficed to support this huge body. In the fourth century it everywhere disunited and dismembered itself; the barbarians entered on all sides; the provinces no longer resisted, no longer troubled themselves concerning the general destiny. At this time, a singular idea suggested itself to some of the emperors: they desired to try whether hopes of general liberty, a confederation—a system analogous to that which, in the present day, we call representative government—would not better defend the unity of the Roman empire than despotic administration. Here is a rescript of Honorius and Theodosius the younger, addressed, in the year 418, to the prefect of Gaul, the only purpose of which was to attempt to establish in the south of Gaul a sort of representative government, and, with its aid, to maintain the unity of the empire.[5]

"Rescript of the emperors Honorius and Theodosius the younger, addressed, in the year 418, to the prefect of the Gauls, sitting in the town of Arles.

"Honorius and Theodosius, Augusti, to Agricola, prefect of the Gauls:

"Upon the satisfactory statement that your Magnificence has made to us, among other information palpably advantageous to the state, we decree the force of law in perpetuity to the following ordinances, to which the inhabitants of our seven provinces will owe obedience, they being such that they themselves might have desired and demanded them. Seeing that persons in office, or special deputies, from motives of public or private utility, not only from each of the provinces, but also from every town, often present themselves before your Magnificence, either to render accounts or to treat of things relative to the interest of proprietors, we have judged that it would be a seasonable and profitable thing that, from the date of the present year, there should be annually, at a fixed time, an assemblage held in the metropolis—that is, in the town of Arles, for the inhabitants of the seven provinces. By this institution we have in view to provide equally for

5. Through this doomed attempt by later emperors to find a way to renew the strength of the Western Empire, by means of consultation with local élites, Guizot is able to present representative government or "general liberty" as the only serious alternative to adminstrative despotism in an extended territory.

general and particular interests. In the first place, by the meeting of the most notable of the inhabitants in the illustrious presence of the prefect, if motives of public order have not called him elsewhere, the best possible information may be gained upon every subject under deliberation. Nothing of that which will have been treated of and decided upon, after a ripe consideration, will escape the knowledge of any of the provinces, and those who shall not have been present at the assembly will be bound to follow the same rules of justice and equity. Moreover, in ordaining that an annual assembly be held in the city of Constantine,* we believe that we are doing a thing not only advantageous to the public good, but also adapted to multiply social relations. Indeed, the city is so advantageously situated, strangers come there in such numbers, and it enjoys such an extensive commerce, that everything finds its way there which grows or is manufactured in other places. All admirable things that the rich East, perfumed Arabia, delicate Assyria, fertile Africa, beautiful Spain, valiant Gaul produce, abound in this place with such profusion, that whatever is esteemed magnificent in the various parts of the world seems there the produce of the soil. Besides, the junction of the Rhône with the Tuscan sea approximates and renders almost neighbours those countries which the first traverses, and the second bathes in its windings. Thus, since the entire earth places at the service of this city all that it has most worthy—since the peculiar productions of all countries are transported hither by land, by sea, and by the course of rivers, by help of sails, of oars, and of wagons—how can our Gaul do otherwise than behold a benefit in the command which we give to convoke a public assembly in a city, wherein are united, as it were, by the gift of God, all the enjoyments of life, and all the facilities of commerce?

"The illustrious prefect Petronius,† through a laudable and reasonable motive, formerly commanded that this custom should be observed; but as the practice thereof was interrupted by the confusion of the times, and by the reign of usurpers, we have resolved to revive it in vigour by the authority

---

* Constantine the Great had a singular liking for the town of Arles. It was he who established there the seat of the seat of the Gaulish prefecture; he desired also that it should bear his name, but custom prevailed against his wish.

† Petronius was prefect of the Gauls between the years 402 and 408.

of our wisdom. Thus, then, dear and beloved cousin Agricola, your illustrious Magnificence, conforming yourself to our present ordinance, and to the custom established by your predecessors, will cause to be observed throughout the provinces the following rules:

"'Let all persons, who are honoured with public functions, or who are proprietors of domains, and all judges of provinces, be informed that, each year, they are to assemble in council in the city of Arles, between the ides of August and those of September, the days of convocation and of sitting being determined at their pleasure.

"'Novem Populinia and the second Aquitaine, being the most distant provinces, should their judges be detained by indispensable occupations, may send deputies in their place, according to custom.

"'Those who shall neglect to appear at the place assigned and at the time appointed, shall pay a fine, which, for the judges, shall be five pounds of gold, and three pounds for the members of the *curiae** and other dignitaries.'

"We propose, by this means, to confer great advantages and favour on the inhabitants of our provinces. We feel, also, assured of adding to the ornaments of the city of Arles, to the fidelity of which we are so much indebted, according to our brother and patrician.[†]

"Given on the 15th of the calends of May; received at Arles on the 10th of the calends of June."

The provinces and the towns refused the benefit; no one would nominate the deputies, no one would go to Arles. Centralization and unity were contrary to the primitive character of that society; the local and municipal spirit reappeared everywhere, and the impossibility of reconstituting a general society or country became evident. The towns confined themselves, each to its own walls and its own affairs, and the empire fell because none wished to be of the empire, because citizens desired to be only of their own city. Thus we again discover, at the fall of the Roman empire, the same fact which we have detected in the cradle of Rome, namely, the predominance of the municipal form and spirit. The Roman world had

---

* The municipal bodies of Roman towns were called *curiae,* and the members of those bodies, who were very numerous, were called *curiales.*

[†] Constantine, the second husband of Placidius, whom Honorius had chosen for colleague in 421.

returned to its first condition; towns had constituted it; it dissolved; and towns remained.

In the municipal system we see what ancient Roman civilization has bequeathed to modern Europe; that system was very irregular, much weakened, and far inferior, no doubt, to what it had been in earlier times; but, nevertheless, the only real, the only constituted system which had outlived all the elements of the Roman world.

When I say *alone,* I make a mistake. Another fact, another idea equally survived: the idea of the empire, the name of emperor, the idea of imperial majesty, of an absolute and sacred power attached to the name of emperor. These are the elements which Roman has transmitted to European civilization; upon one hand, the municipal system, its habits, rules, precedents, the principle of freedom; on the other, a general and uniform civil legislation, the idea of absolute power, of sacred majesty, of the emperor, the principle of order and subjection.

But there was formed at the same time, in the heart of the Roman society, a society of a very different nature, founded upon totally different principles, animated by different sentiments, a society which was about to infuse into modern European society elements of a character wholly different; I speak of the *Christian church.* I say, the Christian church, and not Christianity. At the end of the fourth and at the beginning of the fifth century, Christianity was no longer merely an individual belief, it was an institution; it was constituted; it had its government, a clergy, an hierarchy calculated for the different functions of the clergy, revenues, means of independent action, rallying points suited for a great society, provincial, national, and general councils, and the custom of debating in common upon the affairs of the society. In a word, Christianity, at this epoch, was not only a religion, it was also a church.

Had it not been a church, I cannot say what might have happened to it amid the fall of the Roman empire. I confine myself to simply human considerations; I put aside every element which is foreign to the natural consequences of natural facts: had Christianity been, as in the earlier times, no more than a belief, a sentiment, an individual conviction, we may believe that it would have sunk amidst the dissolution of the empire, and the invasion of the barbarians. In later times, in Asia and in all the north of Africa, it sunk under an invasion of the same nature, under the invasion of the Moslem barbarians; it sunk then, although it subsisted in the form of an institution, or constituted church. With much more reason might the same thing have happened at the moment of the fall of the Roman empire. There existed, at that time, none of those means by which, in the present day, moral influences establish themselves or offer resistance, independently of institutions; none of those means whereby a pure truth, a pure idea obtains a great empire over minds, governs actions, and determines events.[6] Nothing of the kind existed in the fourth century to give a like authority to ideas and to personal sentiments. It is clear that a society strongly organized and strongly governed, was indispensable to struggle against such a disaster, and to issue victorious from such a storm. I do not think that I say more than the truth in affirming that at the end of the fourth and the commencement of the fifth centuries it was the Christian church that saved Christianity; it was the church with its institutions, its magistrates, and its power, that vigorously resisted the internal dissolution of the empire and barbarism; that conquered the barbarians and became the bond, the medium, and the principle of civilization between the Roman and barbarian worlds. It is, then, the condition of the church rather than that of religion, properly so called, that we must look to, in order to discover what Christianity has, since then, added to modern civilization, and what new elements it has introduced therein. What was the Christian church at that period?

When we consider, always under a purely human point of view, the various revolutions which have accomplished themselves during the development of Christianity, from the time of its origin up to the fifth century; if, I repeat, we consider it simply as a community and not as a religious creed, we find that it passed through these essentially different states.

In the very earliest period, the Christian society presents itself as a simple association of a common creed and common sentiments; the first Christians united to enjoy together the same emotions, and the same religious convictions. We find among them no system of determinate doctrines, no rules, no discipline, no body of magistrates.

6. Still another theme in liberal polemic during the Great Debate of the 1820s was the central importance of publicity and freedom of information for the proper operation of representative government.

Of course, no society, however newly born, however weakly constituted it may be, exists without a moral power which animates and directs it. In the various Christian congregations there were men who preached, taught, and morally governed the congregation, but there was no formal magistrate, no recognized discipline; a simple association caused by a community of creed and sentiments was the primitive condition of the Christian society.

In proportion as it advanced—and very speedily, since traces are visible in the earliest monuments—a body of doctrines, of rules, of discipline, and of magistrates, began to appear; one kind of magistrates were called πρεσβυτεροι, or *ancients,* who became the priests; another, επισκοποι, or inspectors, or superintendents, who became bishops; a third διακονοι, or deacons, who were charged with the care of the poor, and with the distribution of alms.

It is scarcely possible to determine what were the precise functions of these various magistrates; the line of demarcation was probably very vague and variable, but what is clear is that an establishment was organized. Still, a peculiar character prevails in this second period: the preponderance and rule belonged to the body of the faithful. It was the body of the faithful which prevailed, both as to the choice of functionaries, and as to the adoption of discipline, and even doctrine. The church government and the Christian people were not as yet separated. They did not exist apart from, and independently of, one another; and the Christian people exercised the principal influence in the society.

In the third period all was different. A clergy existed who were distinct from the people, a body of priests who had their own riches, jurisdiction, and peculiar constitution; in a word, an entire government, which in itself was a complete society, a society provided with all the means of existence, independently of the society to which it had reference, and over which it extended its influence. Such was the third stage of the constitution of the Christian church; such was the form in which it appeared at the beginning of the fifth century. The government was not completely separated from the people; there has never been parallel kind of government, and less in religious matters than in any others; but in the relations of the clergy to the faithful, the clergy ruled almost without control.

The Christian clergy had moreover another and very different source
of influence. The bishops and the priests became the principal municipal
magistrates. You have seen, that of the Roman empire there remained,
properly speaking, nothing but the municipal system. It had happened,
from the vexations of despotism and the ruin of the towns, that the *curiales,*
or members of the municipal bodies, had become discouraged and apathetic; on the contrary, the bishops, and the body of priests, full of life and
zeal, offered themselves naturally for the superintendence and direction of
all matters. We should be wrong to reproach them for this, to tax them with
usurpation; it was all in the natural course of things; the clergy alone were
morally strong and animated; they became everywhere powerful. Such is
the law of the universe.[7]

The marks of this revolution are visible in all the legislation of the emperors at this period. If you open the code, either of Theodosius or of Jus-
tinian, you will find numerous regulations which remit municipal affairs to
the clergy and the bishops. Here are some of them:

"*Cod. Just. I. 1. tit. IV., de episcopali audientiâ.* § 26.—With respect to the
yearly affairs of cities, whether they concern the ordinary revenues of the
city, either from funds arising from the property of the city, or from private
gifts or legacies, or from any other source; whether public works, or depôts
of provisions, or aqueducts, or the maintenance of baths, or ports, or the
construction of walls or towers, or the repairing of bridges or roads, or trials
in which the city may be engaged in reference to public or private interests,
we ordain as follows:—The very pious bishop, and three notables chosen
from amongst the first men of the city, shall meet together; they shall, each
year, examine the works done; they shall take care that those who conduct
them, or who have conducted them, shall regulate them with precision,
render their accounts, and show that they have duly performed their engagements in the administration, whether of the public monuments, or of

---

7. Guizot uses his analysis of the way Christian bishops became the leading municipal
figures and magistrates as the Western Empire collapsed, to argue that moral influence—
influence resting on assent, on the hearts and minds of the ruled—is the only reliable or
lasting form of influence. In that sense one could say that Guizot's historical presupposi-
tions were more "idealist" than "materialist."

the sums appointed for provisions or baths, or of expenses in the maintenance of roads, aqueducts, or any other work.

"*Ibid.* § 30.—With regard to the guardianship of young persons of the first or second age, and of all those for whom the law appoints guardians, if their fortune does not exceed 500 *aurei,* we ordain that the nomination of the president of the province shall not be waited for, as this gives rise to great expenses, particularly if the said president do not reside in the city in which it is necessary to provide the guardianship. The nomination of guardians shall in such case be made by the magistrate of the city. . . . . . in concert with the very pious bishop and other person or persons invested with public offices, if there be more than one.

"*Ibid. I. 1. tit. LV., de defensoribus,* § 8.—We desire that the defenders of the cities, being well instructed in the holy mysteries of the orthodox faith, be chosen and instituted by the venerable bishops, the priests, the notables, the proprietors, and the *curiales.* As regards their installation, it shall be referred to the glorious power of the pretorian prefect, in order that their authority may have infused into it more solidity and vigour from the letters of admission of his Magnificence."

I might cite a great number of other laws, and you would everywhere meet with the fact which I have mentioned: between the municipal system of the Romans, and that of the middle ages, the municipal-ecclesiastic system interposed; the preponderance of the clergy in the affairs of the city succeeded that of the ancient municipal magistrates, and p receded the organization of the modern municipal corporations.

You perceive what prodigious power was thus obtained by the Christian church, as well by its own constitution, as by its influence upon the Christian people, and by the part which it took in civil affairs. Thus, from that epoch, it powerfully assisted in forming the character and furthering the development of modern civilization. Let us endeavour to sum up the elements which it from that time introduced into it.

And first of all there was an immense advantage in the presence of a moral influence, of a moral power, of a power which reposed solely upon convictions and upon moral creeds and sentiments, amidst the deluge of material power which at this time inundated society. Had the Christian church not existed, the whole world must have been abandoned to purely material force. The church alone exercised a moral power. It did more: it sustained, it spread abroad the idea of a rule, of a law superior to all human laws. It proposed, for the salvation of humanity, the fundamental belief, that there exists, above all human laws, a law which is denominated, according to periods and customs, sometimes reason, sometimes the divine law, but which, everywhere and always, is the same law under different names.

In short, with the church originated a great fact, the separation of spiritual and temporal power. This separation is the source of liberty of conscience; it is founded upon no other principle but that which is the foundation of the most perfect and extended freedom of conscience. The separation of temporal and spiritual power is based upon the idea that physical force has neither right nor influence over souls, over conviction, over truth. It flows from the distinction established between the world of thought and the world of action, between the world of internal and that of external facts. Thus this principle of liberty of conscience for which Europe has struggled so much, and suffered so much, this principle which prevailed so late, and often, in its progress, against the inclination of the clergy, was enunciated, under the name of the separation of temporal and spiritual power, in the very cradle of European civilization; and it was the Christian church which, from the necessity imposed by its situation of defending itself against barbarism, introduced and maintained it.

The presence, then, of a moral influence, the maintenance of a divine law, and the separation of the temporal and spiritual powers, are the three grand benefits which the Christian church in the fifth century conferred upon the European world.

Even at that time, however, all its influences were not equally salutary. Already, in the fifth century, there appeared in the church certain unwholesome principles, which have played a great part in the development of our civilization. Thus, at this period, there prevailed within it the separation of governors and the governed, the attempt to establish the independence of governors as regards the governed, to impose laws upon the governed, to possess their mind, their life, without the free consent of their reason and of their will. The church, moreover, endeavoured to render the theocratic principle predominant in society, to usurp the temporal power, to reign

exclusively. And when it could not succeed in obtaining temporal dominion, in inducing the prevalence of the theocratic principle, it allied itself
with temporal princes, and, in order to share, supported their absolute
power, at the expense of the liberty of the people.[8]

Such were the principles of civilization which Europe in the fifth century
derived from the church and from the Empire. It was in this condition that
the barbarians found the Roman world, and came to take possession of it.
In order to fully understand all the elements which met and mixed in the
cradle of our civilization, it only remains for us to study the barbarians.

When I speak of the barbarians, you understand that we have nothing to
do here with their history; narrative is not our present business. You know
that at this period, the conquerors of the Empire were nearly all of the same
race; they were all Germans, except some Sclavonic tribes, the Alani, for
example. We know also that they were all in pretty nearly the same stage of
civilization. Some difference, indeed, might have existed between them in
this respect, according to the greater or less degree of connexion which the
different tribes had had with the Roman world. Thus no doubt the Goths
were more advanced, possessed milder manners than the Franks. But in
considering matters under a general point of view, and in their results as regards ourselves, this original difference of civilization among the barbarous
people is of no importance.

It is the general condition of society among the barbarians that we need
to understand. But this is a subject with which, at the present day, it is
very difficult to make ourselves acquainted. We obtain without much difficulty a comprehension of the Roman municipal system, of the Christian
church; their influence has been continued up to our own days. We find
traces of it in numerous institutions and actual facts; we have a thousand
means of recognizing and explaining them. But the customs and social
condition of the barbarians have completely perished. We are compelled

---

8. Guizot's strictures on the growth of Papal and ecclesiastical power, on the separation
of the clergy from the people in the early middle ages, obviously had important Protestant
and Reformation roots. The Reformers had always liked to contrast the simplicity and
"democracy" of the primitive Church with the decadent and exploitative Church of the
later middle ages.

to make them out either from the earliest historical monuments, or by an effort of the imagination.

There is a sentiment, a fact, which, before all things, it is necessary that we should well understand, in order to represent faithfully to oneself the barbaric character: the pleasure of individual independence; the pleasure of enjoying oneself with vigour and liberty, amidst the chances of the world and of life; the delights of activity without labour; the taste for an adventurous career, full of uncertainty, inequality, and peril. Such was the predominating sentiment of the barbarous state, the moral want which put in motion these masses of human beings. In the present day, locked up as we are in so regular a society, it is difficult to realize this sentiment to oneself with all the power which it exercised over the barbarians of the fourth and fifth centuries. There is only one work, which, in my opinion, contains this characteristic of barbarism, stamped in all its energy: *The History of the Conquest of England by the Normans,* of M. Thierry, the only book wherein the motives, tendencies, and impulses which actuate men in a social condition, bordering on barbarism, are felt and reproduced with a really Homeric faithfulness. Nowhere else do we see so well the nature of a barbarian and of the life of a barbarian. Something of this sort is also found, though, in my opinion, in a much lower degree, with much less simplicity, much less truth, in Cooper's romances upon the savages of America.[9] There is something in the life of the American savages, in the relations and the sentiments they bear with them in the middle of the woods, that recalls, up to a certain point, the manners of the ancient Germans. No doubt these pictures are somewhat idealized, somewhat poetic; the dark side of the barbaric manners and life is not presented to us in all its grossness. I speak not only of the evils induced by these manners upon the social state, but of the internal and individual condition of the barbarian himself. There was,

9. Doubtless Guizot was influenced by an enormous European vogue for the novels of James Fenimore Cooper in the 1820s. Cooper's rather idealized accounts of the savage independence of the North American Indians, their hatred of constraint, probably helped to suggest a comparison with the Germanic invaders of the Western Roman Empire. The comparison fascinated some of Guizot's audience, notably the young Alexis de Tocqueville. One of Tocqueville's hopes when visiting the United States in 1831–2 was that he would be able to observe at first hand "a social condition" which had once played such an important part in European history but now survived chiefly in the Americas.

within this passionate want of personal independence, something more gross and more material than one would be led to conceive from the work of M. Thierry; there was a degree of brutality and of apathy which is not always exactly conveyed by his recitals. Nevertheless, when we look to the bottom of the question, notwithstanding this alloy of brutality, of materialism, of dull, stupid selfishness, the love of independence is a noble and a moral sentiment, which draws its power from the moral nature of man; it is the pleasure of feeling oneself a man, the sentiment of personality, of human spontaneity in its free development.

It was through the German barbarians that this sentiment was introduced into European civilization; it was unknown in the Roman world, unknown in the Christian church, and unknown in almost all the ancient civilizations. When you find liberty in ancient civilizations, it is political liberty, the liberty of the citizen: man strove not for his personal liberty, but for his liberty as a citizen: he belonged to an association, he was devoted to an association, he was ready to sacrifice himself to an association.[10] It was the same with the Christian church: a sentiment of strong attachment to the Christian corporation, of devotion to its laws, and a lively desire to extend its empire; or rather, the religious sentiment induced a reaction of man upon himself, upon his soul, an internal effort to subdue his own liberty, and to submit himself to the will of his faith. But the sentiment of personal independence, a love of liberty displaying itself at all risks, without any other motive but that of satisfying itself; this sentiment, I repeat, was unknown to the Roman and to the Christian society. It was by the barbarians that it was brought in and deposited in the cradle of modern civilization, wherein it has played so conspicuous a part, has produced such worthy results, that it is impossible to help reckoning it as one of its fundamental elements.

10. Here Guizot draws on Benjamin Constant's important essay *On Ancient and Modern Liberty* (1819). In this essay Constant tries to subdue the pre-Revolutionary enthusiasm (associated especially with Rousseau's) for the ancient *polis* or city-state by demonstrating that the modern conception of liberty—as a private sphere of choice protected by individual rights—differs radically from the ancient conception of liberty as citizens sharing in public decision-making and the exercise of power.

There is a second fact, a second element of civilization, for which we are equally indebted to the barbarians: this is military clientship; the bond which established itself between individuals, between warriors, and which, without destroying the liberty of each, without even in the beginning destroying, beyond a certain point, the equality which almost completely existed between them, nevertheless founded an hierarchical subordination, and gave birth to that aristocratical organization, which afterwards became feudalism. The foundation of this relation was the attachment of man to man, the fidelity of individual to individual, without external necessity, and without obligation based upon the general principles of society. In the ancient republics you see no man attached freely and especially to any other man; they were all attached to the city. Among the barbarians it was between individuals that the social bond was formed; first by the relation of the chief to his companion, when they lived in the condition of a band wandering over Europe; and, later, by the relation of suzerain to vassal. This second principle, which has played so great a part in the history of modern civilization, this devotion of man to man, came to us from the barbarians; it is from their manners that it has passed into ours.

I ask you, was I wrong in saying at the beginning, that modern civilization, even in its cradle, had been as varied, as agitated, and as confused as I have endeavoured to describe it to you in the general picture I have given you of it? Is it not true that we have now discovered, at the fall of the Roman empire, almost all the elements which unite in the progressive development of our civilization? We have found, at that time, three wholly different societies: the municipal society, the last remains of the Roman empire; the Christian society; and the Barbaric society. We find these societies very variously organized, founded upon totally different principles, inspiring men with wholly different sentiments; we find the craving after the most absolute independence side by side with the most complete submission; military patronage side by side with ecclesiastical dominion; the spiritual and temporal powers everywhere present; the canons of the church, the learned legislation of the Romans, the almost unwritten customs of the barbarians; everywhere the mixture, or rather the co-existence of the most diverse races, languages, social situations, manners, ideas, and impressions. Herein I think we have a sufficient proof of the faithfulness of the general character under which I have endeavoured to present our civilization to you.

No doubt, this confusion, this diversity, this struggle, have cost us very dear; these have been the cause of the slow progress of Europe, of the storms and sufferings to which she has been a prey. Nevertheless, I do not think we need regret them. To people, as well as to individuals, the chance of the most complete and varied development, the chance of an almost unlimited progress in all directions, compensates of itself alone for all that it may cost to obtain the right of casting for it. And, all things considered, this state, so agitated, so toilsome, so violent, has availed much more than the simplicity with which other civilizations present themselves; the human race has gained thereby more than it has suffered.

We are now acquainted with the general features of the condition in which the fall of the Roman empire left the world; we are acquainted with the different elements which were agitated and became mingled, in order to give birth to European civilization. Henceforth we shall see them advancing and acting under our eyes. In the next lecture I shall endeavour to show what they became, and what they effected in the epoch which we are accustomed to call the times of barbarism; that is to say, while the chaos of invasion yet existed.

THIRD LECTURE

Object of the lecture—All the various systems pretend to be legitimate—What is political legitimacy?—Co-existence of all systems of government in the fifth century—Instability in the condition of persons, properties, and institutions—There were two causes of this, one material, the continuation of the invasion; the other moral, the selfish sentiment of individuality peculiar to the barbarians—The germs of civilization have been the necessity for order, the recollections of the Roman empire, the Christian church, and the barbarians—Attempts at organization by the barbarians, by the towns, by the church of Spain, by Charlemagne, and Alfred—The German and Arabian invasions cease—The feudal system begins.

I HAVE PLACED BEFORE YOU the fundamental elements of European civilization, tracing them to its very cradle, at the moment of the fall of the Roman empire. I have endeavoured to give you a glimpse beforehand of their diversity, and their constant struggle, and to show you that no one of them succeeded in reigning over our society, or at least in reigning over it so completely as to enslave or expel the others. We have seen that this was the distinguishing character of European civilization. We now come to its history at its commencement, in the ages which it is customary to call the barbarous.

At the first glance we cast upon this epoch, it is impossible not to be struck with a fact which seems to contradict what we have lately said. When you examine certain notions which are accredited concerning the antiquities of modern Europe, you will perceive that the various elements of our civilization, the monarchical, theocratical, aristocratical, and democratical principles, all pretend that European society originally belonged to them, and that they have only lost the sole dominion by the usurpations of contrary principles. Question all that has been written, all that has been said upon this subject, and you will see that all the systems whereby our beginnings are sought to be represented or explained, maintain the exclusive predominance of one or other of the elements of European civilization.

Thus there is a school of feudal publicists, of whom the most celebrated is M. de Boulainvilliers, who pretend that, after the fall of the Roman empire, it was the conquering nation, subsequently become the nobility, which possessed all powers and rights; that society was its domain; that kings and peoples have despoiled it of this domain; that aristocratic organization was the primitive and true form of Europe.

Beside this school, you will find that of the monarchists, the abbé Dubos, for instance, who maintain, on the contrary, that it was to royalty European society belonged. The German kings, say they, inherited all the rights of the Roman emperors; they had even been called in by the ancient nations, the Gauls among others; they alone ruled legitimately; all the acquisitions of the aristocracy were only encroachments upon monarchy.

A third party presents itself, that of the liberal publicists, republicans, democrats, or whatever you like to call them. Consult the abbé de Mably; according to him, it is to the system of free institutions, to the association of free men, to the people properly so called, that the government of society devolved from the period of the fifth century: nobles and kings enriched themselves with the spoils of primitive freedom; it sank beneath their attacks, indeed, but it reigned before them.

And above all these monarchical, aristocratical, and popular pretensions, rises the theocratical pretension of the church, who affirms, that in virtue of her very mission, of her divine title, society belonged to her; that she alone had the right to govern it; that she alone was the legitimate queen of the European world, won over by her labours to civilization and to truth.

See then the position in which we are placed! We fancied we had shown that no one of the elements of European civilization had exclusively ruled in the course of its history; that those elements had existed in a constant state of vicinity, of amalgamation, of combat, and of compromise; and yet, at our very first step, we meet with the directly contrary opinion, that, even in its cradle, in the bosom of barbaric Europe, it was such or such a one of their elements which alone possessed society. And it is not only in a single country, but in all the countries of Europe, that, beneath slightly different forms, at different periods, the various principles of our civilization have manifested these irreconcilable pretensions. The historical schools we have just characterized, are to be met with everywhere.

This is an important fact—important not in itself, but because it reveals other facts which hold a conspicuous place in our history. From this simultaneous setting forth of the most opposite pretensions to the exclusive possession of power in the first age of modern Europe, two remarkable facts become apparent. The first the principle, the idea of political legitimacy; an idea which has played a great part in the course of European civilization. The second the veritable and peculiar character of the condition of barbaric Europe, of that epoch with which we are at present especially concerned.

I shall endeavour to demonstrate these two facts, to deduce them successively from this combat of primitive pretensions which I have just described.

What do the various elements of European civilization, the theocratical, monarchical, aristocratical, and popular elements pretend to, when they wish to appear the first who possessed society in Europe? Do they not thus pretend to have been alone legitimate? Political legitimacy is evidently a right founded upon antiquity, upon duration; priority in time is appealed to as the source of the right, as the proof of the legitimacy of power. And observe, I pray you, that this pretension is not peculiar to any one system, to any one element of our civilization; it extends to all. In modern times we are accustomed to consider the idea of legitimacy as existing in only one system, the monarchical. In this we are mistaken; it is discoverable in all. You have already seen that all the elements of our civilization have equally desired to appropriate it. If we enter into the subsequent history of Europe, we shall find the most different social forms and governments equally in possession of their character of legitimacy. The Italian and Swiss aristocracies and democracies, the republic of San Marino, as well as the greatest monarchies of Europe, have called themselves, and have been regarded as, legitimate; the former, like the latter, have founded their pretension to legitimacy upon the antiquity of their institutions, and upon the historical priority and perpetuity of their system of government.

If you leave Europe and direct your attention to other times and other countries, you everywhere meet with this idea of political legitimacy; you find it attaching itself everywhere to some portion of the government, to some institution, form, or maxim. There has been no country, and no time, in which there has not existed a certain portion of the social system, public powers, which has not attributed to itself, and in which has not been recognized this character of legitimacy, derived from antiquity and long duration.

What is this principle? what are its elements? how has it introduced itself into European civilization?

At the origin of all powers, I say of all without any distinction, we meet with physical force. I do not mean to state that force alone has founded them all, or that if, in their origin, they had not had other titles than that of force, they would have been established. Other titles are manifestly necessary; powers have become established in consequence of certain social expediences, of certain references to the state of society, manners, and opinions. But it is impossible to avoid perceiving that physical force has stained the origin of all the powers of the world, whatever may have been their character and form.

Yet none will have anything to say to this origin; all powers, whatever they may be, reject it; none will admit themselves the offspring of force. An unconquerable instinct warns governments that force does not found right, and that if force was their origin, their right could never be established. This, then, is the reason why, when we go back to early times, and there find the various systems and powers a prey to violence, all exclaim, "I was anterior to all this, I existed previously, in virtue of other titles; society belonged to me before this state of violence and struggle in which you meet with me; I was legitimate, but others contested and seized my rights."

This fact alone proves that the idea of force is not the foundation of political legitimacy, but that it reposes upon a totally different basis. What, indeed, is done by all these systems in thus formally disavowing force? They themselves proclaim that there is another kind of legitimacy, the true foundation of all others, the legitimacy of reason, justice, and right; and this is the origin with which they desire to connect themselves. It is because they wish it not to be supposed that they are the offspring of force, that they pretend to be invested in the name of their antiquity, with a different title. The first characteristic, then, of political legitimacy, is to reject physical force as a source of power, and to connect it with a moral idea, with a moral force, with the idea of right, of justice, and of reason. This is the fundamental element from which the principle of political legitimacy has issued. It has issued thence by the help of antiquity and long duration. And in this manner:

After physical force has presided at the birth of all governments, of all societies, time progresses; it alters the works of force, it corrects them, corrects them by the very fact that a society endures, and is composed of men. Man carries within himself certain notions of order, justice, and reason, a certain desire to induce their prevalence, to introduce them into the circumstances among which he lives; he labours unceasingly at this task; and if the social condition in which he is placed continues, he labours always with a certain effect. Man places reason, morality, and legitimacy in the world in which he lives.[1]

Independently of the work of man, by a law of Providence which it is impossible to mistake, a law analogous to that which regulates the material world, there is a certain measure of order, reason, and justice, which is absolutely necessary to the duration of a society. From the single fact of its duration, we may conclude that a society is not wholly absurd, insensate, and iniquitous; that it is not utterly deprived of that element of reason, truth, and justice, which alone gives life to societies. If, moreover, the society develops itself, if it becomes more vigorous and more powerful, if the social condition from day to day is accepted by a greater number of men, it is because it gathers by the action of time more reason, justice, and right; because circumstances regulate themselves, step by step, according to true legitimacy.

---

1. Here again Guizot draws on Maine de Biran's distinction between "active" and "passive" experience by arguing that man "places reason, morality and legitimacy in the world in which he lives." There is an important parallel here with the emphasis in late eighteenth-century German philosophy and historiography on man as a social being who creates cultures. But Maine de Biran's framework, and *a fortiori* Guizot's, is more individualist, less preoccupied with the people or *volk*.

Thus the idea of political legitimacy penetrates the world, and men's minds, from the world. It has for its foundation and first origin, in a certain measure at least, moral legitimacy, justice, reason, and truth, and afterwards the sanction of time, which gives cause for believing that reason has won entrance into facts, and that true legitimacy has been introduced into the external world. At the epoch which we are about to study, we shall find force and falsehood hovering over the cradle of royalty, of aristocracy, of democracy, and of the church herself; you will everywhere behold force and falsehood reforming themselves, little by little, under the hand of time, right and truth taking their places in civilization. It is this introduction of right and truth into the social state, which has developed, step by step, the idea of political legitimacy; it is thus that it has been established in modern civilization.

When, therefore, attempts have at different times been made to raise this idea as the banner of absolute power, it has been perverted from its true origin. So far is it from being the banner of absolute power, that it is only in the name of right and justice that it has penetrated and taken root in the world. It is not exclusive; it belongs to no one in particular, but springs up wherever right develops itself. Political legitimacy attaches itself to liberty as well as to power; to individual rights, as well as to the forms according to which public functions are exercised. We shall meet with it, in our way, in the most contrary systems; in the feudal system, in the municipalities of Flanders and Germany, in the Italian republics, no less than in monarchy. It is a character spread over the various elements of modern civilization, and which it is necessary to understand thoroughly on entering upon its history.

The second fact which clearly reveals itself in the simultaneous pretensions of which I spoke in the beginning, is the true character of the so called barbarian epoch. All the elements of European civilization pretend at this time to have possessed Europe; it follows that none of them predominated. When a social form predominates in the world, it is not so difficult to recognize it. On coming to the tenth century we shall recognize, without hesitation, the predominance of the feudal system; in the seventeenth century we shall not hesitate to affirm that the monarchical system prevails; if we look to the municipalities of Flanders, to the Italian republics, we shall immediately declare the empire of the democratic principle. When there is really any predominating principle in society, it is impossible to mistake it.

The dispute which has arisen between the various systems that have had a share in European civilization, upon the question, which predominated at its origin, proves, then, that they all co-existed, without any one of them prevailing generally enough, or certainly enough to give to society its form and its name.

Such, then, is the character of the barbarian epoch; it was the chaos of all elements, the infancy of all systems, an universal turmoil, in which even strife was not permanent or systematic. By examining all the aspects of the social state at this period, I might show you that it is impossible anywhere to discover a single fact, or a single principle, which was anything like general or established. I shall confine myself to two essential points: the condition of individuals, and the condition of institutions. That will be enough to paint the entire society.

At this period we meet with four classes of persons—1. The free men; that is to say, those who depended upon no superior, upon no patron, and who possessed their property and regulated their life in complete liberty, without any bond of obligation to any other man. 2. The *leudes, fideles, anstrustions,* &c., bound at first by the relation of companion to chief, and afterwards by that of vassal to suzerain, to another man, towards whom, on account of a grant of lands, or other gifts, they had contracted the obligation of service. 3. The freedman. 4. The slaves.

But were these various classes fixed? Did men, when once they were inclosed in their limits, remain there? Had the relations of the various classes anything of regularity and permanence? By no means. You constantly behold freemen who leave their position to place themselves in the service of some one, receiving from him some gift or other, and passing into the class of *leudes;* others you see who fall into the class of slaves. Elsewhere *leudes* are seen struggling to separate themselves from their patrons, to again become independent, to re-enter the class of freemen. Everywhere you behold a movement, a continual passage of one class into another; an uncertainty, a general instability in the relations of the classes; no man remaining in his position, no position remaining the same.

Landed properties were in the same condition. You know that these were distinguished as allodial, or wholly free, and beneficiary, or subject to certain obligations with regard to a superior: you know how an attempt has been made to establish, in this last class of properties, a precise and defined system; it has been said that the benefices were at first given for a certain determinate number of years, afterwards for life, and that finally they became hereditary. A vain attempt! All these kinds of tenure existed without order and simultaneously; we meet, at the same moment, with benefices for a fixed time, for life, and hereditary; the same lands, indeed, passed in a few years through these different states. There was nothing more stable in the condition of lands than in that of individuals. On all sides was felt the laborious transition of the wandering to the sedentary life, of personal relations to the combined relations of men and properties, or to real relations. During this transition all is confused, local, and disordered.[2]

In the institutions we find the same instability, the same chaos. Three systems of institutions co-existed: royalty; aristocratic institutions, or the dependence of men and lands one upon another; and free institutions, that is to say, the assemblies of free men deliberating in common. None of these systems was in possession of society; none of them prevailed over the others. Free institutions existed, but the men who should have taken part in the assemblies rarely attended them. The signorial jurisdiction was not more regularly exercised. Royalty, which is the simplest of institutions, and the easiest to determine, had no fixed character; it was partly elective, partly hereditary. Sometimes the son succeeded the father; sometimes a selection was made from the family; sometimes it was a simple election of a distant relation, or of a stranger. In no system will you find anything fixed; all institutions, as well as all social situations, existed together, became confounded, and were continually changing.

In states the same fluctuation prevailed: they were erected and suppressed, united and divided; there were no boundaries, no governments,

---

2. The emphasis on property relations and class structure in Guizot—the more "materialist" aspect of his historiography—is of course what especially influenced Karl Marx in the 1840s. It is only if the influence of Maine de Biran's voluntarist philosophy on Guizot's conception of historical explanation is ignored, that Guizot can be seen as a proto-Marxist. But that does serious injustice to the complexity of his argument.

no distinct people; but a general confusion of situations, principles, facts, races, and languages: such was barbarous Europe.

Within what limits is this strange period bounded? Its origin is well marked; it begins with the fall of the Roman empire. But when did it conclude? In order to answer this question, we must learn to what this condition of society is to be attributed, what were the causes of this barbarism.

I think I can perceive two principal causes: the one material, arising from without, in the course of events; the other moral, originating from within, from man himself.

The material cause was the continuation of the invasion. We must not fancy that the invasion of the barbarians ceased in the fifth century; we must not think that, because Rome was fallen, we shall immediately find the barbaric kingdoms founded upon its ruins, or that the movement was at an end. This movement lasted long after the fall of the empire; the proofs of this are manifest.

See the Frank kings, even of the first race, called continually to make war beyond the Rhine; Clotaire, Dagobert constantly engaged in expeditions into Germany, fighting against the Thuringians, Danes, and Saxons, who occupied the right bank of the Rhine. Wherefore? Because these nations wished to cross the river, to come and take their share of the spoils of the empire. Whence, about the same time, those great invasions of Italy by the Franks established in Gaul, and principally by the eastern or Austrasian Franks? They attacked Switzerland; passed the Alps; entered Italy. Why? Because they were pressed, on the north-east, by new populations; their expeditions were not merely forays for pillage, they were matters of necessity; they were disturbed in their settlements, and went elsewhere to seek their fortune. A new Germanic nation appeared upon the stage, and founded in Italy the kingdom of the Lombards. In Gaul, the Frank dynasty changed; the Carlovingians succeeded the Merovingians. It is now acknowledged that this change of dynasty was, to say the truth, a fresh invasion of Gaul by the Franks, a movement of nations, which substituted the eastern for the western Franks. The change was completed; the second race now governed. Charlemagne commenced against the Saxons what the Merovingians had done against the Thuringians; he was incessantly engaged in war against the nations beyond the Rhine. Who urged these on?

The Obotrites, the Wiltzes, the Sorabes, the Bohemians, the entire Sclavonic race which pressed upon the Germanic, and from the sixth to the ninth century compelled it to advance towards the west. Everywhere to the north-east the movement of invasion continued and determined events.

In the south, a movement of the same nature exhibited itself: the Moslem Arabs appeared. While the Germanic and Sclavonic people pressed on along the Rhine and Danube, the Arabs began their expeditions and conquests upon all the coasts of the Mediterranean.

The invasion of the Arabs had a peculiar character. The spirit of conquest and the spirit of proselytism were united. The invasion was to conquer a territory and disseminate a faith. There was a great difference between this movement and that of the Germans. In the Christian world, the spiritual and temporal powers were distinct. The desire of propagating a creed and making a conquest, did not co-exist in the same men. The Germans, when they became converted, preserved their manners, sentiments, and tastes; terrestrial passions and interests continued to rule them; they became Christians, but not missionaries. The Arabs, on the contrary, were both conquerors and missionaries; the power of the sword and that of the word, with them, were in the same hands. At a later period, this character determined the unfortunate turn taken by Mussulman civilization; it is in the combination of the spiritual and temporal powers, in the confusion of moral and material authority, that the tyranny which seems inherent in this civilization originated. This I conceive to be the cause of the stationary condition into which that civilization is everywhere fallen. But the fact did not make its appearance at first; on the contrary, it added prodigious force to the Arab invasion. Undertaken with moral passions and ideas, it immediately obtained a splendour and a greatness which was wanting to the German invasion; it exhibited far more energy and enthusiasm, and far differently influenced the minds of men.

Such was the state of Europe, from the fifth to the ninth century: pressed on the south by the Mahometans, on the north by the Germans and the Sclavonic tribes, it was scarcely possible that the reaction of this double invasion should do other than hold the interior of Europe in continual disorder. The populations were constantly being displaced, and forced one upon the other; nothing of a fixed character could be established;

the wandering life recommenced on all sides. There was, no doubt, some difference in this respect in the different states: the chaos was greater in Germany than in the rest of Europe, Germany being the focus of the movement; France was more agitated than Italy. But in no place could society settle or regulate itself; barbarism continued on all sides, from the same cause that had originated it.

So much for the material cause, that which arose from the course of events. I now come to the moral cause, which sprang from the internal condition of man, and which was no less powerful.

After all, whatever external events may be, it is man himself who makes the world; it is in proportion to the ideas, sentiments, and dispositions, moral and intellectual, of man, that the world becomes regulated and progressive; it is upon the internal condition of man that the visible condition of society depends.

What is required to enable men to found a society with anything of durability and regularity? It is evidently necessary that they should have a certain number of ideas sufficiently extended to suit that society, to apply to its wants, to its relations. It is necessary, moreover, that these ideas should be common to the greater number of the members of the society; finally, that they should exercise a certain empire over their wills and actions.

It is clear, that if men have no ideas extending beyond their own existence, if their intellectual horizon is confined to themselves, if they are abandoned to the tempest of their passions and their wills, if they have not among them a certain number of notions and sentiments in common, around which to rally, it is clear, I say, that between them no society is possible, and that each individual must be a principle of disturbance and dissolution to any association which he may enter.

Wherever individuality predominates almost exclusively, wherever man considers no one but himself, and his ideas do not extend beyond himself, and he obeys nothing but his own passions, society (I mean a society somewhat extended and permanent) becomes for him almost impossible. Such, however, was the moral condition of the conquerors of Europe, at the time upon which we are now occupied. I remarked in my last lecture that we are indebted to the Germans for an energetic sentiment of individual liberty, of human individuality. But in a state of extreme barbarism and ignorance, this sentiment becomes selfishness in all its brutality, in all its insociability. From the fifth to the eighth century it was at this point among the Germans. They cared only for their own interests, their own passions, their own will: how could they be reconciled to a condition even approximating to the social? Attempts were made to prevail upon them to enter it; they attempted to do so themselves. But they immediately abandoned it by some act of carelessness, some burst of passion, some want of intelligence. Constantly did society attempt to form itself; constantly was it destroyed by the act of man, by the absence of the moral conditions under which alone it can exist.

Such were the two determining causes of the barbarous state. So long as these were prolonged, barbarism endured. Let us see how and when they at last terminated.

Europe laboured to escape from this condition. It is in the nature of man, even when he has been plunged into such a condition by his own fault, not to desire to remain in it. However rude, however ignorant, however devoted to his own interests and to his own passions he may be, there is within him a voice and an instinct, which tells him that he was made for better things, that he has other powers, another destiny. In the midst of disorder, the love of order and of progress pursues and harasses him. The need of justice, foresight, development, agitates him even under the yoke of the most brutal selfishness. He feels himself impelled to reform the material world, and society, and himself; and he labours to do this, though unaware of the nature of the want which urges him. The barbarians aspired after civilization, while totally incapable of it, nay more, detesting it from the instant that they became acquainted with its law.

There remained, moreover, considerable wrecks of the Roman civilization. The name of the Empire, the recollection of that great and glorious society, disturbed the memories of men, particularly of the senators of towns, of bishops, priests, and all those who had had their origin in the Roman world.

Among the barbarians themselves, or their barbaric ancestors, many had been witnesses of the grandeur of the Empire; they had served in its armies, they had conquered it. The image and name of Roman civilization had an imposing influence upon them, and they experienced the desire of imitating, of reproducing, of preserving something of it. This was another cause which urged them to quit the condition of barbarism I have described.

There was a third cause which suggests itself to every mind; I mean the Christian church. The church was a society regularly constituted, having its principles, its rules, and its discipline, and experiencing an ardent desire to extend its influence and conquer its conquerors. Among the Christians of this period, among the Christian clergy, there were men who had thought upon all moral and political questions, who had decided opinions and energetic sentiments upon all subjects, and a vivid desire to propagate and give them empire. Never has any other society made such efforts to influence the surrounding world, and to stamp thereon its own likeness, as were made by the Christian church between the fifth and the tenth centuries.[3] When we come to study its particular history, we shall see all that it has done. It attacked barbarism, as it were, at every point, in order to civilize by ruling over it.

Finally, there was a fourth cause of civilization, a cause which it is impossible fitly to appreciate, but which is not therefore the less real, and this is the appearance of great men. No one can say why a great man appears at a certain epoch, and what he adds to the development of the world; that is a secret of Providence: but the fact is not therefore less certain. There are men whom the spectacle of anarchy and social stagnation strikes and revolts, who are intellectually shocked therewith as with a fact which ought not to exist, and are possessed with an unconquerable desire of changing it, a desire of giving some rule, somewhat of the general, regular, and permanent to the world before them. A terrible and often tyrannical power, which commits a thousand crimes, a thousand errors, for human weakness attends it; a power, nevertheless, glorious and salutary, for it gives to humanity, and with the hand of man, a vigorous impulse forward, a mighty movement.

These different causes and forces led, between the fifth and ninth centuries, to various attempts at extricating European society from barbarism.

3. Guizot's emphasis on the role of the Christian Church in "civilizing" the Germanic tribes invading Western Europe is part of his enterprise of combating the anti-clericalism which had dominated eighteenth-century French thought and led by the 1820s to the association of Christianity with the forces of social reaction and obscurantism.

The first attempt, which, although but slightly effective, must not be overlooked, since it emanated from the barbarians themselves, was the drawing up of the barbaric laws: between the sixth and eighth centuries the laws of almost all the barbarous people were written. Before this they had not been written; the barbarians had been governed simply by customs, until they established themselves upon the ruins of the Roman empire. We may reckon the laws of the Burgundians, of the Salian and Ripuarian Franks, of the Visigoths, of the Lombards, the Saxons, the Frisons, the Bavarians, the Alemanni, &c. Here was manifestly a beginning of civilization; an endeavour to bring society under general and regular principles. The success of this attempt could not be great: it was writing the laws of a society which no longer existed, the laws of the social state of the barbarians before their establishment upon the Roman territory, before they had exchanged the wandering for the sedentary life, the condition of nomade warriors for that of proprietors. We find, indeed, here and there, some articles concerning the lands which the barbarians had conquered, and concerning their relations with the ancient inhabitants of the country; but the foundation of the greater part of their laws is the ancient mode of life, the ancient German condition; they were inapplicable to the new society, and occupied only a trifling place in its development.

At the same time, another kind of attempt was made in Italy and the south of Gaul. Roman society had not so completely perished there as elsewhere; a little more order and life remained in the cities. There civilization attempted to lift again its head. If, for example, we look to the kingdom of the Ostrogoths in Italy under Theodoric, we see even under the dominion of a barbarous king and nation the municipal system, taking breath, so to speak, and influencing the general course of events. Roman society had acted upon the Goths, and had to a certain degree impressed them with its likeness. The same fact is visible in the south of Gaul. It was at the commencement of the sixth century that a Visigoth king of Toulouse, Alaric, caused the Roman laws to be collected, and published a code for his Roman subjects under the name of the *Breviarium Aniani*.

In Spain it was another power—namely, that of the church, which tried to revive civilization. In place of the ancient German assemblies, the assemblies of warriors, it was the council of Toledo which prevailed in Spain;

and although distinguished laymen attended this council, the bishops had dominion there. Look at the law of the Visigoths; you will see that it is not a barbarous law; it was evidently compiled by the philosophers of the time, the clergy. It abounds in general ideas, in theories, theories wholly foreign to barbarous manners. Thus: you know that the legislation of the barbarians was a personal legislation—that is to say, that the same law applied only to men of the same race. The Roman law governed the Romans, the Frank law governed the Franks; each people had its law, although they were united under the same government and inhabited the same territory. This is what is called the system of personal legislation, in opposition to that of real legislation fixed upon the territory. Well, the legislation of the Visigoths was not personal, but fixed upon the territory. All the inhabitants of Spain, Visigoths and Romans, were subject to the same law. Continue your investigation, and you will find yet more evident traces of philosophy. Among the barbarians, men had, according to their relative situations, a determinate value; the barbarian, the Roman, the freeman, the vassal, &c., were not held at the same price, there was a tariff of their lives. The principle of the equal value of men in the eye of the law was established in the law of the Visigoths. Look to the system of procedure, and you find, in place of the oath of *compurgatores,* or the judicial combat, the proof by witnesses, and a rational investigation of the matter in question, such as might be prosecuted in a civilized society. In short, the whole Visigoth law bears a wise, systematic, and social character. We may perceive herein the work of the same clergy who prevailed in the councils of Toledo, and so powerfully influenced the government of the country.

In Spain, then, up to the great invasion of the Arabs, it was the theocratic principle which attempted the revival of civilization.

In France the same endeavour was the work of a different power; it came from the great men, above all from Charlemagne.[4] Examine his reign under its various aspects; you will see that his predominating idea was the design of civilizing his people. First, let us consider his wars. He was constantly

4. In discussing the role of "great men," and especially that of Charlemagne, in European history, Guizot evidently has parallels with Napoleon's recent career in mind. That parallel he develops at length in his lectures on the *History of Civilization in France* (1828–30).

in the field, from the south to the north-east, from the Ebro to the Elbe or the Weser. Can you believe that these were mere wilful expeditions, arising simply from the desire of conquest? By no means. I do not mean to say that all that he did is to be fully explained, or that there existed much diplomacy or strategic skill in his plans; but he obeyed a great necessity—a strong desire of suppressing barbarism. He was engaged during the whole of his reign in arresting the double invasion—the Mussulman invasion on the south, and the German and Sclavonic invasion on the north. This is the military character of the reign of Charlemagne; his expedition against the Saxons had no other origin and no other purpose.

If you turn from his wars to his internal government, you will there meet with a fact of the same nature—the attempt to introduce order and unity into the administration of all the countries which he possessed. I do not wish to employ the word *kingdom* nor the word *state*; for these expressions convey too regular a notion, and suggest ideas which are little in harmony with the society over which Charlemagne presided. But this is certain, that being master of an immense territory, he felt indignant at seeing all things incoherent, anarchical, and rude, and desired to alter their hideous condition. First of all he acted by means of his *missi dominici*, whom he dispatched into the various parts of his territory, in order that they might observe circumstances and reform them, or give an account of them to him. He afterwards worked by means of general assemblies, which he held with much more regularity than his predecessors had done. At these assemblies he caused all the most considerable persons of the territory to be present. They were not free assemblies, nor did they at all resemble the kind of deliberations with which we are acquainted; they were merely a means taken by Charlemagne of being well informed of facts, and of introducing some order and unity among his disorderly populations.

Under whatever point of view you consider the reign of Charlemagne, you will always find in it the same character, namely, warfare against the barbarous state, the spirit of civilization; this is what appears in his eagerness to establish schools, in his taste for learned men, in the favour with which he regarded ecclesiastical influence, and in all that he thought proper to do, whether as regarded the entire society or individual man.

An attempt of the same kind was made somewhat later in England by King Alfred.

Thus the different causes to which I have directed attention, as tending to put an end to barbarism, were in action in some part or other of Europe from the fifth to the ninth century.

None succeeded. Charlemagne was unable to found his great empire, and the system of government which he desired to establish therein. In Spain, the church succeeded no better in establishing the theocratic principle. In Italy and in the south of Gaul, although Roman civilization often attempted to rise again, it was not till afterwards, towards the end of the tenth century, that it really re-acquired any vigour. Up to that time all efforts to terminate barbarism proved abortive; they supposed that men were more advanced than they truly were; they all desired, under various forms, a society more extended or more regular than was compatible with the distribution of power and the condition of men's minds. Nevertheless, they had not been wholly useless. At the beginning of the tenth century, neither the great empire of Charlemagne nor the glorious councils of Toledo were any longer spoken of; but barbarism had not the less arrived at its extreme term—two great results had been obtained.

I. The movement of the invasions on the north and south had been arrested: after the dismemberment of the empire of Charlemagne, the states established on the right bank of the Rhine opposed a powerful barrier to the tribes who continued to urge their way westward. The Normans prove this incontestably; up to this period, if we except the tribes which cast themselves upon England, the movement of maritime invasions had not been very considerable. It was during the ninth century that it became constant and general. And this was because invasions by land were become very difficult, society having, on this side, acquired more fixed and certain frontiers. That portion of the wandering population which could not be driven back, was constrained to turn aside and carry on its roving life upon the sea. Whatever evils were done in the west by Norman expeditions, they were far less fatal than invasions by land; they disturbed dawning society far less generally.

In the south, the same fact declared itself. The Arabs were quartered in Spain; warfare continued between them and the Christians, but it no longer entailed the displacement of the population. Saracenic bands still, from time to time, infested the coasts of the Mediterranean; but the grand progress of Islamism had evidently ceased.

II. At this period we see the wandering life ceasing, in its turn, throughout the interior of Europe; populations established themselves; property became fixed; and the relations of men no longer varied from day to day, at the will of violence or chance. The internal and moral condition of man himself began to change; his ideas and sentiments, like his life, acquired fixedness; he attached himself to the places which he inhabited, to the relations which he had contracted there, to those domains which he began to promise himself that he would bequeath to his children, to that dwelling which one day he will call his castle, to that miserable collection of colonists and slaves which will one day become a village. Everywhere little societies, little states, cut, so to speak, to the measure of the ideas and the wisdom of man, formed themselves. Between these societies was gradually introduced the bond, of which the customs of barbarism contained the germ, the bond of a confederation which did not annihilate individual independence. On the one hand, every considerable person established himself in his domains, alone with his family and servitors; on the other hand, a certain hierarchy of services and rights became established between these warlike proprietors scattered over the land. What was this? The feudal system rising definitively from the bosom of barbarism. Of the various elements of our civilization, it was natural that the Germanic element should first prevail; it had strength on its side, it had conquered Europe; from it Europe was to receive its earliest social form and organization. This is what happened. Feudalism, its character, and the part played by it in the history of European civilization, will be the subject-matter of my next lecture; and, in the bosom of that victorious feudal system, we shall meet, at every step, with the other elements of our civilization—royalty, the church, municipal corporations; and we shall foresee without difficulty that they are not destined to sink beneath this feudal form, to which they become assimilated, while struggling against it, and while waiting the hour when victory shall visit them in their turn.

FOURTH LECTURE

Object of the lecture—Necessary alliance between facts and doctrines—Preponderance of the country over the towns—Organization of a small feudal society—Influence of feudalism upon the character of the possessor of the fief, and upon the spirit of family—Hatred of the people towards the feudal system—The priest could do little for the serfs—Impossibility of regularly organizing feudalism: 1. No powerful authority; 2. No public power; 3. Difficulty of the federative system—The idea of the right of resistance inherent in feudalism—Influence of feudalism favourable to the development of the individual, unfavourable to social order.

W E H A V E S T U D I E D the condition of Europe after the fall of the Roman empire, in the first period of modern history, the barbarous. We have seen that, at the end of this epoch, and at the commencement of the tenth century, the first principle, the first system that developed itself and took possession of European society, was the feudal system; we have seen that feudalism was the first-born of barbarism. It is, then, the feudal system which must now be the object of our study.

I scarcely think it necessary to remind you that it is not the history of events, properly speaking, which we are considering. It is not my business to recount to you the destinies of feudalism. That which occupies us is the history of civilization; this is the general and hidden fact which we seek under all the external facts which envelop it.

Thus events, social crises, the various states through which society has passed, interest us only in their relations to the development of civilization; we inquire of them solely in what respects they have opposed or assisted it, what they have given to it, and what they have refused it. It is only under this point of view that we are to consider the feudal system.

In the commencement of these lectures we defined the nature of civilization; we attempted to investigate its elements; we saw that it consisted, on the one hand, in the development of man himself, of the individual, of humanity; on the other hand, in that of his external condition, in the development of society. Whenever we find ourselves in the presence of an event, of a system, or of a general condition of the world, we have this double question to ask of it, what has it done for or against the development of man, for or against the development of society?

You understand beforehand, that, during our investigations, it is impossible that we should not meet upon our way most important questions of moral philosophy. When we desire to know in what an event or a system has contributed to the development of man and of society, it is absolutely needful that we should be acquainted with the nature of the true development of society, and of man; that we should know what developments are false and illegitimate, perverting instead of ameliorating, causing a retrogressive instead of a progressive movement.

We shall not seek to escape from this necessity. Not only should we thereby mutilate and lower our ideas and the facts, but the actual state of the world imposes upon us the necessity of freely accepting this inevitable alliance of philosophy and history. This is precisely one of the characteristics, perhaps the essential characteristic of our epoch. We are called upon to consider, to cause to progress together, science and reality, theory and practice, right and fact.[1] Up to our times, these two powers have existed separately; the world has been accustomed to behold science and practice following different roads, without recognizing each other, or, at least, without meeting. And when doctrines and general ideas have desired to amalgamate with events and influence the world, they have only succeeded under the form and by means of the arm of fanaticism. The empire of human societies, and the direction of their affairs, have hitherto been shared between two kinds of influences: upon one hand, the believers, the men of general ideas and principles, the fanatics; on the other, men strangers to all

1. Guizot's insistence on the importance of joining theory and fact is, in effect, his way of justifying the use of sociological models to get beneath the surface of events to their causes. That is what is distinctive about "philosophical history" as opposed to narrative history.

rational principles, who govern themselves merely according to circumstances, practicians, free-thinkers, as the seventeenth century called them. This condition of things is now ceasing; neither fanatics nor free-thinkers will any longer have dominion. In order now to govern and prevail with men, it is necessary to be acquainted with general ideas and circumstances; it is necessary to know how to value principles and facts, to respect virtue and necessity, to preserve oneself from the pride of fanatics, and the not less blind scorn of free-thinkers. To this point have we been conducted by the development of the human mind and the social state: upon one hand, the human mind, exalted and freed, better comprehends the connexion of things, knows how to look around on all sides, and makes use of all things in its combinations; on the other hand, society has perfected itself to that degree, that it can be compared with the truth; that facts can be brought into juxta-position with principles, and yet, in spite of their still great imperfections, not inspire by the comparison invincible discouragement or distaste. I shall thus obey the natural tendency, convenience, and the necessity of our times, in constantly passing from the examination of circumstances to that of ideas, from an exposition of facts to a question of doctrines. Perhaps, even, there is in the actual disposition of men's minds, another reason in favour of this method. For some time past a confirmed taste, I might say a sort of predilection, has manifested itself among us, for facts, for practical views, for the positive aspect of human affairs. We have been to such an extent a prey to the despotism of general ideas, of theories; they have, in some respects, cost us so dear, that they are become the objects of a certain degree of distrust. We like better to carry ourselves back to facts, to special circumstances, to applications. This is not to be regretted; it is a new progress, a great step in knowledge, and towards the empire of truth; provided always that we do not allow ourselves to be prejudiced and carried away by this disposition; that we do not forget that truth alone has a right to reign in the world; that facts have no value except as they tend to explain, and to assimilate themselves more and more to the truth; that all true greatness is of thought; and that all fruitfulness belongs to it. The civilization of our country has this peculiar character, that it has never wanted intellectual greatness; it has always been rich in ideas; the power of the human mind has always been great in French society; greater, perhaps, than in any other. We must not lose this high privilege; we must not fall into the somewhat subordinate and material state which characterizes other societies. Intelligence and doctrines must occupy in the France of the present day, at least the place which they have occupied there hitherto.

We shall, then, by no means avoid general and philosophical questions; we shall not wander in search of them, but where facts lead us to them, we shall meet them without hesitation or embarrassment. An occasion of doing so will more than once present itself, during the consideration of the feudal system in its relations to the history of European civilization.

A good proof that, in the tenth century, the feudal system was necessary, was the only possible social state, is the universality of its establishment. Wherever barbarism ceased, everything took the feudal form. At the first moment, men saw in it only the triumph of chaos; all unity, all general civilization vanished; on all sides they beheld society dismembering itself; and, in its stead, they beheld a number of minor, obscure, isolated, and incoherent societies erect themselves. To contemporaries, this appeared the dissolution of all things, universal anarchy. Consult the poets and the chroniclers of the time; they all believed themselves at the end of the world. It was, nevertheless, the beginning of a new and real society, the feudal, so necessary, so inevitable, so truly the only possible consequence of the anterior state, that all things entered into it and assumed its form. Elements, the most foreign to this system, the church, municipalities, royalty, were compelled to accommodate themselves to it; the churches became suzerains and vassals, cities had lords and vassals, royalty disguised itself under the form of suzerainship. All things were given in fief, not only lands, but certain rights, the right, for instance, of felling in forests, and of fishing. The churches gave in fief their perquisites, from their revenues from baptisms, the churchings of women. Water and money were given in fief. Just as all the general elements of society entered into the feudal frame, so the smallest details, and the most trifling facts of common life, became a part of feudalism.

In beholding the feudal form thus taking possession of all things, we are tempted to believe, at first, that the essential and vital principle of feudalism everywhere prevailed. But this is a mistake. In borrowing the feudal form, the elements and institutions of society which were not analogous to the feudal system, did not renounce their own nature or peculiar principles. The feudal church did not cease to be animated and governed, at bottom, by the theocratic principle; and it laboured unceasingly, sometimes in concert with the royal power, sometimes with the pope, and sometimes with the people, to destroy this system, of which, so to speak, it wore the livery. It was the same with royalty and with the corporations; in the one the monarchical, in the other the democratical principle, continued, at bottom, to predominate. Notwithstanding their feudal livery, these various elements of European society constantly laboured to deliver themselves from a form which was foreign to their true nature, and to assume that which corresponded to their peculiar and vital principle.

Having shown the universality of the feudal form, it becomes very necessary to be on our guard against concluding from this the universality of the feudal principle, and against studying feudalism indifferently, whenever we meet with its physiognomy. In order to know and comprehend this system thoroughly, to unravel and judge its effects in reference to modern civilization, we must examine it where the form and principle are in harmony; we must study it in the hierarchy of lay possessors of fiefs, in the association of the conquerors of the European territory. There truly resided feudal society which we shall now try to enter.

I spoke just now of the importance of moral questions, and of the necessity of not avoiding them. But there is a totally opposite kind of consideration, which has generally been too much neglected; I mean the material condition of society, the material changes introduced into mankind's method of existing, by a new fact, by a revolution, by a new social state. We have not always sufficiently considered these things; we have not always sufficiently inquired into the modifications introduced by these great crises of the world, into the material existence of men, into the material aspect of their relations. These modifications have more influence upon the entire society than is supposed. Who does not know how much the influence of climates has been studied, and how much importance was attached to it by Montesquieu. If we regard the immediate influence of climate upon men, perhaps it is not so extensive as has been supposed; it is, at all events, very vague and difficult to be appreciated. But the indirect influence of climate, that which, for example, results from the fact, that, in a warm country, men live in the open air, while, in a cold country, they shut themselves up in their houses, that, in one case, they nourish themselves in one manner, in the other, in another, these are facts of great importance, facts which by the simple difference of material life, act powerfully upon civilization. All great revolutions lead to modifications of this sort in the social state, and these are very necessary to be considered.

The establishment of the feudal system produced one of these modifications, of unmistakeable importance; it altered the distribution of the population over the face of the land.[2] Hitherto the masters of the soil, the sovereign population, had lived united in more or less numerous masses of men, whether sedentarily in cities, or wandering in bands through the country. In consequence of the feudal system, these same men lived isolated, each in his own habitation, and at great distances from one another. You will immediately perceive how much influence this change was calculated to exercise upon the character and course of civilization. The social preponderance, the government of society, passed suddenly from the towns to the country; private property became of more importance than public property; private life than public life. Such was the first and purely material effect of the triumph of feudal society. The further we examine into it, the more will the consequence of this single fact be unfolded to our eyes.

Let us investigate this society in itself, and see what part it has played in the history of civilization. First of all, let us take feudalism in its most simple, primitive, and fundamental element; let us consider a single possessor of a fief in his domain, and let us see what will become of all those who form the little society around him.

He establishes himself upon an isolated and elevated spot, which he takes care to render safe and strong; there he constructs what he will call his castle. With whom does he establish himself? With his wife and children; perhaps some freemen, who have not become proprietors, attach

2. Guizot's analysis of dramatic changes in the distribution of population in feudal Europe, with its spread over rural areas instead of a concentration in cities or wandering bands, belongs to the more "materialist" aspect of his argument and may also have influenced Marx. Guizot evidently considers the distribution of population more important than Montesquieu's emphasis on climate.

themselves to his person, and continue to live with him, at his table. These are the inhabitants of the interior of the castle. Around and at its foot, a little population of colonists and serfs gather together, who cultivate the domains of the possessor of the fief. In the centre of this lower population religion plants a church; it brings hither a priest. In the early period of the feudal system, this priest was commonly at the same time the chaplain of the castle and the pastor of the village; by and bye these two characters separated; the village had its own pastor, who lived there, beside his church. This, then, was the elementary feudal society, the feudal molecule, so to speak. It is this element that we have first of all to examine. We will demand of it the double question which should be asked of all our facts: What has resulted from it in favour of the development, 1. of man himself, 2. of society?

We are perfectly justified in addressing this double question to the little society which I have just described, and in placing faith in its replies; for it was the type and faithful image of the entire feudal society. The lord, the people on his domains, and the priest; such is feudalism upon the great as well as the small scale, when we have taken from it royalty and the towns, which are distinct and foreign elements.

The first fact that strikes us in contemplating this little society, is the prodigious importance which the possessor of the fief must have had, both in his own eyes, and in the eyes of those who surrounded him. The sentiment of personality, of individual liberty, predominated in the barbaric life. But here it was wholly different; it was no longer only the liberty of the man, of the warrior; it was the importance of the proprietor, of the head of the family, of the master, that came to be considered. From this situation an impression of immense superiority must have resulted; a superiority quite peculiar, and very different from everything that we meet with in the career of other civilizations. I will give the proof of this. I take in the ancient world some great aristocratical position, a Roman patrician, for instance: like the feudal lord, the Roman patrician was head of a family, master, superior. He was, moreover, the religious magistrate, the pontiff in the interior of his family. Now, his importance as a religious magistrate came to him from without; it was not a purely personal and individual importance; he received it from on high; he was the delegate of the Divinity; the interpreter of the religious creed. The Roman patrician was, besides, the member of a corporation which lived united on the same spot, a member of the senate; this again was an importance which came to him from without, from his corporation, a received, a borrowed importance. The greatness of the ancient aristocrats, associated as it was with a religious and political character, belonged to the situation, to the corporation in general, rather than to the individual. That of the possessor of the fief was purely individual; it was not derived from any one; all his rights, all his power, came to him from himself. He was not a religious magistrate; he took no part in a senate; it was in his person that all his importance resided; all that he was, he was of himself, and in his own name. What a mighty influence must such a situation have exerted on its occupant! What individual haughtiness, what prodigious pride—let us say the word—what insolence, must have arisen in his soul! Above himself there was no superior of whom he was the representative or interpreter; there was no equal near him; no powerful and general law which weighed upon him; no external rule which influenced his will; he knew no curb but the limits of his strength and the presence of danger. Such was the necessary moral result of this situation upon the character of man.

I now proceed to a second consequence, mighty also, and too little noticed, namely, the particular turn taken by the feudal family spirit.

Let us cast a glance over the various family systems.[3] Take first of all the patriarchal system of which the Bible and oriental records offer the model. The family was very numerous; it was a tribe. The chief, the patriarch, lived therein in common with his children, his near relations, the various generations which united themselves around him, all his kindred, all his servants; and not only did he live with them all, but he had the same interests, the same occupations, and he led the same life. Was not this the condition of Abraham, of the patriarchs, and of the chiefs of the Arab tribes, who still reproduce the image of the patriarchal life?

Another family system presents itself, namely, the *clan,* a petty society, whose type we must seek for in Scotland or Ireland. Through this system,

---

3. Guizot's discussion of different family types is just one example of the way in which he drew on the social theory of the Scottish Enlightenment.

very probably, a large portion of the European family has passed. This is no longer the patriarchal family. There is here a great difference between the situation of the chief and that of the rest of the population. They did not lead the same life: the greater portion tilled and served; the chief was idle and warlike. But they had a common origin; they all bore the same name; and their relations of kindred, ancient traditions, the same recollections, the same affections, established a moral tie, a sort of equality between all the members of the clan.

These are the two principal types of the family society presented by history. But have we here the feudal family? Obviously not. It seems, at first, that the feudal family bears some relation to the clan; but the difference is much greater than the resemblance. The population which surrounded the possessor of the fief were totally unconnected with him; they did not bear his name; between them and him there was no kindred, no bond, moral or historical. Neither did it resemble the patriarchal family. The possessor of the fief led not the same life, nor did he engage in the same occupations with those who surrounded him; he was an idler and a warrior, whilst the others were labourers. The feudal family was not numerous; it was not a tribe; it reduced itself to the family, properly so called, namely, to the wife and children; it lived separated from the rest of the population, shut up in the castle. The colonists and serfs made no part of it; the origin of the members of this society was different, the inequality of their situation immense. Five or six individuals, in a situation at once superior to and estranged from the rest of the society, that was the feudal family. It was of course invested with a peculiar character. It was narrow, concentrated, and constantly called upon to defend itself against, to distrust, and, at least, to isolate itself from, even its retainers. The interior life, domestic manners, were sure to become predominant in such a system. I am aware that the brutality of the passions of a chief, his habit of spending his time in warfare or the chase, were a great obstacle to the development of domestic manners. But this would be conquered; the chief necessarily returned home habitually; he always found there his wife and children, and these well nigh only; these would alone constitute his permanent society—they would alone share his interests, his destiny. Domestic life necessarily, therefore, acquired great sway. Proofs of this abound. Was it not within the bosom of the feudal family that the importance of women developed itself? In all the ancient societies, I do not speak of those where the family spirit did not exist, but of those wherein it was very powerful, in the patriarchal life for instance, women did not hold at all so considerable a place as they acquired in Europe under the feudal system. It was to the development and necessary preponderance of domestic manners in feudalism, that they chiefly owed this change, this progress in their condition. Some have desired to trace the cause to the peculiar manners of the ancient Germans; to a national respect which, it is said, they bore towards women amidst their forests. Upon one sentence of Tacitus, German patriotism has built I know not what superiority, what primitive and uneradicable purity of German manners, as regards the relations of the two sexes.[4] Mere fancies! Phrases similar to that of Tacitus, concerning sentiments and usages analogous to those of the ancient Germans, are to be found in the recitals of a crowd of observers of savage or barbarous people. There is nothing primitive therein, nothing peculiar to any particular race. It was in the effects of a strongly marked social position, in the progress and preponderance of domestic manners, that the importance of women in Europe originated; and the preponderance of domestic manners became, very early, an essential characteristic of the feudal system.

A second fact, another proof of the empire of domestic life, equally characterizes the feudal family: I mean the hereditary spirit, the spirit of perpetuation, which evidently predominated therein. The hereditary spirit is inherent in the family spirit; but nowhere has it so strongly developed itself as under the feudal system. This resulted from the nature of the property with which the family was incorporated. The fief was unlike other properties: it constantly demanded a possessor to defend it, serve it, acquit himself of the obligations inherent in the domain, and thus maintain it in its rank amidst the general association of the masters of the soil. Thence resulted a sort of identification between the actual possessor of the fief and the fief itself, and all the series of its future possessors.

4. Guizot here uses sociological models to combat what he sees as the unduly romantic "myths" associated with some German accounts of their own national origins and customs. In his view, theories of social and economic change can offer a useful corrective to the "distortions" introduced by national pride.

This circumstance greatly contributed to fortify and make closer the family ties, already so powerful by the very nature of the feudal family.

I now issue from the seignorial dwelling, and descend amidst the petty population that surrounds it. Here all things wear a different aspect. The nature of man is so good and fruitful, that when a social situation endures for any length of time, a certain moral tie, sentiments of protection, benevolence, and affection, inevitably establish themselves among those who are thus approximated to one another, whatever may be the conditions of approximation. It happened thus with feudalism. No doubt, after a certain time, some moral relations, some habits of affection, became contracted between the colonists and the possessor of the fief. But this happened in spite of their relative position, and not by reason of its influence. Considered in itself, the position was radically wrong. There was nothing morally in common between the possessor of the fief and the colonists; they constituted part of his domain; they were his property; and under this name, property, were included all the rights which, in the present day, are called rights of public sovereignty, as well as the rights of private property, the right of imposing laws, of taxing, and punishing, as well as that of disposing of and selling. As far as it is possible that such should be the case where men are in presence of men, between the lord and the cultivators of his lands there existed no rights, no guarantees, no society.

Hence, I conceive, the truly prodigious and invincible hatred with which the people at all times have regarded the feudal system, its recollections, its very name. It is not a case without example for men to have submitted to oppressive despotisms, and to have become accustomed to them; nay, to have willingly accepted them. Theocratic and monarchical despotisms have more than once obtained the consent, almost the affections, of the population subjected to them. But feudal despotism has always been repulsive and odious; it has oppressed the destinies, but never reigned over the souls of men. The reason is, that in theocracy and monarchy, power is exercised in virtue of certain words which are common to the master and to the subject; it is the representative, the minister of another power superior to all human power; it speaks and acts in the name of the Divinity or of a general idea, and not in the name of man himself, of man alone. Feudal despotism was altogether different; it was the power of the individual over the individual; the dominion of the personal and capricious will of a man. This is, perhaps, the only tyranny of which, to his eternal honour, man will never willingly accept. Whenever, in his master, he beholds a mere man, from the moment that the will which oppresses him appears a merely human and individual will, like his own, he becomes indignant, and supports the yoke wrathfully. Such was the true and distinguishing character of feudal power; and such was also the origin of the antipathy which it has ever inspired.

The religious element which was associated with it was little calculated to ease the burden. I do not conceive that the influence of the priest, in the little society which I have just described, was very great, nor that he succeeded much in legitimating the relations of the inferior population with the lord. The church has exerted a very great influence upon European civilization, but this it has done by proceedings of a general character, by changing, for instance, the general dispositions of men. When we enter closely into the petty feudal society, properly so called, we find that the influence of the priest, between the colonists and the lord, scarcely amounted to anything. Most frequently he was himself rude and subordinate as a serf, and very little in condition or disposition to combat the arrogance of the lord. No doubt, called, as he was, to sustain and develop somewhat of moral life in the inferior population, he was dear and useful to it on this account; he spread through it somewhat of consolation and of life; but, I conceive, he could and did very little to alleviate its destiny.

I have examined the elementary feudal society; I have placed before you the principal consequences which necessarily flowed from it, whether to the possessor of the fief himself, or his family, or the population congregated around him. Let us now go forth from this narrow inclosure. The population of the fief was not alone upon the land; there were other societies, analogous or different, with which it bore relation. What influence did the general society to which that population belonged, necessarily exercise upon civilization?

I will make a brief remark, before answering this question: It is true that the possessor of the fief and the priest belonged, one and the other, to a general society; they had, at a distance, numerous and frequent relations. It was not the same with the colonists, the serfs: every time that, in order to designate the population of the country at this period, we make use of a general word, which seems to imply one and the same society, the word *people,* for example, we do not convey the truth. There was for this population no general society; its existence was purely local. Beyond the territory which they inhabited, the colonists had no connexion with any thing or person. For them there was no common destiny, no common country; they did not form a people. When we speak of the feudal association as a whole, it is only the possessors of the fiefs that are concerned.

Let us see what were the relations of the petty feudal society with the general society with which it was connected, and to what consequences these relations necessarily led as regards the development of civilization.

You are acquainted with the nature of the ties which united the possessors of the fiefs among themselves, with the obligations of service, on the one hand, of protection on the other. I shall not enter into a detail of these obligations; it suffices that you have a general idea of their character. From these obligations there necessarily arose within the mind of each possessor of a fief, a certain number of moral ideas and sentiments, ideas of duty, sentiments of affection. The fact is evident that the principle of fidelity, of devotion, of loyalty to engagements, and all sentiments connected therewith, were developed and sustained by the relations of the possessors of the fiefs between themselves.

These obligations, duties, and sentiments, endeavoured to convert themselves into rights and institutions. Every one knows that feudalism desired legally to determine what were the services due from the possessor of the fief towards his suzerain; what were the services which he might expect in return; in what cases the vassal owed pecuniary or military aid to his suzerain; in what forms the suzerain ought to obtain the consent of his vassals, for services to which they were not compelled by the simple tenure of their fiefs. Attempts were made to place all their rights under the guarantee of institutions, which aimed at insuring their being respected. Thus, the seignorial jurisdictions were destined to render justice between the possessors of the fiefs, upon claims carried before their common suzerain. Thus, also, each lord who was of any consideration assembled his vassals in a parliament, in order to treat with them concerning matters which required their consent or their concurrence. In short, there existed a collection of political, judicial, and military means, with which attempts were made to organize the feudal system, converting the relations between the possessors of fiefs into rights and institutions.

But these rights and these institutions had no reality, no guarantee.

If one is asked, what is meant by a guarantee, a political guarantee, one is led to perceive that its fundamental character is the constant presence, in the midst of the society, of a will, of a power disposed and in a condition to impose a law upon particular wills and powers, to make them observe the common rule, and respect the general right.

There are only two systems of political guarantees possible: it is either necessary there should be a particular will and power so superior to all others, that none should be able to resist it, and that all should be compelled to submit to it as soon as it interferes; or else that there should be a public will and power, which is the result of agreement, of the development of particular wills, and which, once gone forth from them, is in a condition to impose itself upon, and to make itself respected equally by all.

Such are the two possible systems of political guarantees: the despotism of one or of a body, or free government. When we pass systems in review, we find that all of them come under one or other of these heads.

Well, neither one nor the other existed, nor could exist, under the feudal system.

No doubt the possessors of the fiefs were not all equal among themselves; there were many of superior power, many powerful enough to oppress the weaker. But there was no one, beginning from the first of the suzerains, the king, who was in condition to impose law upon all the others, and make himself obeyed. Observe that all the permanent means of power and action were wanting: there were no permanent troops, no permanent taxes, no permanent tribunals. The social powers and institutions had, after a manner, to recommence and create themselves anew every time they were required. A tribunal was obliged to be constructed for every process, an army whenever there was a war to be made, a revenue whenever money was wanted; everything was occasional, accidental, and special; there was no means of central, permanent, and independent government. It is plain that, in such a system, no individual was in a condition to impose his will upon others, or to cause the general rights to be respected by all.

On the other hand, resistance was as easy as repression was difficult. Shut up in his castle, having to do only with a small number of enemies, easily finding, among vassals of his own condition, the means of coalition, and of assistance, the possessor of the fief defended himself with the greatest facility.

Thus, then, we see that the first system of guarantees, the system which places them in the intervention of the strongest, was not possible under feudalism.

The other system, that of a free government, a public power, was equally impracticable; it could never have arisen in the bosom of feudalism. The reason is sufficiently simple. When we speak, in the present day, of a public power, of that which we call the rights of sovereignty, the right of giving laws, taxing, and punishing, we all think that those rights belong to no one, that no one has, on his own account, a right to punish others, and to impose upon them a charge, a law. Those are rights which belong only to society in the mass, rights which are exercised in its name, which it holds not of itself, but receives from the Highest. Thus, when an individual comes before the powers invested with these rights, the sentiment which, perhaps without his consciousness, reigns in him is, that he is in the presence of a public and legitimate power, which possesses a mission for commanding him, and he is submissive beforehand and internally. But it was wholly otherwise under feudalism. The possessor of the fief, in his domain, was invested with all the rights of sovereignty over those who inhabited it; they were inherent to the domain, and a part of his private property. What are at present public rights were then private rights; what is now public power was then private power. When the possessor of a fief, after having exercised sovereignty in his own name, as a proprietor over all the population amidst which he lived, presented himself at an assembly, a parliament held before his suzerain, a parliament not very numerous, and composed in general of men who were his equals, or nearly so, he did not bring with him, nor did he carry away the idea of a public power. This idea was in contradiction to all his existence, to all that he had been in the habit of doing in the interior of his own domains. He saw there only men who were invested with the same rights as himself, who were in the same situation, and, like him, acted in the name of their personal will. Nothing in the most elevated department of the government, in what we call public institutions, conveyed to him, or forced him to recognize this character of superiority and generality, which is inherent to the idea that we form to ourselves of public powers. And if he was dissatisfied with the decision, he refused to agree with it, or appealed to force for resistance.

Under the feudal system, force was the true and habitual guarantee of right, if, indeed, we may call force a guarantee. All rights had perpetual recourse to force to make themselves recognized or obeyed. No institution succeeded in doing this; and this was so generally felt that institutions were rarely appealed to. If the seignorial courts and parliaments of vassals had been capable of influence, we should have met with them in history more frequently than we do, and found them exerting more activity; their rarity proves their invalidity.

At this we must not be astonished; there is a reason for it, more decisive and deeply seated than those which I have described.

Of all systems of government and political guarantee, the federative system is certainly the most difficult to establish and to render prevalent; a system which consists in leaving in each locality and each particular society all that portion of the government which can remain there, and in taking from it only that portion which is indispensable to the maintenance of the general society, and carrying this to the centre of that society, there to constitute of it a central government.[5] The federative system, logically the most simple, is, in fact, the most complex. In order to reconcile the degree of local independence and liberty which it allows to remain, with the degree of general order and submission which it demands and supposes in certain cases, a very advanced degree of civilization is evidently requisite; it is necessary that the will of man, that individual liberty should concur in the establishment and maintenance of this system, much more than in that of any other, for its means of coercion are far less than those of any other.

---

5. In the course of the Great Debate of the 1820s the Doctrinaires had reformulated the political problem facing modern democratic societies into the following question: can a balance be found between central power and local autonomy? As a result, their writings reveal a growing interest in federalism as a political system—an interest which helped to stimulate Tocqueville's journey to the United States.

The federative system, then, is that which evidently requires the greatest development of reason, morality, and civilization, in the society to which it is applied.[6] Well, this, nevertheless, was the system which feudalism endeavoured to establish; the idea of general feudalism, in fact, was that of a federation. It reposed upon the same principles on which are founded, in our day, the federation of the United States of America, for example. It aimed at leaving in the hands of each lord all that portion of government and sovereignty which could remain there, and to carry to the suzerain, or to the general assembly of barons, only the least possible portion of power, and that only in cases of absolute necessity. You perceive the impossibility of establishing such a system amidst ignorance, amidst brutal passions—in short, in a moral state so imperfect as that of man under feudalism. The very nature of government was contradictory to the ideas and manners of the very men to whom it was attempted to be applied. Who can be astonished at the ill success of these endeavours at organization?

We have considered feudal society, first, in its most simple and fundamental element, then in its entirety. We have examined, under these two points of view, that which it necessarily did, that which naturally flowed from it, as to its influence upon the course of civilization. I conceive that we have arrived at this double result:

First, feudalism has exerted a great, and, on the whole, a salutary influence upon the internal development of the individual; it has awakened in men's minds ideas, energetic sentiments, moral requirements, fine developments of character and passion.

Secondly, under the social point of view, it was unable to establish either legal order or political guarantees; it was indispensable to the revival in Europe of society, which had been so entirely dissolved by barbarism,

---

6. Here Guizot's argument reveals how his account of the development of "civilization" is also a theory of progress, which puts the restoration of a degree of local autonomy at the end of a process which had, earlier, involved the radical centralization of governmental power. The free concurrence of wills, upon which a balance between central power and local autonomy depends, requires moral and intellectual developments which were not present earlier in European history. This argument had been adumbrated by Guizot in his *History of Representative Government in Europe* (1822).

that it was incapable of a more regular and more extended form; but the feudal form, radically bad in itself, could neither regulate nor extend itself. The only political right which the feudal system caused to assert itself in European society was the right of resistance—I do not say legal resistance, that could not have place in a society so little advanced. The progress of society consists precisely in substituting, on the one hand, public powers for particular wills; on the other, legal for individual resistance. In this consists the grand aim, the principal perfection of the social order; much latitude is left to personal liberty; then, when that liberty fails, when it becomes necessary to demand from it an account of itself, appeal is made to public reason alone, to determine the process instituted against the liberty of the individual. Such is the system of legal order and of legal resistance. You perceive, without difficulty, that under feudalism there existed nothing of this sort. The right of resistance which the feudal system maintained and practised was the right of personal resistance—a terrible, unsocial right, since it appeals to force and to war, which is the destruction of society itself; a right which, nevertheless, should never be abolished from the heart of man, for its abolition is the acceptation of servitude. The sentiment of the right of resistance had perished in the disgrace of Roman society, and could not rise anew from its wreck; it could not come more naturally, in my opinion, from the principle of the Christian society. To feudalism we are indebted for its re-introduction into the manners of Europe. It is the boast of civilization to render it always useless and inactive; it is the boast of the feudal system to have constantly professed and defended it.

Such, if I do not deceive myself, is the result of an examination of feudal society, considered in itself, in its general elements, and independently of historical development. If we pass on to facts, to history, we shall see that what has happened is what might have been looked for; that the feudal system has done what it was fitted to do; that its destiny has been in conformity with its nature. Events may be adduced in proof of all the conjectures and inferences which I have drawn from the very nature of this system.

Cast a glance upon the general history of feudalism between the tenth and thirteenth centuries; it is impossible to mistake the great and salutary influence exerted by it upon the development of sentiments, characters, and ideas. We cannot look into the history of this period without meeting with a crowd of noble sentiments, great actions, fine displays of humanity, born evidently in the bosom of feudal manners. Chivalry, it is true, does not resemble feudalism—nevertheless, it is its daughter: from feudalism issued this ideal of elevated, generous, loyal sentiments. It says much in favour of its parentage.

Turn your eyes to another quarter: the first bursts of European imagination, the first attempts of poetry and of literature, the first intellectual pleasures tasted by Europe on its quitting barbarism, it is under the shelter, under the wings of feudalism, in the interior of the feudal castles, that all these were born. This kind of development of humanity requires a movement in the soul, in life, leisure, a thousand conditions which are not to be met with in the laborious, melancholy, coarse, hard existence of the common people. In France, in England, in Germany, it is with the feudal times that the first literary recollections, the first intellectual enjoyments of Europe connect themselves.

On the other, if we consult history upon the social influence of feudalism, its answers will always be in harmony with our conjectures; it will reply that the feudal system has been as much opposed to the establishment of general order as to the extension of general liberty. Under whatever point of view you consider the progress of society, you find the feudal system acting as an obstacle. Therefore, from the earliest existence of feudalism, the two forces which have been the grand motive powers of the development of order and liberty—on one hand the monarchical power, the popular power on the other; royalty, and the people—have attacked and struggled against it unceasingly. Some attempts have, at different times, been made to regulate it, and construct out of it a state somewhat legal and general: in England, such attempts were made by William the Conqueror and his sons; in France, by Saint Louis; in Germany, by many of the emperors. All attempts, all efforts have failed. The very nature of feudal society was repugnant to order and legality. In modern ages, some men of intellect have attempted to re-establish feudalism as a social system; they have desired to discover therein a legal, regulated, and progressive state; they have made of it an age of gold. But ask them to assign the age of gold to some particular place or time, and they can do no such thing:

it is an Utopia without a date, a drama for which we find, in past times, neither theatre nor actors. The cause of this error is easy to discover, and it equally explains the mistake of those who cannot pronounce the name of feudalism without cursing it. Neither one party nor the other has taken the pains to consider the double aspect under which feudalism presents itself; to distinguish, on the one hand, its influence upon the individual development of man, upon sentiments, characters, and passions, and, on the other, its influence upon the social state. The one party has not been able to persuade itself that a social system, in which so many beautiful sentiments, so many virtues are found—in which they behold the birth of all literatures, and in which manners assume a certain elevation and nobility—can have been so bad and fatal as it is pretended. The other party has only seen the wrong done by feudalism to the mass of the population, the obstacles opposed by it to the establishment of order and liberty; and this party has not been able to believe that fine characters, great virtues, and any progress, can have resulted from it. Both have mistaken the double element of civilization; they have not understood that it consists of two developments, of which the one may, in time, produce itself independently of the other; although, after the course of centuries, and by means of a long series of circumstances, they must reciprocally call forth and lead to each other.

For the rest, that which feudalism was in theory it was in fact; that to which theory pointed as likely to result from it, has resulted from it. Individuality and energy of personal existence, such was the predominating trait among the conquerors of the Roman world; the development of individuality necessarily resulted, before all things, from the social system which was founded by and for themselves. That which man himself brings to a social system, at the moment of his entrance, his internal and moral qualities, powerfully influence the situation in which he establishes himself. The situation, in turn, re-acts upon these qualities, and strengthens and develops them. The individual predominated in the German society; it was for the benefit of the development of the individual that feudal society, the daughter of German society, exerted its influence. We shall again find the same fact in the different elements of civilization; they have remained faithful to their principle; they have advanced and urged on the world in the direction which they first entered. In our next lecture, the history of the church and of its influence, from the fifth to the twelfth century, upon European civilization, will furnish us with another and a striking illustration of this fact.

FIFTH LECTURE

*Object of the lecture—Religion is a principle of association—
Constraint is not of the essence of government—Conditions of the
legitimacy of government: 1. The power must be in the hands of
the most worthy; 2. The liberty of the governed must be respected—
The church being a corporation, and not a caste, fulfilled the first of
these conditions—Of the various methods of nomination and election
that existed therein—It wanted the other condition, on account of
the illegitimate extension of authority, and on account of the abusive
employment of force—Movement and liberty of spirit in the bosom of
the church—Relations of the church with princes—The independence
of spiritual power laid down as a principle—Pretensions and efforts
of the church to usurp the temporal power.*

WE HAVE EXAMINED the nature and influence of the feudal system; it is with the Christian church, from the fifth to the twelfth century, that we are now to occupy ourselves: I say, with the *church*; and I have already laid this emphasis, because it is not with Christianity properly speaking, with Christianity as a religious system, but with the church as an ecclesiastical society, with the Christian clergy, that I propose to engage your attention.

In the fifth century, this society was almost completely organized; not that it has not since then undergone many and important changes; but we may say that, at that time, the church, considered as a corporation, as a government of Christian people, had attained a complete and independent existence.

One glance is enough to show us an immense difference between the state of the church and that of the other elements of European civilization in the fifth century. I have mentioned, as the fundamental elements of our civilization, the municipal and feudal systems, royalty, and the church. The municipal system, in the fifth century, was no more than the wreck of the Roman empire, a shadow without life or determinate form. The feudal system had not yet issued from the chaos. Royalty existed only in name. All the civil elements of modern society were in either decay or infancy. The church alone was, at the same time, young and constituted; it alone had acquired a definite form, and preserved all the vigour of early age; it alone possessed, at once, movement and order, energy and regularity, that is to say, the two great means of influence. Is it not, let me ask you, by moral life, by internal movement, on the one hand, and by order and discipline on the other, that institutions take possession of society? The church, moreover, had mooted all the great questions which interest man; it busied itself with all the problems of his nature, and with all the chances of his destiny. Thus its influence upon modern civilization has been very great, greater, perhaps, than even its most ardent adversaries, or its most zealous defenders have supposed. Occupied with rendering it services, or with combating it, they have regarded it only in a polemical point of view, and have therefore, I conceive, been unable either to judge it with equity, or to measure it in all its extent.

The Christian church in the fifth century presents itself as an independent and constituted society, interposed between the masters of the world, the sovereigns, the possessors of the temporal power on the one hand, and the people on the other, serving as a bond between them, and influencing all.

In order completely to know and comprehend its action, we must therefore consider it under three aspects: first of all we must regard it in itself, make an estimate of what it was, of its internal constitution, of the principles which predominated in it, and of its nature; we must then examine it in its relation to the temporal sovereignties, kings, lords, and others; lastly, in its relations to the people. And when from this triple examination we shall have deduced a complete picture of the church, of its principles, its situation, and the influence which it necessarily exercised, we shall verify our assertions by an appeal to history; we shall find out whether the facts and events, properly so called, from the fifth to the twelfth century, are in harmony with the results to which we have been led by the study of the nature of the church, and of its relations, both with the masters of the world and with the people.

First of all, let us occupy ourselves with the church in itself, with its internal condition, and its nature.

The first fact which strikes us, and perhaps the most important, is its very existence, the existence of a religious government, of a clergy, of an ecclesiastical corporation, of a priesthood, of a religion in the sacerdotal state.

With many enlightened men, these very words, a body of priesthood, a religious government, appear to determine the question. They think that a religion which ends in a body of priests, a legally constituted clergy, in short, a governed religion, must be, taking all things together, more injurious than useful. In their opinion, religion is a purely individual relation of man to God; and that whenever the relation loses this character, whenever an external authority comes between the individual and the object of religious creeds—namely, God—religion is deteriorated, and society in danger.[1]

We cannot dispense with an examination of this question. In order to ascertain what has been the influence of the Christian church, we must know what ought to be, by the very nature of the institution, the influence of a church and of a clergy. In order to appreciate this influence, we must find out, first of all, whether religion is, in truth, purely individual, whether it does not provoke and give birth to something more than merely a private relation between each man and God; or whether it necessarily becomes a source of new relations between men, from which a religious society and a government of that society necessarily flow.

If we reduce religion to the religious sentiment properly so called, to that sentiment which is very real, though somewhat vague and uncertain as to its object, and which we can scarcely characterize otherwise than by naming it—to this sentiment which addresses itself sometimes to external

1. Guizot is implicitly criticizing the views of some Romantic writers, especially those of Chateaubriand and Constant, who sought to base religion exclusively on individual sentiment or feeling. Guizot's Calvinist background makes such an interpretation seem to him grossly inadequate to the intellectual and moral issues which religious doctrine and precept seek to address.

nature, sometimes to the innermost recesses of the soul, to-day to poetry, to-morrow to the mysteries of the future, which, in a word, wanders every-where, seeking everywhere to satisfy itself, and fixing itself nowhere—if we reduce religion to this sentiment, it seems evident to me that it should remain purely individual. Such a sentiment may provoke a momentary association between men; it can, it even ought to take pleasure in sym-pathy, nourishing and strengthening itself thereby. But by reason of its fluctuating and doubtful character, it refuses to become the principle of a permanent and extensive association, to adapt itself to any system of pre-cepts, practices, and forms; in short, to give birth to a religious society and government.

But either I deceive myself strangely, or this religious sentiment is not the complete expression of the religious nature of man. Religion, I con-ceive, is a different thing, and much more than this.

In human nature and in human destiny there are problems of which the solution lies beyond this world, which are connected with a class of things foreign to the visible world, and which inveterately torment the soul of man, who is fixedly intent upon solving them. The solution of these prob-lems, creeds, dogmas, which contain that solution, or, at least, flatter them-selves that they do, these constitute the first object and the first source of religion.

Another path leads men to religion. To those among you who have prosecuted somewhat extended philosophical studies, it is, I conceive, suf-ficiently evident at present that morality exists independently of religious ideas; that the distinction of moral good and evil, the obligation to shun the evil, and to do the good, are laws, which, like the laws of logic, man dis-covers in his own nature, and which have their principle in himself, as they have their application in his actual life. But these facts being decided, the independence of morality being admitted, a question arises in the human mind—Whence comes morality? To what does it lead? Is this obligation to do good, which subsists of itself, an isolated fact, without author and aim? Does it not conceal from, or rather, does it not reveal to man a destiny which is beyond this world? This is a spontaneous and inevitable question, by which morality, in its turn, leads man to the door of religion, and discov-ers to him a sphere from which he had not borrowed morality.

Thus, in the problems of our nature, upon one hand, and in the necessity of discovering a sanction, origin, and aim for morality, on the other, we find assured and fruitful sources of religion, which thus presents itself under aspects very different from that of a mere instrument, as it has been described; it presents itself as a collection—1st, of doctrines called forth by problems which man discovers within himself; 2nd, of precepts which correspond to those doctrines, and give to natural morality a meaning and a sanction; 3rd, of promises which address themselves to the hopes of humanity in the future. This is what truly constitutes religion; this is what it is at bottom, and not a mere form of sensibility, a flight of the imagination, a species of poetry.

Reduced in this manner to its true elements and to its essence, religion no longer appears as a purely individual fact, but as a powerful and fruitful principle of association. Consider it as a system of creeds and dogmas: truth belongs to no one; it is universal, absolute; men must seek and profess it in common. Consider the precepts that associate themselves with doctrines: an obligatory law for one is such for all; it must be promulgated, it must bring all men under its empire. It is the same with the promises made by religion in the name of its creeds and precepts: they must be spread abroad, and all men must be called to gather the fruits of them. From the essential elements of religion, then, you see that the religious society is born; indeed, it flows therefrom so infallibly that the word which expresses the most energetic social sentiment, the most imperious necessity of propagating ideas and extending a society, is the word *proselytism,* a word which applies above all to religious creeds, and, indeed, seems to be almost exclusively consecrated to them.

The religious society being once born, when a certain number of men become united in common religious creeds, under the law of common religious precepts, and in common religious hopes, that society must have a government. There is no society which can survive a week, an hour, without a government. At the very instant in which the society forms itself, and even by the very fact of its formation, it calls forth a government, which proclaims the common truth, the bond of the society, and promulgates and supports the precepts which originate in that truth. The necessity for a power, for a government over the religious society, as over every other,

is implied in the fact of the existence of that society. And not only is government necessary, but it naturally forms itself. I must not pause for any
time to explain how government originates and establishes itself in society
in general. I shall confine myself to saying that, when things follow their
natural laws, when external force does not mix itself up with them, power
always flies to the most capable, to the best, to those who will lead society towards its aim. In a warlike expedition, the bravest obtain the power.
Is research or skilful enterprise the object of an association? the most capable will be at the head of it. In all things, when the world is left to its
natural course, the natural inequality of men freely displays itself, and each
takes the place which he is capable of occupying. Well, as regards religion,
men are no more equal in talents, faculties, and power, than in the other
cases; such a one will be better able than any other to expound religious
doctrines, and to cause them to be generally adopted; some other bears
about him more authority to induce the observance of religious precepts;
a third will excel in sustaining and animating religious emotions and hopes
in the souls of men. The same inequality of faculties and influence which
gives rise to power in civil society, originates it equally in religious society.
Missionaries arise and declare themselves like generals. Thus, as, on one
hand, religious government necessarily flows from the nature of religious
society, so, on the other, it naturally develops itself therein by the mere effect of the human faculties and their unequal partition. Therefore, from the
moment at which religion is born in man, religious society develops itself;
and from the moment at which religious society appears, it gives rise to its
government.

But now a fundamental objection arises: there is nothing in this case
to ordain or impose; nothing coercive. There is no room for government,
since unlimited liberty is required to exist.

It is, I conceive, a very rude and petty idea of government in general,
to suppose that it resides solely, or even principally, in the force which it
exerts to make itself obeyed in its coercive element.

I leave the religious point of view; I take civil government. I pray you
follow with me the simple course of facts. The society exists: there is something to be done, no matter what, in its interest and name; there is a law
to make, a measure to take, a judgment to pronounce. Assuredly there is

likewise a worthy manner of fulfilling these social wants; a good law to make, a good measure to take, a good judgment to pronounce. Whatever may be the matter in hand, whatever may be the interest in question, there is in every case a truth that must be known, a truth which must decide the conduct of the question.

The first business of government is to seek this truth, to discover what is just, reasonable, and adapted to society. When it has found it, it proclaims it. It becomes then necessary that it should impress it upon men's minds; that the government should make itself approved of by those upon whom it acts; that it should persuade them of its reasonableness. Is there anything coercive in this? Assuredly not. Now, suppose that the truth which ought to decide concerning the affair, no matter what, suppose, I say, that this truth once discovered and proclaimed, immediately all understandings are convinced, all wills determined, that all recognize the reasonableness of the government, and spontaneously obey it; there is still no coercion, there is no room for the employment of force. Is it that the government did not exist? is it that, in all this, there was no government? Evidently there was a government, and it fulfilled its task.[2] Coercion comes then only when the resistance of individual will occurs, when the idea, the proceeding which the government has adopted, does not obtain the approbation and voluntary submission of all. The government then employs force to make itself obeyed; this is the necessary result of human imperfection, an imperfection which resides at once in the governing power and in the society. There will never be any way of completely avoiding it; civil governments will ever be compelled to have recourse, to

---

2. This discussion of the educational role of government, its moral and intellectual function, shows Guizot trying to find a middle way between Hobbes's theory of the state in *Leviathan*, with its almost exclusive emphasis on the coercive role of government, and Rousseau's *Social Contract*, in which realizing the General Will (or justice) makes coercion almost redundant. While avoiding the extremes of Rousseau's doctrine, Guizot is at pains to emphasize that government *is* conceivable apart from command and coercion. Lurking in his argument is a Protestant critique of the structure of the Catholic Church, with Papal authority having triumphed over the conciliar movement which had, in the fifteenth century, sought to introduce something like representative government and free discussion into the Church.

a certain extent, to coercion. But governments are evidently not consti-tuted by coercion: whenever they can dispense with it, they do, and to the great profit of all: indeed, their highest perfection is to dispense with it, and to confine themselves to methods purely moral, to the action which they exert upon the understanding; so that the more the government dis-penses with coercion, the more faithful it is to its true nature, the better it fulfils its mission. It is not thereby reduced in power or contracted, as is vulgarly supposed; it acts only in another manner, and in a manner which is infinitely more general and powerful. Those governments which make the greatest use of coercion, succeed not nearly so well as those which employ it scarcely at all.

In addressing itself to the understanding, in determining the will, in act-ing by purely intellectual means, the government, instead of reducing, ex-tends and elevates itself; it is then that it accomplishes the most and the greatest things. On the contrary, when it is obliged incessantly to employ coercion, it contracts and lessens itself, and effects very little, and that little very ill.

Thus the essence of government does not reside in coercion, in the em-ployment of force; but that which above all things constitutes it, is a system of means and powers, conceived with the design of arriving at the discov-ery of what is applicable to each occasion; at the discovery of truth, which has a right to rule society, in order that afterwards the minds of men may be brought to open themselves to it, and adopt it voluntarily and freely. The necessity for, and the actual existence of a government are thus perfectly conceivable, when there is no occasion for coercion, when even it is abso-lutely interdicted.

Well, such is the government of the religious society. Undoubtedly, co-ercion is interdicted to it; undoubtedly, the employment of force by it is illegitimate, whatever may be its aim, for the single reason that its exclu-sive territory is the human conscience: but not the less, therefore, does it subsist; not the less has it to accomplish all the acts I have mentioned. It must discover what are the religious doctrines which solve the prob-lems of the human destiny; or, if there exists already a general system of creeds whereby those problems are solved, it must discover and exhibit the consequences of that system, as regards each particular case; it must promulgate and maintain the precepts which correspond to its doctrines; it must preach and teach them, in order that, when the society wanders from them, it may bring it back. There must be no coercion; the duties of this government are, examining, preaching, and teaching religious virtues; and, at need, admonishing or censuring. Suppress coercion as completely as you will, you will yet behold all the essential questions of the organization of a government arise and claim solutions. For example, the question whether a body of religious magistrates is necessary, or whether it is possible to trust to the religious inspiration of individuals (a question which is debated between the majority of religious societies and the Quakers), will always exist, it will always be necessary to discuss it. In like manner, the question, whether, when it has been agreed that a body of religious magistrates is necessary, we should prefer a system of equality, of religious ministers equal among themselves, and deliberating in common, to an hierarchical constitution, with various degrees of power; this question will never come to an end, because you deny all coercive power to ecclesiastical magistrates, whosoever they may be. Instead, then, of dissolving religious society in order that we may have the right of destroying religious government, we must rather recognize that the religious society forms itself naturally, that the religious government flows as naturally from the religious society, and that the problem to be solved is to ascertain under what conditions this government should exist, what are its foundations, principles, and conditions of legitimacy. This is the real investigation which is imposed by the necessary existence of a religious government as of all others.

The conditions of legitimacy are the same for the government of a religious society as for that of any other; they may be reduced to two: the first, that the power should attach itself to and remain constantly in the hands of the best and most capable, as far, at least, as human imperfection will allow of its doing so; that the truly superior people who exist dispersed among the society should be sought for there, brought to light, and called upon to unfold the social law, and to exercise power: the second, that the power legitimately constituted, should respect the legitimate liberties of those over whom it exercises itself. In these two conditions, a good system of forming and organizing power, and a good system of guarantees of liberty, consists the worth of government in general, whether religious or civil; all governments ought to be judged according to this criterion.[3]

Instead, then, of taunting the church, or the government of the Christian world, with its existence, we should find out how it was constituted, and whether its principles corresponded with the two essential conditions of all good government. Let us examine the church in this two-fold view.

As regards the formation and transmission of power in the church, there is a word which is often used in speaking of the Christian clergy, and which I wish to discard; it is the word *caste.* The body of ecclesiastical magistrates has often been called a caste. Look round the world; take any country in which castes have been produced, in India or Egypt; you will see everywhere that the caste is essentially hereditary; it is the transmission of the same position, and the same power, from father to son. Wherever there is no inheritance, there is no caste, there is a corporation; the spirit of a corporation has its inconveniences, but it is very different from the spirit of the caste. The word *caste,* cannot be applied to the Christian church. The celibacy of the priests prevents the Christian church from ever becoming a caste.

You already see, to a certain extent, the consequences of this difference. To the system of caste, to the fact of inheritance, monopoly is inevitably attached. This results from the very definition of the word caste. When the same functions and the same powers become hereditary in the same families, it is evident that privilege must have been attached to them, and that no one could have acquired them independently of his origin. In fact, this was what happened; wherever the religious government fell into the hands of a caste, it became a matter of privilege; no one entered into it but those who belonged to the families of the caste. Nothing resembling this is met with in the Christian church; and not only is there no resemblance found, but the church has continually maintained the principle of the equal admissibility of all men to all her duties and dignities, whatever

---

3. Guizot spells out two criteria for legitimate government—(1) giving power to a "natural aristocracy" or open political élite; and (2) respecting individual rights or freedoms. The first criterion grew out of the Doctrinaires' analysis of the difference between the development of French and British institutions. In contrast to France, where the feudal aristocracy degenerated into a caste, Britain had seen its feudal aristocracy open out into a governing class founded on wealth and education as well as birth.

may have been their origin. The ecclesiastical career, particularly from the fifth to the twelfth century, was open to all. The church recruited herself from all ranks, alike from the inferior as well as the superior; more often indeed from the inferior. Around her all was disposed of under the system of privilege; she alone maintained the principle of equality and competition; she alone called all who were possessed of legitimate superiority to the possession of power.[4] This was the first great consequence which naturally resulted from her being a body, and not a caste.

Again, there is an inherent spirit in castes, the spirit of immobility. This assertion needs no proof. Open any history, and you will see the spirit of immobility imprinted upon all societies, whether political or religious, where the system of castes dominated. The fear of progress, it is true, was introduced at a certain epoch, and up to a certain point, in the Christian church. But we cannot say that it has dominated there; we cannot say that the Christian church has remained immovable and stationary; for many long ages she has been in movement and progress; sometimes provoked by the attacks of an external opposition, sometimes impelled from within, by desires of reform and internal development. Upon the whole, it is a society which has continually changed and marched onwards, and which has a varied and progressive history. There can be no doubt that the equal admission of all men to the ecclesiastical functions, that the continual recruiting of the church according to principles of equality, has powerfully contributed to maintain, and incessantly re-animate within it, its life and movement, to prevent the triumph of the spirit of immobility.

How could the church who thus admitted all men to power assure herself of their right to it? How could she discover and bring to light, from the heart of society, the legitimate superiorities which were to share the government?

Two principles were in vigour in the church: first, the election of the inferior by the superior—the choice, the nomination; secondly, the election

4. Guizot focuses on the rule of celibacy for clergy to show how the medieval Church retained a legitimacy, by remaining open to talent, in the midst of a feudal society otherwise founded on privilege and birthright—that is, on injustice. The theme of social mobility is thus introduced as one of the prerequisites for a liberal society and representative government.

of the superior by the subordinates—that is, an election properly so called, what we understand as such in the present day.

The ordination of priests, for instance, the power of making a man a priest, belonged to the superior alone. The choice was exercised by the superior over the inferior. So, in the collation of certain ecclesiastical benefices, among others, benefices attached to the feudal concessions, it was the superior—king, pope, or lord—who nominated the incumbent; in other cases, the principle of election, properly so called, was in force. The bishops had long been, and at the epoch which occupies us were still very often, elected by the body of the clergy; sometimes even the congregations interfered. In the interior of monasteries, the abbot was elected by the monks. At Rome, the popes were elected by the college of cardinals, and at one time even the whole of the Roman clergy took part in the election. You thus see the two principles—the choice of the inferior by the superior, and the election of the superior by the subordinate—acknowledged and acted upon in the church, especially at the epoch under consideration. It was by one or other of these means that she nominated the men called upon to exercise a portion of the ecclesiastical power.

Not only were these two principles co-existent, but being essentially different, there was a struggle between them. After many centuries and many vicissitudes, the nomination of the inferior by the superior gained the mastery in the Christian church; but as a general thing, from the fifth to the twelfth century, it was the other principle, the choice of the superior by the subordinate, which still prevailed. And do not be surprised at the co-existence of two principles so dissimilar. Regard society in general, the natural course of the world, the manner in which power is transmitted in it, you will see that this transmission is brought into force sometimes according to one of these principles and sometimes according to the other. The church did not originate them; she found them in the providential government of human things, and thence she borrowed them. There is truth and utility in each of them; their combination will often be the best means of discovering the legitimate power. It is a great misfortune, in my opinion, that one of these two, the choice of the inferior by the superior, should have gained the mastery in the church; the second, however, has never entirely disappeared; and under various names, with more or less success, it has been reproduced in all epochs, so as at all events to enter protest and interrupt prescription.

The Christian church derived, at the epoch which occupies us, immense strength from its respect for equality and legitimate superiorities. It was the most popular society, the most accessible and open to all kinds of talent, to all the noble ambitions of human nature. Thence arose its power, much more than from its riches, or from the illegitimate means which it has too often employed.

As regards the second condition of a good government, respect for liberty, there was much to wish for in the church.

Two evil principles met in it; the one avowed, and, as it were, incorporated in the doctrines of the church; the other introduced into it by human weakness, and not as a legitimate consequence of doctrines.

The first was the denial of the right of individual reason, the pretension to transmit creeds down through the whole religious society, without any one having the right to judge for himself. It was easier to lay down this principle than to make it actually prevail. A conviction does not enter into the human intellect unless the intellect admits it; it must make itself acceptable. In whatever form it presents itself, and whatever name it evokes, reason weighs it; and if the creed prevail, it is from being accepted by reason. Thus, under whatever form they may be concealed, the action of the individual reason is always exerted upon the ideas which are sought to be imposed upon it. It is very true that reason may be altered; it may to a certain extent abdicate and mutilate itself; it may be induced to make an ill use of its faculties, or not to put in force all the use of them to which it has a right; such, indeed, has been the consequence of the ill principle admitted by the church; but as regards the pure and complete influence of this principle, it never has been, and never can be, put into full force.

The second evil principle is the right of constraint which the church arrogates to herself—a right contrary to the very nature of religious society, to the very origin of the church, and her primitive maxims—a right which has been disputed by many of the most illustrious fathers, St. Ambrose, St. Hilary, St. Martin, but which has, notwithstanding, prevailed and become a dominant fact. The pretension of forcing to believe, if two such words can stand in juxta-position, or of physically punishing belief, the persecution of heresy, contempt for the legitimate liberty of human thought, this is an error which was introduced into the church even before the fifth century; and dearly has it cost her.

If, then, we consider the church in relation to the liberty of her members, we perceive that her principles in this respect were less legitimate and less salutary than those which presided at the formation of the ecclesiastical power. It must not be supposed, however, that an evil principle radically vitiates an institution, nor even that it is the cause of all the evil which it carries in its breast. Nothing more falsifies history than logic: when the human mind rests upon an idea, it draws from it every possible consequence, makes it produce all the effect it is capable of producing, and then pictures it in history with the whole retinue. But things do not happen in this way; events are not so prompt in their deductions as the human mind. There is in all things a mixture of good and evil so profound and invincible, that wherever you penetrate, when you descend into the most hidden elements of society or the soul, you find there these two orders of existent facts developing themselves side by side, combating without exterminating one another. Human nature never goes to the extremity either of evil or good; it passes incessantly from one to the other, erecting itself at the moment when it seems most likely to fall, and weakening at the moment when its walk seems firmest. We shall find here that character of discordance, variety, and strife, which I have remarked as being the fundamental characteristic of European civilization. There is still another general fact which characterizes the government of the church, and of which it is necessary to take notice.

At the present day, when the idea of government presents itself to us, whatever it may be, we know that there is no pretension of governing other than the external actions of man—the civil relations of men among themselves; governments profess to apply themselves to nothing more. With regard to human thought, human conscience, and morality, properly so called, with regard to individual opinions and private manners, they do not interfere; these fall within the domain of liberty.

The Christian church did or wished to do directly the contrary; she undertook to govern the liberty, private manners, and opinions of individuals.

She did not make a code like ours, to define only actions at once morally culpable and socially dangerous, and only punishing them in proportion as they bore this two-fold character. She made a catalogue of all actions morally culpable, and under the name of sins she punished all with the intention of repressing all; in a word, the government of the church did not address itself, like modern governments, to the external man, to the purely civil relations of men among themselves; it addressed itself to the internal man, to the thought and conscience, that is to say, to all that is most private to him, most free and rebellious against constraint. The church, then, from the very nature of her enterprise, together with the nature of some of the principles upon which she founded her government, was in danger of becoming tyrannical, and of employing illegitimate force. But at the same time the force encountered a resistance which it could not vanquish. However little movement and space are left them, human thought and liberty energetically re-act against all attempts to subdue them, and at every moment compel the very despotism which they endure to abdicate. Thus it happened in the bosom of the Christian church. You have seen the proscription of heresy, the condemnation of the right of inquiry, the contempt for individual reason, and the principle of the imperative transmission of doctrines upon authority. Well! Show one society in which individual reason has been more boldly developed than in the church! What are sects and heresies, if they are not the fruit of individual opinions? Sects and heresies, all the signs of opposition in the church, are the incontestable proof of the moral life and activity which reigned in it; a life tempestuous and painful, overspread with perils, errors, crimes, but noble and powerful, and one that has given rise to the finest developments of mind and intellect. Leave the opposition, look into the ecclesiastical government itself; you will find it constituted and acting in a manner very different from what some of its principles seem to indicate. It denied the right of inquiry, and wished to deprive individual reason of its liberty; and yet it is to reason that it incessantly appeals, and liberty is its dominant fact. What are its institutions and means of action? provincial councils, national councils, general councils, a continual correspondence, the incessant publication of letters, admonitions, and writings. Never did a government proceed to such an extent by discussion and common deliberation. We might suppose ourselves in the heart of the Greek schools of philosophy; and yet it was no mere discussion, or seeking for truth that was at issue; it involved questions of authority, of adopting measures, of promulgating decrees; in fine, of a government. But such in the very heart of this government was the energy of intellectual life, that it became the dominant and universal fact, to which all others gave way; and what shone forth on all sides, was the exercise of reason and liberty.

I am far from inferring that these bad principles which I have attempted to set forth, and which, in my opinion, existed in the system of the church, remained in it without effect. At the epoch which now occupies us, they already bore but too bitter fruit, and were destined at a later period to bear fruit still more bitter: but they have not accomplished all the evil of which they were capable, they have not stifled all the good which grew in the same soil. Such was the church, considered in itself, in its internal construction and nature. I now pass to its relations with the sovereigns, the masters of temporal power. This is the second point of view under which I promised to consider it.

When the Empire fell—when, instead of the ancient Roman system, the government, in the midst of which the church had taken birth, with which she had developed, and had ancient ties as well as habits in common, she found herself exposed to those barbarian kings and chiefs who wandered over the land, or remained fixed in their castles, and to whom neither traditions, creeds, nor sentiments, could unite her; her danger was great, and as great was her terror.

A single idea became dominant in the church: this was to take possession of the newcomers, to convert them. The relations between the church and the barbarians had, at first, scarcely any other aim. In influencing the barbarians, it was necessary that their senses and their imagination should be appealed to. We therefore find at this epoch a great augmentation in the number, pomp, and variety of the ceremonies of worship. The chronicles prove that this was the chief means by which the church acted upon the barbarians; she converted them by splendid spectacles.[5] When they were

5. Guizot's interpretation of the growth of ecclesiastical ritual and pomp in order to impress the barbarian invaders of Europe can, again, be seen as quasi-Protestant, in so far as it suggests that the growth of civilization ought in due course to make it possible once again to dispense with such semi-barbarous rites.

established and converted, and when there existed some ties between them and the church, she did not cease to run many dangers on their part. The brutality and recklessness of the barbarians were such, that the new creeds and sentiments with which they were inspired exercised but little empire over them. Violence soon reassumed the upper hand, and the church, like the rest of society, was its victim. For her defence she proclaimed a principle formerly laid down under the Empire, although more vaguely—this was the separation of the spiritual from the temporal power, and their reciprocal independence. It was by the aid of this principle that the church lived freely in connexion with the barbarians; she maintained that force could not act upon the system of creeds, hopes, and religious promises; that the spiritual world and the temporal world were entirely distinct. You may at once see the salutary consequences resulting from this principle. Independently of its temporal utility to the church, it had this inestimable effect, of bringing about, on the foundation of right, the separation of powers, and of controlling them by means of each other. Moreover, in sustaining the independence of the intellectual world, as a general thing, in its whole extent, the church prepared the way for the independence of the individual intellectual world—the independence of thought. The church said that the system of religious creeds could not fall under the yoke of force; and each individual was led to apply to his own case the language of the church. The principle of free inquiry, of liberty of individual thought, is exactly the same as that of the independence of general spiritual authority, with regard to temporal power.

Unhappily, it is easy to pass from the desire for liberty to the lust for domination. It thus happened within the bosom of the church; by the natural development of ambition and human pride, the church attempted to establish, not only the independence of spiritual power, but also its domination over temporal power. But it must not be supposed that this pretension had no other source than in the weaknesses of human nature; there were other more profound sources which it is of importance to know.

When liberty reigns in the intellectual world; when thought and human conscience are not subjected to a power which disputes their right to debate and decide, or employs force against them; when there is no visible and constituted spiritual government, claiming and exercising the right to dictate opinions; then the idea of the domination of the spiritual over the temporal order is impossible. Nearly such is the present state of the world. But when there exists, as there did exist in the tenth century, a government of the spiritual order; when thought and conscience come under laws, institutions, and powers, which arrogate to themselves the right of commanding and constraining them; in a word, when spiritual power is constituted, when it actually takes possession of human reason and conscience, in the name of right and force, it is natural that it should be led to assume the domination over the temporal order, that it should say: "How! I have right and influence over that which is most elevated and independent in man; over his thought, his internal will, and his conscience, and shall I not have right over his exterior, material, and passing interests! I am the interpreter of justice and truth, and am I not allowed to regulate worldly affairs according to justice and truth?" In very virtue of this reasoning, the spiritual order was sure to attempt the usurpation of the temporal order. And this was the more certain from the fact that the spiritual order embraced every development of human thought at that time; there was but one science, and that was theology; but one spiritual order, the theological; all other sciences, rhetoric, arithmetic, even music, all was comprised in theology.

The spiritual power, thus finding itself at the head of all the activity of human thought, naturally arrogated to itself the government of the world. A second cause tended as powerfully to this end—the frightful state of the temporal order, the violence and iniquity which prevailed in the government of temporal societies.

We, for many centuries, have spoken at our ease of the rights of temporal power; but at the epoch under consideration, the temporal was mere force, ungovernable brigandage. The church, however imperfect her notions still were concerning morality and justice, was infinitely superior to such a temporal government as this; the cries of the people continually pressed her to take its place. When a pope, or the bishops, proclaimed that a prince had forfeited his rights, and that his subjects were absolved from their oath of fidelity, this intervention, without doubt subject to various abuses, was often, in particular cases, legitimate and salutary. In general, when liberty has failed mankind, it is religion that has had the charge of replacing it. In the tenth century, the people were not in a state to defend themselves, and so make their rights available against civil violence: religion, in the name of Heaven, interfered. This is one of the causes which have most contributed to the victories of the theocratical principle.

There is a third, which I think is too seldom remarked: the complexity of situation of the heads of the church, the variety of aspects under which they have presented themselves in society. On one hand, they were prelates, members of the ecclesiastical order, and part of the spiritual power, and by this title independent; on the other, they were vassals, and, as such, engaged in the bonds of civil feudalism. This is not all; besides being vassals, they were subjects; some portion of the ancient relations between the Roman emperors, and the bishops, and the clergy, had now passed into those between the clergy and the barbarian sovereigns. By a series of causes which it would be too tedious to develop, the bishops had been led to regard, up to a certain point, the barbarian sovereigns as the successors of the Roman emperors, and to attribute to them all their prerogatives. The chiefs of the clergy, then, had a three-fold character: an ecclesiastical character, and as such, an independent one; a feudal character, one, as such, bound to certain duties, and holding by certain services; and, lastly, the character of a simple subject, and as such, bound to obey an absolute sovereign. Now mark the result. The temporal sovereigns, who were not less covetous and ambitious than the bishops, availed themselves of their rights as lords or sovereigns, to encroach upon the spiritual independence, and to seize upon the collation of benefices, the nomination of bishops, &c. The bishops, on their side, often entrenched themselves in their spiritual independence, in order to escape their obligations as vassals or subjects; so that, on either hand, there was an almost inevitable tendency which led the sovereigns to destroy spiritual independence, and the heads of the church to make spiritual independence a means of universal domination.

The result has been shown in facts of which no one is ignorant: in the quarrels concerning investitures, and in the struggle between the priesthood and the empire. The various situations of the heads of the church, and the difficulty of reconciling them, were the real sources of the uncertainty and contest of these pretensions.

Lastly, the church had a third relation with the sovereigns, which was for her the least favourable and the most unfortunate of them all. She laid claim to coaction, to the right of restraining and punishing heresy; but she had no means of doing this; she had not at her disposal a physical force; when she had condemned the heretic, she had no means of executing judgment upon him. What could she do? She invoked the aid of what was called the secular arm; she borrowed the force of civil power, as a means of coaction. And she thereby placed herself, in regard to civil power, in a situation of dependence and inferiority. A deplorable necessity to which she was reduced by the adoption of the evil principle of coaction and persecution.

It remains for me to make you acquainted with the relations of the church with the people; what principles were prevalent in them, and what consequences have thence resulted to civilization in general. I shall afterwards attempt to verify the inductions we have here drawn from the nature of its institutions and principles, by means of history, facts, and the vicissitudes of the destiny of the church from the fifth to the twelfth century.

SIXTH LECTURE

Object of the lecture—Separation of the governing and the governed party in the church—Indirect influence of the laity upon the clergy—The clergy recruited from all conditions of society—Influence of the church upon the public order and upon legislation—The penitential system—The development of the human mind is entirely theological—The church usually ranges itself on the side of power—Not to be wondered at; the aim of religions is to regulate human liberty—Different states of the church, from the fifth to the twelfth century—1st. The imperial church—2nd. The barbaric church; development of the separating principle of the two powers; the monastic order—3rd. The feudal church; attempts at organization; want of reform; Gregory VII—The theocratical church—Regeneration of the spirit of inquiry; Abailard—Movement of the boroughs—No connexion between these two facts.

W E   W E R E   U N A B L E, at our last meeting, to terminate the inquiry into the state of the church from the fifth to the twelfth century. After having decided that it should be considered under three principal aspects—first, in itself alone, in its internal constitution, and in its nature as a distinct and independent society; next, in its relations to the sovereign and the temporal power; and lastly, in its relations with the people—we have only accomplished the two first divisions of this task. It now remains for me to make you acquainted with the church in its relations with the people. I shall afterwards endeavour to draw from this three-fold inquiry a general idea of the influence of the church upon European civilization from the fifth to the twelfth century. And lastly, we will verify our assertions by an examination of the facts, by the history of the church itself at that epoch.

You will easily understand that, in speaking of the relations of the church with the people, I am forced to confine myself to very general terms. I cannot enter into detail of the practices of the church, or of the daily relations of the clergy with the faithful. It is the dominant principles and overall effects of the system and of the conduct of the church towards the Christian people, that I have to place before you.

The characteristic fact, and, it must so be called, the radical vice of the relations of the church with the people, is the separation of the governing and the governed, the non-influence of the governed in their government, the independence of the Christian clergy with regard to the faithful.

This evil must have been provoked by the state of man and of society, for we find it introduced into the Christian church at a very early period. The separation of the clergy and the Christian people was not entirely consummated at the epoch under consideration; there was, on certain occasions, in the election of bishops for instance, at least in some cases, a direct intervention of the Christian people in its government. But this intervention became by degrees more weak, and of more rare occurrence; it was from the second century of our era that it began visibly and rapidly to decline. The tendency to the isolation and independence of the clergy is, in a measure, the history of the church itself, from its very cradle. From thence, it cannot be denied, arose the greater portion of those abuses which, at this epoch, and still more at a later period, have cost so dear to the church. We must not, however, impute them solely to this, nor regard this tendency to isolation as peculiar to the Christian clergy. There is in the very nature of religious society a strong inclination to raise the governing far above the governed, to attribute to the former something distinct and divine. This is the effect of the very mission with which they are charged, and of the character under which they present themselves to the eyes of people, and such an effect is more grievous in the religious society than in any other. What is it that is at stake with the governed? Their reason, their conscience, their future destiny, that is to say, all that is most near to them, most individual, and most free. We can conceive, to a certain point, that although great evil may result therefrom, a man may abandon to an external authority the direction of his material interests, and his temporal destiny. We can understand the philosopher, who, when they came to tell him that his house was on fire, answered, "Go and inform my wife; I do not meddle in the household affairs." But, when it extends to the conscience, the thought, and the internal existence, to the abdication of self-government, to the delivering oneself to a foreign power, it is truly a moral suicide, a servitude a hundredfold worse than that of the body, or than that of the soil. Such, however, was the evil which, without prevailing entirely, as I shall immediately show, gradually usurped the Christian church in its relations with the faithful. You have already seen that, for the clergy themselves, and in the very heart of the church, there was no guarantee for liberty. It was far worse beyond the church, and among the laity. Among ecclesiastics, there was, at least, discussion, deliberation, and a display of individual faculties; there the excitement of contest supplied, in some measure, the want of liberty. There was none of this between the clergy and the people. The laity took part in the government of the church as mere spectators. Thus we see springing up and prevailing at a very early period, the idea that theology and religious questions and affairs, are the privileged domain of the clergy; that the clergy alone have the right, not only of deciding, but of taking part therein at all; that in any case the laity can have no kind of right to interfere. At the period under consideration, this theory was already in full power; centuries, and terrible revolutions were necessary to conquer it, to bring back within the public domain, religious questions and knowledge.

In principle, then, as well as in fact, the legal separation of the clergy and the Christian people was almost consummated before the twelfth century.

I would not have you suppose, however, that even at this epoch the Christian people were entirely without influence in its government. The legal intervention was wanting, but not influence—that is almost impossible in any government, still more so in a government founded upon a belief common both to the governing and the governed. Wherever this community of ideas is developed, or wherever a similar intellectual movement prevails with the government and the people, there must necessarily exist a connexion between them, which no vice in the organization can entirely destroy. To explain myself clearly, I will take an example near to us, and from the political order: at no epoch in the history of France has the French people had less legal influence on its government, by means of institutions, than in the seventeenth and eighteenth centuries, under Louis XIV and Louis XV.

No one is ignorant that at this period nearly all official and direct influence of the country in the exercise of authority had perished; yet there can be no doubt that the people and the country then exercised upon the government far more influence than in other times—in the times, for instance, when the states-general were so often convoked, when the parliament took so important a part in politics, and when the legal participation of the people in power was much greater.

It is because there is a force which cannot be inclosed by laws, which, when necessary, can dispense with institutions: it is the force of ideas, of the public mind and opinion. In France, in the seventeenth and eighteenth centuries, there was a public opinion which was much more powerful than at any other epoch. Although deprived of the means of acting legally upon the government, it acted indirectly by the empire of ideas, which were common alike to the governing and the governed, and by the impossibility which the governing felt of taking no note of the opinion of the governed. A similar fact happened in the Christian church from the fifth to the twelfth century; the Christian people, it is true, were deficient in legal action, but there was a great movement of mind in religious matters—this movement brought the laity and the ecclesiastics into conjunction, and by this means the people influenced the clergy.

In all cases in the study of history, it is necessary to hold, as highly valuable, indirect influences; they are much more efficacious, and sometimes more salutary, than is generally supposed. It is natural that men should wish their actions to be prompt and evident, should desire the pleasure of participating in their success, power, and triumph. This is not always possible, not always even useful. There are times and situations in which indirect and unseen influences are alone desirable and practicable. I will take another example from the political order. More than once, especially in 1641, the English parliament, like many other assemblies in similar crises, has claimed the right of nominating directly the chief officers of the crown, the ministers, councillors of state, &c.; it regarded this direct action in the government as an immense and valuable guarantee. It has sometimes exercised this prerogative, and always with bad success. The selections were ill concerted, and affairs ill governed. But how is it in England at the present day? Is it not the influence of parliament which decides the formation of the ministry, and the nomination of all the great officers of the crown? Certainly; but then it is an indirect and general influence, instead of a special intervention. The end at which England has long aimed is gained, but by different means; the first means which were tried had never acted beneficially.

There is a reason for this, concerning which I ask your permission to detain you for a moment. Direct action supposes, in those to whom it is confided, far more enlightenment, reason, and prudence: as they are to attain the end at once, and without delay, it is necessary that they should be certain of not missing that end. Indirect influences, on the contrary, are only exercised through obstacles, and after tests which restrain and rectify them; before prospering, they are condemned to undergo discussion, and to see themselves opposed and controlled; they triumph but slowly, and, in a measure, conditionally. For this reason, when minds are not sufficiently advanced and ripened to guarantee their direct action being taken with safety, indirect influences, although often insufficient, are still preferable. It was thus that the Christian people influenced their government, very incompletely, in much too limited an extent, I am convinced—but still they influenced it.

There was also another cause of approximation between the church and the people; this was the dispersion, so to speak, of the Christian clergy amongst all social conditions. Almost everywhere, when a church has been constituted independently of the people whom it governed, the body of priests has been formed of men nearly in the same situation; not that great inequalities have not existed among them, but, upon the whole, the government has appertained to colleges of priests living in common, and governing, from the depths of the temple, the people under their law. The Christian church was quite differently organized. From the miserable habitation of the serf, at the foot of the feudal castle, to the king's palace itself, everywhere there was a priest, a member of the clergy. The clergy was associated with all human conditions. This diversity in the situation of the Christian priests, this participation in all fortunes, has been a grand principle of union between the clergy and the laity, a principle which has been wanting in most churches invested with power. The bishops and chiefs of the Christian clergy were, moreover, as you have seen, engaged in the feudal organization, and were members, at one and the same time, of a civil and of an ecclesiastical hierarchy. Hence it was that the same interests, habits, and manners, became common to both the civil and religious orders. There has been much complaint, and with good reason, of bishops who have gone to war, of priests who have led the life of laymen. Of a verity, it was a great abuse, but still an abuse far less grievous than was, elsewhere, the existence of those priests who never left the temple, and whose life was totally separated from that of the community. Bishops, in some way mixed up in civil discords, were far more serviceable than priests who were total strangers to the population, to all its affairs and its manners. Under this connexion, there was established between the clergy and the Christian people a parity of destiny and situation, which, if it did not correct, at least lessened the evil of the separation between the governing and the governed.

This separation being once admitted, and its limits determined (the attainment of which object I have just attempted), let us investigate the manner in which the Christian church was governed, and in what way it acted upon the people under its command. On the one hand, how it tended to the development of man, and the internal progress of the individual; and on the other, how it tended to the amelioration of the social condition.

As regards the development of the individual, I do not think, correctly speaking, that, at the epoch under consideration, the church troubled itself much in the matter; it endeavoured to inspire the powerful of the world with milder sentiments, and with more justice in their relations with the weak; it maintained in the weak a moral life, together with sentiments and desires of a more elevated order than those to which their daily destiny condemned them. Still, for the development of the individual, properly so called, and for increasing the worth of man's personal nature, I do not think that at this period the church did much, at all events not among the laity. What it did effect was confined to the ecclesiastical society; it concerned itself much with the development of the clergy, and the instruction of the priests; it had for them schools, and all the institutions which the deplorable state of society permitted. But they were ecclesiastical schools destined only for the instruction of the clergy; beyond this, the church acted only indirectly and by very dilatory means upon the progress of ideas and manners. It doubtless provoked general activity of mind, by the career which it opened to all those whom it judged capable of serving it; but this was all that it did at this period towards the intellectual development of the laity.

It worked more, I believe, and that in a more efficacious manner, towards the amelioration of the state of society. There can be no doubt that it struggled resolutely against the great vices of the social state, against slavery, for instance. It has often been repeated, that the abolition of slavery among modern people is entirely due to Christians. That I think is saying too much: slavery existed for a long period in the heart of Christian society, without it being particularly astonished or irritated. A multitude of causes, and a great development in other ideas and principles of civilization, were necessary for the abolition of this iniquity of all iniquities. It cannot be doubted, however, that the church exerted its influence to restrain it.[1] We have an undeniable proof of this. The greater part of the forms of enfranchisement, at various epochs, were based upon religious principles: it is in the name of religious ideas, upon hopes of the future, and upon the religious equality of mankind, that enfranchisement has almost always been pronounced.

The church worked equally for the suppression of a crowd of barbarous customs, and for the amelioration of the criminal and civil legislation. You know how monstrous and absurd this legislation then was, despite some principles of liberty in it; you also know what ridiculous proofs, such as judicial combat, and even the simple oaths of a few men, were considered as the only means of arriving at the truth. The church endeavoured to substitute in their stead more rational and legitimate means. I have already spoken of the difference which may be observed between the laws of the Visigoths,

1. By presenting a moderate version of the claim that Christianity had destroyed slavery, Guizot seeks to "save" the contribution of the Church and reiterates themes which had figured in meetings of the *Society for Christian Morality*, the society he had directed in the later 1820s and which became an important centre of opposition to the ultra-royalist government of Villèle. Once again, Guizot's argument is that the Church, far from being the enemy of the modern world, has played a crucial role in creating it.

issued chiefly from the councils of Toledo, and other barbarous laws. It is impossible to compare them without being struck by the immense superiority of the ideas of the church in matters of legislation, justice, and in all that interests the search for truth and the destiny of mankind. Doubtless many of these ideas were borrowed from the Roman legislation; but had not the church preserved and defended them, if it had not worked their propagation, they would, doubtless, have perished. For example, as regards the employment of the oath in legal procedure; open the law of the Visigoths, and you will see with what wisdom it is used:

"Let the judge, that he may understand the cause, first interrogate the witnesses, and afterwards examine the writings, to the end that the truth may be discovered with more certainty, and that the oath may not be needlessly administered. The search for truth requires that the writings on either side be carefully examined, and that the necessity for the oath, suspended over the heads of the parties, arrive unexpectedly. Let the oath be administered only in those cases when the judge can discover no writings, proof, or other certain evidence of the truth." (*For. Jud.* 1. ii. tit. i. 21.)

In criminal matters, the relation between the punishments and the offences is determined according to philosophical and moral notions, which are very just. One may there recognize the efforts of an enlightened legislator struggling against the violence and want of reflection of barbarous manners. The chapter, *De coede et morte hominum,* compared with laws corresponding thereto in other nations, is a very remarkable example. Elsewhere, it is the damage done which seems to constitute the crime, and the punishment is sought in the material reparation of pecuniary composition. Here the crime is reduced to its true, veritable, and moral element, the intention. The various shades of criminality, absolutely involuntary homicide, homicide by inadvertency, provoked homicide, homicide with or without premeditation, are distinguished and defined nearly as correctly as in our codes, and the punishments vary in just proportion. The justice of the legislator went still further. He has attempted, if not to abolish, at least to lessen the diversity of legal value, established among men by the laws of barbarism. The only distinction which he kept up, was that of the free man and the slave. As regards free men, the punishment varies neither according to the origin nor the rank of the deceased, but solely according to the various degrees of moral culpability of the murderer. With regard to slaves, although not daring to deprive the master of all right to life and death, he at least attempted to restrain it, by subjecting it to a public and regular procedure. The text of the law deserves citation.

"If no malefactor or accomplice in a crime, should go unpunished, with how much more reason should we condemn those who have committed homicide lightly and maliciously! Therefore, as masters, in their pride, often put their slaves to death, without fault on their part, it is right that this licence should be entirely extirpated, and we ordain that the present law be perpetually observed by all. No master or mistress can put to death without public trial any of their male or female slaves, nor any person dependent upon them. If a slave, or any other servant, shall commit any crime which will render him liable to capital punishment, his master, or accuser, shall immediately inform the judge, or the count, or the duke, of the place where the crime was committed. After an investigation into the affair, if the crime be proved, let the culprit undergo, either through the judge or his own master, the sentence of death which he merits: provided, however, that if the judge will not put the accused to death, he shall draw up a capital sentence against him in writing; and then it shall be in the power of the master either to kill him or spare his life. At the same time, if the slave by a fatal audacity, resisting his master, shall strike, or attempt to strike, him with a weapon or stone, and if the master, while defending himself, should kill the slave in his rage, the master shall not receive the punishment due to a homicide; but it must be proved that this really was the fact, and that, by the testimony or oath of the slaves, male or female, who may have been present, and by the oath of the author of the deed himself. Whoever in pure malice, whether with his own hand or by that of another, shall kill his slave without public judgment, shall be reckoned infamous, and declared incapable of bearing testimony, and shall pass the remainder of his life in exile or penitence, and his goods shall fall to his nearest heir, to whom the law accords the inheritance." (*For. Jud.* 1. vi. tit. v. 1. 12.)

There is one fact in the institutions of the church, which is generally not sufficiently remarked: it is the penitential system, a system so much the more curious to study in the present day, from its being, as regards the principles and applications of the penal law, exactly in accordance with the ideas of modern philosophy. If you study the nature of the punishments of the church, and the public penances which were its principal mode of chastisement, you will see that the chief object is to excite repentance in the soul of the culprit, and moral terror in the beholders, by the example. There was also another idea mixed with it, that of expiation. I know not, as a general thing, if it be possible to separate the idea of expiation from that of punishment, and whether there is not in all punishment, independently of the necessity of provoking repentance in the culprit, and of deterring those who might be tempted to become so, a secret and imperious want to expiate the wrong committed. But, leaving aside this question, it is evident that repentance and example are the ends proposed by the church in its whole penitential system. Is not this, also, the end of a truly philosophical legislation? Is it not in the name of these principles, that the most enlightened jurists of this and the past century have advocated the reform of the European penal legislation? Open their works, those of Bentham for instance, and you will be surprised by all the resemblances which you will meet with between the penal means therein proposed, and those employed by the church.[2] They certainly did not borrow them from her, nor could she have foreseen that one day her example would be invoked to aid the plans of the least devout of philosophers. Lastly, she strove by all sorts of means to restrain violence and continual warfare in society. Every one knows what was the *truce of God,* and numerous measures of a similar kind, by which the church struggled against the employment of force, and strove to introduce more order and gentleness into society. These facts are so well known, that it is needless for me to enter into details. Such are the principal points which I have to place before you concerning the relations between the church and the people. We have considered it under the three aspects which I first announced; and have gained an inward and outward knowledge of it, both in its internal constitution and its two-fold position. It now remains for us to deduce from our knowledge, by means of induction and conjecture, its general influence upon European civilization. This,

2. This suggestive, even provocative use of the analogy between the penitential system of the Church and "progressive" moral philosophy of the eighteenth century, exemplified by Bentham's utilitarianism, is typical of Guizot's strategy for underlining the importance of Christianity in the moral and intellectual formation of Europe.

if I mistake not, is a work almost completed, or at least far advanced; the simple announcement of the dominant facts and principles in the church, show and explain its influence; the results have, in some measure, already passed before your eyes with the causes. If, however, we attempt to reca- pitulate them, we shall, I think, be led to two general assertions.

The first is, that the church must have exercised a very great influence upon the moral and intellectual orders in modern Europe, upon public ideas, sentiments, and manners.

The fact is evident; the moral and intellectual development of Europe has been essentially theological. Survey history from the fifth to the twelfth century; it is theology that possessed and directed the human spirit; all opinions are impressed by theology; philosophical, political, and histori- cal questions, are all considered under a theological point of view. So all- powerful is the church in the intellectual order, that even the mathematical and physical sciences are held in submission to its doctrines. The theologi- cal spirit is, in a manner, the blood which ran in the veins of the European world, down to Bacon and Descartes. For the first time, Bacon in England, and Descartes in France, carried intelligence beyond the path of theology.

The same fact is evident in all branches of literature; theological habits, sentiments, and language, are manifest at every step.

Upon the whole, this influence has been salutary; not only has it sus- tained and fertilized the intellectual movement in Europe, but the system of doctrines and precepts, under the name of which it implanted the move- ment, was far superior to anything with which the ancient world was ac- quainted. There was at the same time movement and progress.

The situation of the church, moreover, gave an extent and a variety to the development of the human mind in the modern world, which it had not possessed previously. In the east, intellect is entirely religious; in Greek society, it is exclusively human; in the one, humanity, properly so called, that is, its actual nature and destiny, vanishes; in the other, it is man him- self, his actual passions, sentiments, and interests which occupy the whole stage. In the modern world, the religious spirit is mixed up with everything, but it excludes nothing. Modern intellect has at once the stamp of human- ity and of divinity. Human sentiments and interests occupy an important place in our literature; and yet the religious character of man, that portion of his existence which links him to another world, appears in every step; so that the two great sources of man's development, humanity and religion, have flowed at one time, and that abundantly; and despite all the evil and abuses with which it is mixed, despite many acts of tyranny, regarded from an intellectual point of view, the influence of the church has tended more to develop than compress, more to extend than to confine.

Under a political point of view, it is otherwise. There can be no doubt that in softening sentiments and manners, in crying down and exploding numerous barbarous customs, the church has powerfully contributed to the amelioration of the social state; but in the political order, properly so called, as regards the relations between the government and the subject, between power and liberty, I do not think that, upon the whole, her influence has been beneficial. Under this relation, the church has always presented itself as the interpreter and defender of two systems, the theocratic or the Roman imperial system, that is, of despotism, sometimes under a religious, and sometimes under a civil form. Take all her institutions, and all her legislation; take her canons and procedure; and you will always find, as the dominant principle, theocracy or the empire. If weak, the church sheltered herself under the absolute power of the emperors; if strong, she claimed the same absolutism on her own account, in the name of her spiritual power. We must not confine ourselves to particular facts or special instances. The church has, doubtless, often invoked the rights of the people against the bad government of the sovereigns; and often even approved of, and provoked insurrection; has often maintained, in face of the sovereign, the rights and interests of the people. But when the question of political guarantees has arisen between power and liberty, when the question was of establishing a system of permanent institutions, which might truly place liberty beyond the invasions of power, the church has generally ranged upon the side of despotism.

One need not be much astonished at this, nor charge the clergy with too great a degree of human weakness, nor suppose it a vice peculiar to the Christian church. There is a more profound and powerful cause. What does a religion pretend to? It pretends to govern the human passions and the human will. All religion is a restraint, a power, a government. It comes in the name of divine law, for the purpose of subduing human nature. It is human liberty, then, with which it chiefly concerns itself; it is human liberty which resists it, and which it wishes to overcome. Such is the enterprise of religion, such its mission and its hope.

It is true, that although human liberty is what religions concern themselves with, although they aspire to the reformation of the will of man, they have no moral means of acting upon him but through himself, by his own will. When they act by external means, by force, seduction, or any means, in fact, which are foreign to the free concurrence of man, when they treat him as they would water or wind, as a material power, they do not attain their end, they neither reach nor govern the human will. For religions to accomplish what they attempt, they must make themselves acceptable to liberty itself; it is needful that man should submit, but he must do so voluntarily and freely, and must preserve his liberty in the very heart of his submission. This is the double problem which religions are called upon to solve.

This they have too often overlooked; they have considered liberty as an obstacle, not as a means; they have forgotten the nature of the force to which they address themselves, and have treated the human soul as they would a material force. It is in following this error that they have almost always been led to range themselves on the side of power and despotism against human liberty, regarding it only as an adversary, and taking more pains to subdue than to secure it. If religions had turned their means of action to good account, if they had not allowed themselves to be carried away by a natural but deceitful inclination, they would have seen that it is necessary to guarantee liberty in order to regulate it morally; that religion cannot, nor ought to act except by moral means; they would have respected the will of man in applying themselves to govern it. This they have too often forgotten, and religious power has ended in itself suffering as much as liberty.

I will go no further in the examination of the general consequence of the influence of the church upon European civilization. I have recapitulated them in this two-fold result; a great and salutary influence upon the social and moral order, an influence rather unfortunate than beneficial on the political order, properly so called. We have now to verify our assertions by facts, to verify by history that which we have deduced from the mere nature and situation of the ecclesiastical society. Let us see what was the fate of the Christian church from the fifth to the twelfth century, and whether the principles which I have placed before you, and the results which I have attempted to draw from them, were really developed, as I have ventured to describe.

You should be careful not to suppose that these principles and consequences have appeared at the same periods, and with the same distinctness that I have represented them. It is a great and too common an error, when considering the past at the distance of many centuries, to forget the moral chronology, to forget (singular obliviousness!) that history is essentially successive. Take the life of a man, of Cromwell, Gustavus Adolphus, or Cardinal Richelieu. He enters upon his career, he moves and progresses; he influences great events, and he in his turn is influenced by them; he arrives at the goal. We then know him; but it is in his whole, it is, as it were, such as he has issued after much labour from the workshop of Providence. But at starting he was not what he has thus become; he has never been complete and finished at any single period of his life; he has been formed progressively. Men are formed morally as physically; they change daily; their being modifies itself without ceasing; the Cromwell of 1650 was not the Cromwell of 1640. There is always a groundwork of individuality; it is always the same man who perseveres; but how changed are his ideas, sentiments, and will! What things has he lost, and acquired! At whatever moment we look upon the life of man, there is no time when it has been what we shall see it when its term is attained.

It is here, however, that most historians have fallen into error; because they have gained one complete idea of man, they see him such throughout the whole course of his career. For them, it is the same Cromwell who enters parliament in 1628, and who dies thirty years afterwards in the palace of Whitehall. And with regard to institutions and general influences, they incessantly commit the same error. Let us guard against it; I have represented to you the principles of the church in their entirety, and the development of the consequences. But remember that historically the picture is not correct; all has been partial and successive, cast here and there over space and time. We must not expect to find this uniformity, this prompt and systematic connexion, in the recital of facts. Here we shall see one principle springing up, there another; all will be incomplete, unequal, and dispersed. We must come to modern times, to the end of the career, before we shall find the entire result. I shall now place before you the various states through which the church passed between the fifth and the twelfth centuries. We cannot collect an entire demonstration of the assertions which I have placed before you, but we shall see sufficient to enable us to presume they are legitimate.

The first condition in which the church appears at the fifth century is the imperial state, the church of the Roman empire. When the Roman empire was on the decline, the church thought herself at the term of her career, and that her triumph was accomplished. It is true, she had completely vanquished paganism. The last emperor who took the rank of sovereign pontiff, which was a pagan dignity, was the emperor Gratian, who died at the end of the fourth century. Gratian was called sovereign pontiff, like Augustus and Tiberius. The church likewise thought herself at the end of her struggle with the heretics, especially with the Arians, the chief heretics of the day. The emperor Theodosius, towards the end of the fourth century, instituted against them a complete and severe legislation. The church then enjoyed the government and the victory over its two most formidable enemies. It was at this moment that she saw the Roman empire fail her, and found herself in the presence of other pagans and heretics, in the presence of the barbarians, Goths, Vandals, Burgundians, and Franks. The fall was immense. You may easily conceive the lively attachment for the empire which must have been preserved in the bosom of the church. Thus we see her strongly adhering to what remained of it—to the municipal system and to absolute power. And when she had converted the barbarians, she attempted to resuscitate the empire; she addressed herself to the barbarous kings, conjured them to become Roman emperors, to take all the rights belonging to them, and enter into the same relations with the church as that which she had maintained with the Roman empire. This was the work of the bishops between the fifth and the sixth centuries, the general state of the church.

This attempt could not be successful; there were no means of reforming the Roman society with barbarians. Like the civil world, the church herself fell into barbarism. This was its second state. When one compares the writings of the ecclesiastical chroniclers of the eighth century with those of preceding ages, the difference is immense. Every wreck of Roman civilization had disappeared, even the language; everything felt itself, as it were, cast into barbarism. On the one hand, barbarians entered the clerical order, and became priests and bishops; and on the other hand, the bishops adopted a life of barbarism, and without quitting their bishoprics, placed themselves at the head of bands, overrunning the country, pillaging, and making war, like the companions of Clovis. You will find in Gregory of Tours mention of several bishops, among others Salonus and Sagittarius, who thus passed their lives.

Two important facts developed themselves in the bosom of this barbarous church. The first is, the separation of spiritual and temporal power. This principle took its rise at this epoch. Nothing could be more natural. The church not having succeeded in resuscitating the absolute power of the Roman empire, and sharing it herself, was forced to seek safety in independence. It was necessary that she should defend herself on all sides, for she was continually threatened. Each bishop and priest saw his barbarous neighbours incessantly interfering in the affairs of the church, to usurp her riches, lands, and power; her only means of defence was to say, "The spiritual order is totally separate from the temporal; you have not the right to interfere in its affairs." This principle, above all others, became the defensive arm of the church against barbarism.

A second important fact belonged to this epoch, the development of the monastic order in the west. It is known that at the commencement of the sixth century, St. Benedict instituted his order among the monks of the west, who were then trifling in number, but who have since prodigiously increased. The monks at this epoch were not members of the clergy, they were still regarded as laymen. No doubt priests, or even bishops, were sought for among them; but it was only at the end of the fifth and beginning of the sixth century, that the monks, in general, were considered as forming a part of the clergy, properly so called. We then find that priests and bishops became monks, believing that by so doing they made a fresh progress in religious life. Thus the monastic order in Europe took all at once a great development. The monks struck the fancy of the barbarians far more than the secular clergy. Their number was as imposing as their singularity of life. The secular clergy, the bishop or simple priest, were common to the imagination of the barbarians, who were accustomed to see, maltreat, and rob them. It was a much more serious affair to attack a monastery, where so many holy men were congregated in one holy place. The monasteries, during the barbaric epoch, were an asylum for the church, as the church was for the laity. Pious men there found a refuge, as in the east they sheltered themselves in the Thebaid, to escape a worldly life and the temptations of Constantinople.

Such are the two great facts in the history of the church, which belong to the barbaric epoch; on one side, the development of the principle of separation between the spiritual and temporal power; on the other, the development of the monastic system in the west.

Towards the end of the barbaric epoch, there was a new attempt to resuscitate the Roman empire made by Charlemagne. The church and the civil sovereign again contracted a close alliance. This was an epoch of great docility, and hence one of great progress for papacy. The attempt again failed, and the empire of Charlemagne fell; but the advantages which the church had gained from his alliance still remained with her. Papacy found herself definitively at the head of Christianity.

On the death of Charlemagne, chaos recommenced; the church again fell into it as did civil society, and only left it to enter the frame of feudalism. This was its third state. By the dissolution of the empire of Charlemagne, there happened almost the same thing in the ecclesiastical order as in the civil order; all unity disappeared, all became local, partial, and individual. There then commenced in the situation of the clergy a struggle which it had never experienced before. This was the struggle between the sentiments and interests of the fief-holder, and the sentiments and interests of the priest. The chiefs of the church were placed between these two positions, each tended to overcome the other; the ecclesiastical spirit was no longer so powerful or so universal; individual interest became more influential, and the desire for independence and the habits of a feudal life, loosened the ties of the ecclesiastical hierarchy. There was then made in the bosom of the church an attempt to remedy the effects of this relaxation. They sought in various quarters, by a system of federation, and by communal assemblies and deliberations, to organize national churches. It is at this epoch, and under the feudal system, that we find the greatest number of councils, convocations, and ecclesiastical assemblies, both provincial and national. It was in France, more especially, that this attempt at unity seemed followed with the greatest ardour. Hincmar, archbishop of Rheims, may perhaps be considered as the representative of this idea. His constant care was to organize the French church; he sought and put in force all the means of correspondence and union which might bring back some unity into the feudal church. We find Hincmar maintaining on the one side the independence of the church with regard to its temporal power, and on the other its independence with regard to the papacy; it was he who, knowing that the pope wished to come into France, and threatened the bishops with excommunication, said, *Si excommunicaturus venerit, excommunicatus abibit.* But this attempt to organize the feudal church succeeded no better than the attempt to organize the imperial church had done. There were no means of establishing unity in this church. Its dissolution was always increasing. Each bishop, prelate, and abbot, isolated himself more and more within his diocese or his monastery. The disorder increased from the same cause. This was the time of the greatest abuses of simony, of the entirely arbitrary disposition of ecclesiastical benefices, and of the greatest looseness of manners among the priests. This disorder greatly shocked the people and the better portion of the clergy. We thence see at an early time, a certain spirit of reform appear in the church, and the desire to seek some authority which could rally all these elements, and impose law upon them. Claude, bishop of Turin, and Agobard, archbishop of Lyons, originated in their dioceses some attempts of this nature; but they were not in a condition to accomplish such a work. There was within the whole church but one force adequate to it, and that was the court of Rome, the papacy. It was, therefore, not long ere it prevailed. The church passed during the course of the eleventh century into its fourth state, that of the theocratical or monastical church. The creator of this new form of church, insofar as a man can create, was Gregory VII.

We are accustomed, to represent to ourselves Gregory VII as a man who wished to render all things immoveable, as an adversary to intellectual development and social progress, and as a man who strove to maintain the world in a stationary or retrograding system. Nothing can be so false.

Gregory VII was a reformer upon the plan of despotism, as were Charlemagne and Peter the Great. He, in the ecclesiastical order, was almost what Charlemagne in France, and Peter the Great in Russia were in the civil order. He wished to reform the church, and through the church to reform society, to introduce therein more morality, more justice, and more law—he wished to effect this through the holy see, and to its profit.

At the same time that he strove to subject the civil world to the church, and the church to papacy, with an aim of reform and progress, and not one of immobility or retrogression, an attempt of the same kind, and a similar movement, was produced in the heart of monasteries. The desire for order, discipline, and moral strictness, was zealously shown. It was at this period that Robert de Molême introduced a severe order at Citeaux. This was the age of St. Norbert and the reform of the prebendaries, of the reform of Cluny, and lastly, of the great reform of St. Bernard. A general ferment reigned in the monasteries; the old monks defended themselves, declared it to be an injurious thing, said that their liberty was in danger, that the manners of the times must be complied with, that it was impossible to return to the primitive church, and treated all the reformers as madmen, dreamers, and tyrants. Open the history of Normandy, by Orderic Vital, and you will continually meet with these complaints.

All therefore seemed tending to the advantage of the church, to its unity and power. While the papacy sought to seize upon the government of the world, and while monasteries reformed themselves in a moral point of view, some powerful though isolated men claimed for human reason its right to be considered as something in man, and its right to interfere in his opinions. The greater part of them did not attack received doctrines nor religious creeds; they only said that reason had a right to test them, and that it did not suffice that they should be affirmed upon authority. John Erigena, Roscelin, and Abailard were the interpreters through whom reason once more began to claim her inheritance; these were the first authors of the movement of liberty which is associated with the movement of reform of Hildebrand and St. Bernard. When we seek the dominant character of this movement, we find that it is not a change of opinion, or a revolt against the system of public creeds—it is simply the right of reasoning claimed on the behalf of reason. The pupils of Abailard asked him, as he himself tells us in his *Introduction to Theology*, "for philosophical argument calculated to satisfy the reason, supplicating him to instruct them, not to repeat what he taught them, but to understand it; because nothing can be believed without being understood, and it is ridiculous to preach things which neither he who professes, nor those whom he teaches, can understand. . . . To what purpose were the study of philosophy, if not to lead to the study of God, to whom all things should be referred? With what view are the faithful permitted to read the writings which treat of the age and the books of the Gentiles, unless to prepare them for understanding the Holy Scriptures, and the necessary capacity for defending them? In this view, it is especially necessary to be aided with all the force of reason, so as to prevent, upon questions so difficult and complicated as are those which form the object of the Christian faith, the subtleties of its enemies from easily contriving to adulterate the purity of our faith."

The importance of this first attempt at liberty, this regeneration of the spirit of inquiry, was soon felt. Although occupied in reforming herself, the church did not the less take the alarm. She immediately declared war against these new reformers, whose methods menaced her more than their doctrines.

This is the great fact which shone forth at the end of the eleventh and beginning of the twelfth century, at the time when the state of the church was that of the theocratical or monastic. At this epoch, for the first time, there arose a struggle between the clergy and the free-thinkers. The quarrels of Abailard and St. Bernard, the councils of Soissons and Sens, where Abailard was condemned, are nothing but the expression of this fact, which holds so important a position in the history of modern civilization. It was the principal circumstance in the state of the church at the twelfth century, at the point at which we shall now leave it.

At the same time, a movement of a different nature was produced, the movement for the enfranchisement of the boroughs. Singular inconsistency of rude and ignorant manners! If it had been said to the citizens who conquered their liberty with so much passion, that there were men who claimed the rights of human reason, the right of free inquiry—men whom the church treated as heretics—they would have instantly stoned or burnt them. More than once did Abailard and his friends run this risk. On

the other hand, those very writers who claimed the rights of human reason, spoke of the efforts for the enfranchisement of the boroughs as of an
abominable disorder, and overthrow of society. Between the philosophical and the communal movement, between the political and the rational
enfranchisement, war seemed to be declared. Centuries were necessary to
effect the reconciliation of these two great powers, and to make them understand that their interests were in common. At the twelfth century, they
had nothing in common.

SEVENTH LECTURE

Object of the lecture—Comparative picture of the state of the boroughs at the twelfth and the eighteenth centuries—Double question—1st. The enfranchisement of the boroughs—State of the towns from the fifth to the tenth century—Their decay and regeneration—Communal insurrection—Charters—Social and moral effects of the enfranchisement of the boroughs—2nd. Internal government of the boroughs—Assemblies of the people—Magistrates—High and low burghership—Diversity of the state of the boroughs in the different countries of Europe.

WE HAVE CONDUCTED, down to the twelfth century, the history of the two great elements of civilization, the feudal system and the church. It is the third of these fundamental elements, I mean the boroughs, which we now have to trace likewise down to the twelfth century, confining ourselves to the same limits which we have observed in the other two.

We shall find ourselves differently situated with regard to the boroughs, from what we were with regard to the church or the feudal system. From the fifth to the twelfth century, the feudal system and the church, although at a later period they experienced new developments, showed themselves almost complete, and in a definitive state; we have watched their birth, increase, and maturity. It is not so with the boroughs. It was only at the end of the epoch which now occupies us, in the eleventh and twelfth centuries, that they take up any position in history; not but that before then they had a history which was deserving of study; nor is it that there were not long before this epoch traces of their existence; but it was only at the eleventh century that they became evidently visible upon the great scene of the world, and as an important element of modern civilization. Thus, in the

132

feudal system and the church, from the fifth to the twelfth century, we have seen the effects born and developed from the causes. Whenever, by way of induction or conjecture, we have deduced certain principles and results, we have been able to verify them by an inquiry into the facts themselves. As regards the boroughs, this facility fails us; we are present only at their birth. At present I must confine myself to causes and origins. What I say concerning the effects of the existence of the boroughs, and their influence in the course of European civilization, I shall say in some measure by way of anticipation. I cannot invoke the testimony of contemporaneous and known facts. It is at a later period, from the twelfth to the fifteenth century, that we shall see the boroughs taking their development, the institution bearing all its fruit, and history proving our assertions. I dwell upon this difference of situation in order to anticipate your objections against the incompleteness and prematurity of the picture which I am about to offer you. I will suppose, that in 1789, at the time of the commencement of the terrible regeneration of France, a burgher of the twelfth century had suddenly appeared among us, and that he had been given to read, provided he knew how, one of the pamphlets which so powerfully agitated mind; for example, the pamphlet of M. Sieyes—"What is the third estate?" His eyes fall upon this sentence, which is the foundation of the pamphlet: "The third estate is the French nation, less the nobility and the clergy." I ask you, what would be the effect of such a phrase upon the mind of such a man? Do you suppose he would understand it? No, he could not understand the words, *the French nation,* because they would represent to him no fact with which he was acquainted, no fact of his age; and if he understood the phrase, if he clearly saw in it this sovereignty attributed to the third estate above all society, of a verity it would appear to him mad, impious, such would be its contradiction to all that he had seen, to all his ideas and sentiments.[1]

Now, ask this astonished burgher to follow you; lead him to one of the French boroughs of this epoch, to Rheims, Beauvais, Laon, or Noyon; a

---

1. This launching of the fascinating comparison of the boroughs and burghers of the twelfth and eighteenth centuries is the point in the text where Guizot's reliance on the categories of atomization and centralization, drawn from the Great Debate, is most obvious and sustained.

different kind of astonishment would seize him: he enters a town; he sees neither towers, nor ramparts, nor burgher militia; no means of defence; all is open, all exposed to the first comer, and the first occupant. The burgher would doubt the safety of this borough; he would think it weak and ill-secured. He penetrates into the interior, and inquires what is passing, in what manner it is governed, and what are its inhabitants. They tell him, that beyond the walls there is a power which taxes them at pleasure, without their consent; which convokes their militia, and sends it to war, without their voice in the matter. He speaks to them of magistrates, of the mayor, and of the aldermen; and he hears that the burghers do not nom-inate them. He learns that the affairs of the borough are not decided in the borough; but that a man belonging to the king, an intendant, admin-isters them, alone and at a distance. Furthermore, they will tell him that the inhabitants have not the right of assembling and deliberating in com-mon upon matters which concern them; that they are never summoned to the public place by the bell of their church. The burgher of the twelfth century would be confounded. First, he was stupified and dismayed at the grandeur and importance that the communal nation, the third estate, at-tributed to itself; and now he finds it on its own hearthstone, in a state of servitude, weakness, and nonentity, far worse than anything which he had experienced. He passes from one spectacle to another utterly different, from the view of a sovereign burghership to that of one entirely powerless. How would you have him comprehend this—reconcile it, so that his mind be not overwhelmed.

Let us, burghers of the nineteenth century, go back to the twelfth, and be present at an exactly corresponding double spectacle. Whenever we regard the general affairs of a country, its state, government, the whole society, we shall see no burghers, hear speak of none; they interfere in nothing, and are quite unimportant. And not only have they no importance in the state, but if we would know what they think of their situation, and how they speak of it, and what their position in regard to their relation with the government of France in general is in their own eyes, we shall find in their language an extraordinary timidity and humility. Their ancient masters, the lords, from whom they forced their franchises, treat them, at least in words, with a haughtiness which confounds us; but it neither astonishes nor irritates them.

Let us enter into the borough itself; let us see what passes there. The scene changes; we are in a kind of fortified place defended by armed burghers: these burghers tax themselves, elect their magistrates, judge and punish, and assemble for the purpose of deliberating upon their affairs. All come to these assemblies; they make war on their own account against their lord; and they have a militia. In a word, they govern themselves; they are sovereigns. This is the same contrast which, in the France of the eighteenth century, so much astonished the burgher of the twelfth; it is only the parts that are changed. In the latter, the burgher nation is all, the borough nothing; in the former, the burghership is nothing, the borough everything.

Assuredly, between the twelfth and the eighteenth centuries, many things must have passed—many extraordinary events, and many revolutions have been accomplished, to bring about, in the existence of a social class, so enormous a change. Despite this change, there can be no doubt but that the third estate of 1789 was, politically speaking, the descendant and heir of the corporations of the twelfth century. This French nation, so haughty and ambitious, which raises its pretensions so high, which so loudly proclaims its sovereignty, which pretends not only to regenerate and govern itself, but to govern and regenerate the world, undoubtedly descends, principally at least, from the burghers who obscurely though courageously revolted in the twelfth century, with the sole end of escaping in some corner of the land from the obscure tyranny of the lords.

Most assuredly it is not in the state of the boroughs in the twelfth century that we shall find the explanation of such a metamorphosis: it was accomplished and had its causes in the events which succeeded it from the twelfth to the eighteenth century; it is there that we shall meet it in its progression. Still the origin of the third estate has played an important part in its history; although we shall not find there the secret of its destiny, we shall, at least, find its germ: for what it was at first is again found in what it has become, perhaps, even to a greater extent than appearances would allow of our presuming. A picture, even an incomplete one, of the state

of the boroughs in the twelfth century, will, I think, leave you convinced
of this.

The better to understand this state, it is necessary to consider the boroughs
from two principal points of view. There are two great questions to resolve:
the first, that of the enfranchisement of the boroughs itself—the question
how the revolution was operated, and from what causes—what change it
brought into the situation of the burghers, what effect it has had upon society in general, upon the other classes, and upon the state. The second question relates only to the government of the boroughs, the internal condition
of the enfranchised towns, the relations of the burghers among themselves,
and the principles, forms, and manners which dominated in the cities.

It is from these two sources, on the one hand, from the change introduced into the social condition of the burghers, and on the other, from
their internal government and their communal condition, that all their influence upon modern civilization originated. There are no facts produced
by this influence, but which should be referred to one or other of these
causes. When, therefore, we shall have summed them up, when we thoroughly understand, on one side, the enfranchisement of the boroughs, and
on the other, the government of the boroughs, we shall be in possession, so
to speak, of the two keys to their history.

Lastly, I shall say a word concerning the various state of the boroughs
throughout Europe. The facts which I am about to place before you do not
apply indifferently to all the boroughs of the twelfth century, to the boroughs of Italy, Spain, England, or France; there are certainly some which
belong to all, but the differences are great and important. I shall point them
out in passing; we shall again encounter them in a later period of civilization, and we will then investigate them more closely.

To understand the enfranchisement of the boroughs, it is necessary to
recall to your minds what was the state of the towns from the fifth to the
eleventh century—from the fall of the Roman empire down to the commencement of the communal revolution. Here, I repeat, the differences
were very great; the state of the towns varied prodigiously in the various
countries of Europe; still there are general facts which may be affirmed of
almost all towns; and I shall try to confine myself to them. When I depart
from this restriction, what I say more especially will apply to the boroughs

of France, and particularly to the boroughs of the north of France, beyond the Rhône and the Loire. These will be the prominent points in the picture which I shall attempt to trace.

After the fall of the Roman empire, from the fifth to the tenth century, the condition of the towns was one neither of servitude nor liberty. One runs the same risk in the employment of words, that I spoke of the other day in the painting of men and events. When a society and a language have long existed, the words take a complete, determined, and precise sense, a legal and official sense, in a manner. Time has introduced into the sense of each term a multitude of ideas, which arise the moment that it is pronounced, and which, not belonging to the same date, are not applicable alike to all times. For example, the words *servitude* and *liberty* call to our minds in the present-day ideas infinitely more precise and complete than the corresponding facts of the eighth, ninth, or tenth century. If we say that, at the eighth century, the towns were in a state of liberty, we say far too much; in the present day we attach a sense to the word *liberty*, which does not represent the fact of the eighth century. We shall fall into the same error if we say that the towns were in a state of servitude, because the word implies an entirely different thing from the municipal facts of that period.

I repeat that, at that time, the towns were neither in a state of servitude nor liberty; they suffered all the ills which accompany weakness; they were a prey to the violence and continual depredations of the strong; but yet, despite all these fearful disorders, despite their impoverishment and depopulation, the towns had preserved, and did still preserve a certain importance: in most of them there was a clergy, a bishop, who by the great exercise of power and his influence upon the population, served as a connecting link between them and their conquerors, and thus maintained the town in a kind of independence, and covered it with the shield of religion. Moreover, there remained in the towns many wrecks of Roman institutions. One meets at this epoch (and many facts of this nature have been collected by M.M. de Savigny and Hullman, Mademoiselle de Lézardière, &c.) with frequent convocations of the senate, of the curia; there is mention made of public assemblies and municipal magistrates. The affairs of the civil order, wills, grants, and a multitude of acts of civil life, were legalized in the curia by its magistrates, as was the case in the Roman municipality. The remains of urban activity and liberty, it is true, gradually disappeared. Barbarism, disorder, and always increasing misfortunes, accelerated the depopulation. The establishment of the masters of the land in the rural districts, and the growing preponderance of agricultural life, were new causes of decay to the towns. The bishops themselves, when they had entered the frame of feudalism, placed less importance on their municipal existence. Finally, when feudalism had completely triumphed, the towns, without falling into the servitude of serfs, found themselves entirely in the hands of a lord, inclosed within some fief, and robbed of all the independence which had been left to them, even in the most barbarous times, in the first ages of the invasion. So that from the fifth century, down to the time of the complete organization of feudalism, the condition of the towns was always upon the decline.

When once feudalism was thoroughly established, when each man had taken his place, and was settled upon his land, when the wandering life had ceased, after some time the towns again began to acquire some importance, and to display anew some activity. It is, as you know, with human activity as with the fecundity of the earth; from the time that commotion ceases, it reappears and makes everything germinate and flourish. With the least glimpse of order and peace, man takes hope, and with hope goes to work. It was thus with the towns; the moment that feudalism was a little fixed, new wants sprang up among the fief-holders, a certain taste for progress and amelioration; to supply this want, a little commerce and industry reappeared in the towns of their domain; riches and population returned to them; slowly, it is true, but still they returned. Among the circumstances which contributed thereto, one, I think, is too little regarded; this is the right of sanctuary in the churches. Before the boroughs had established themselves, before their strength and their ramparts enabled them to offer an asylum to the afflicted population of the country, when as yet they had no safety but that afforded by the church, this sufficed to draw into the towns many unhappy fugitives. They came to shelter themselves in or around the church; and it was not only the case with the inferior class, with serfs and boors, who sought safety, but often with men of importance, rich outlaws. The chronicles of the time are filled with examples of this nature. One sees men, formerly powerful themselves, pursued by a more powerful neighbour, or even by the king himself, who abandon their domains, carrying with them all they can, shut themselves up within a town, and putting themselves under the protection of the church, become citizens. These kind of refugees have not been, I think, without their influence upon the progress of the towns; they introduced into them riches, and elements of a superior population to the mass of their inhabitants. Besides, who knows not, that when once an association is in part formed, men flock to it, both because they find more safety, and also for the mere sake of that sociability which never leaves them?

By the concurrence of all these causes, after the feudal government was in some manner regulated, the towns regained a little strength. Their security, however, did not return to them in the same proportion. The wandering life had ceased, it is true, but the wandering life had been for the conquerors, for the new proprietors of the soil, a principal means of satisfying their passions. When they had wished to pillage, they made an excursion, they went to a distance to seek another fortune, another domain. When each was nearly established, when it became necessary to renounce this conquering vagrancy, there was no cessation of their avidity, their inordinate wants, nor their violent desires. Their weight, then, fell on the people nearest at hand, upon the towns. Instead of going to a distance to pillage, they pillaged at home. The extortions of the nobility upon the burgesses were redoubled from the commencement of the tenth century. Whenever the proprietor of a domain in which a town was situated had any fit of avarice to satisfy, it was upon the burgesses that he exercised his violence. This, above all, was the epoch in which the complaints of the burgesses against the absolute want of security of commerce, burst forth. The merchants, after having made their journeys, were not permitted to enter their towns in peace; the roads and approaches were incessantly beset by the lord and his followers. The time at which industry was recommencing, was exactly that in which security was most wanting. Nothing can irritate a man more than being thus interfered with in his work, and despoiled of the fruits which he had promised himself from it. He is far more annoyed and enraged than when harassed in an existence which has been some time fixed and monotonous, when that which is carried from him has not been the result of his own activity, has not excited in his bosom all the pleasures of hope. There is, in the progressive movement towards fortune of a man or a population, a principle of resistance against injustice and violence far more energetic than in any other situation.[2]

This, then, was the position of the towns during the tenth century; they had more strength, more importance, more riches, and more interests to defend. At the same time, it was more than ever necessary to defend them, because this strength, these interests, these riches, became an object of envy to the lords. The danger and evil increased with the means of resisting them. Moreover, the feudal system gave to all those who participated in it the example of continued resistance; it never presented to the mind the idea of an organized government, capable of ruling and quelling all by imposing its single intervention. It offered, on the contrary, the continuous spectacle of the individual will refusing submission. Such, for the most part, was the position of the possessors of fiefs towards their superiors, of the lesser lords towards the greater; so that at the moment when the towns were tormented and oppressed, when they had new and most important interests to sustain, at that moment they had before their eyes a continual lesson of insurrection. The feudal system has rendered one service to humanity, that of incessantly showing to men the individual will in the full display of its energy. The lesson prospered: in spite of their weakness, in spite of the infinite inequality of condition between them and their lords, the towns arose in insurrection on all sides.

It is difficult to assign an exact date to this event. It is generally said, that the enfranchisement of the commons commenced in the eleventh century; but, in all great events, how many unhappy and unknown efforts occur, before the one which succeeds! In all things, to accomplish its designs, Providence lavishly expends courage, virtues, sacrifices, in a word, man himself; and it is only after an unknown number of unrecorded labours, after a host of noble hearts have succumbed in discouragement, convinced that their cause is lost, it is only then that the cause triumphs. It doubtless happened thus with the commons. Doubtless, in the eighth, ninth, and

2. Guizot here takes up a theme which had been championed by Adam Smith and other thinkers of the Scottish Enlightenment, the close relationship between commerce and liberty. It was a theme used to combat the values of a classical republican tradition which tended to associate "virtue" with warlike qualities and "corruption" with commerce.

tenth centuries, there were many attempts at resistance, and movements towards enfranchisement, which not only were unsuccessful, but of which the memory remained alike without glory or success. It is true, however, that these attempts have influenced posterior events; they re-animated and sustained the spirit of liberty, and prepared the way for the great insurrection of the eleventh century.

I say designedly, insurrection. The enfranchisement of the commons in the eleventh century was the fruit of a veritable insurrection, and a veritable war, a war declared by the population of the towns against their lords. The first fact which is always met with in such histories, is the rising of the burgesses, who arm themselves with the first thing that comes to hand; the expulsion of the followers of the lord who have come to put in force some extortion; or it is an enterprise against the castle; these are always the characteristics of the war. If the insurrection fails, what is done by the conqueror? He orders the destruction of the fortifications raised by the citizens, not only round the town but round each house. One sees at the time of the confederation, after having promised to act in common, and after taking the oath of mutual aid, the first act of the citizen is to fortify himself within his house. Some boroughs, of which at this day the name is entirely obscure, as, for example, the little borough of Vezelay in Nivernois, maintained a very long and energetic struggle against their lord. Victory fell to the abbot of Vezelay; he immediately enjoined the demolition of the fortifications of the citizens' houses; the names of many are preserved, whose fortified houses were thus immediately destroyed.

Let us enter the interior of the habitations of our ancestors; let us study the mode of their construction and the kind of life which they suggest; all is devoted to war, all has the character of war.

This is the construction of a citizen's house in the twelfth century, as far as we can follow it out: there were generally three floors, with one room upon each floor; the room on the ground floor was the common room, where the family took their meals; the first floor was very high up, by way of security; this is the most remarkable characteristic of the construction. On this floor was the room which the citizen and his wife inhabited. The house was almost always flanked by a tower at the angle, generally of a square form; another symptom of war, a means of defence. On the second floor was a room, the use of which is doubtful, but which probably served for the children, and the rest of the family. Above, very often, was a small platform, evidently intended for a place of observation. The whole construction of the house suggests war. This was the evident character, the true name of the movement which produced the enfranchisement of the commons.

When war has lasted a certain time, whoever may be the belligerent powers, it necessarily leads to peace. The treaties of peace between the commons and their adversaries were the charters. The borough charters are mere treaties of peace between the burgesses and their lord.

The insurrection was general. When I say *general,* I do not mean that there was union or coalition between all the citizens in a country: far from it. The situation of the commons was almost everywhere the same; they were everywhere a prey to the same danger, afflicted with the same evil. Having acquired almost the same means of resistance and defence, they employed them at nearly the same epoch. Example, too, may have done something, and the success of one or two boroughs may have been contagious. The charters seem sometimes to have been drawn after the same pattern; that of Noyon, for example, served as a model for those of Beauvais, St. Quentin, &c. I doubt, however, whether example had so much influence as has been supposed. Communications were difficult and rare, and hearsay vague and transient; it is more likely that the insurrection was the result of a similar situation, and of a general and spontaneous movement. When I say, general, I mean to say that it took place almost everywhere; for, I repeat, that the movement was not unanimous and concerted, all was special and local: each borough was insurgent against its lord upon its own account; all passed in its own locality.[3]

The vicissitudes of the struggle were great. Not only did success alternate, but even when peace seemed established, after the charter had been sworn to by each party, it was violated and eluded in every way. The kings

3. Guizot's argument that the "insurrection" of the boroughs or communes from the late eleventh century was not that of a united or self-conscious class, but a series of partial and local events generated by similar social circumstances, prepares the way for his presentation of the eighteenth-century bourgeoisie as a far more inclusive and formidable social class—formidable, above all, because by the later period the bourgeoisie had become conscious of itself as a class sharing interests nationally.

played a great part in the alternations of this struggle. Of this I shall speak in detail when I treat of royalty itself. Its influence in the movement of communal enfranchisement has been sometimes praised, perhaps too highly; sometimes, I think, too much undervalued, and sometimes denied. I shall confine myself at present to saying that it frequently interfered, sometimes invoked by the boroughs and sometimes by the lords; that it has often played contrary parts; that it has acted sometimes on one principle, sometimes on another; that it has unceasingly changed its intentions, designs, and conduct; but that, upon the whole, it has done much, and with more of good than of evil effect.

Despite these vicissitudes, despite the continual violations of the charters, the enfranchisement of the boroughs was consummated in the twelfth century. All Europe, and especially France, which for a century had been covered with insurrections, was covered with charters more or less favourable; the corporations enjoyed them with more or less security, but still they enjoyed them. The fact prevailed, and the right was established.

Let us now attempt to discover the immediate results of this great fact, and what changes it introduced into the condition of the burgesses, in the midst of society.

In the first place, it changed nothing, at least not in the commencement, in the relations of the burgesses with the general government of the country—with what we of the present day call the state; they interfered no more in it than heretofore: all remained local, inclosed within the limits of the fief.

One circumstance, however, should modify this assertion: a bond now began to be established between the citizens and the king. At times, the burgesses had invoked the aid of the king against their lord, or his guarantee, when the charter was promised or sworn to. At other times, the lords had invoked the judgment of the king between themselves and the citizens. At the demand of either one or other of the parties, in a multitude of different causes, royalty had interfered in the quarrel; from thence resulted a frequent relation, and sometimes a rather intimate one, between the burgesses and the king. It was by this relation that the burgesses approached the centre of the state, and began to have a connexion with the general government.

Notwithstanding that all remained local, a new and general class was created by the enfranchisement. No coalition had existed between the citizens; they had, as a class, no common and public existence. But the country was filled with men in the same situation, having the same interests, and the same manners, between whom a certain bond and unity could not fail of being gradually established, which should give rise to the *bourgeoisie*. The formation of a great social class, the bourgeoisie, was the necessary result of the local enfranchisement of the burghers.

It must not be imagined that this class was at this time that which it has since become. Not only has its situation changed, but its elements were entirely different: in the twelfth century it consisted almost entirely of merchants, traders carrying on a petty commerce, and of small proprietors of either land or houses, who had taken up their residence in the town. Three centuries after, the bourgeoisie comprehended besides, advocates, physicians, learned men of all sorts, and all the local magistrates. The bourgeoisie was formed gradually, and of very different elements; as a general thing, in its history no account is given of its succession or diversity. Wherever the bourgeoisie is spoken of, it seems to be supposed that at all epochs it was composed of the same elements. This is an absurd supposition. It is perhaps in the diversity of its composition at different epochs of history that we should look for the secret of its destiny. So long as it did not include magistrates nor men of letters, so long as it was not what it became in the sixteenth century, it possessed neither the same importance nor the same character in the state. To comprehend the vicissitudes of its fortune and power, it is necessary to observe in its bosom the successive rise of new professions, new moral positions, and a new intellectual state. In the twelfth century, I repeat, it was composed of only the small merchants, who retired into the towns after having made their purchases and sales, and of the proprietors of houses and small domains who had fixed their residence there. Here we see the European burgher class in its first elements.

The third great consequence of the enfranchisement of the commons was the contest of classes, a contest which constitutes the fact itself, and which fills modern history. Modern Europe was born from the struggle of the various classes of society. Elsewhere, as I have already observed, this struggle led to very different results: in Asia, for example, one class completely triumphed, and the government of castes succeeded to that of classes, and society sunk into immobility. Thank God, none of this has happened in Europe. None of the classes has been able to conquer or subdue the others; the struggle, instead of becoming a principle of immobility, has been a cause of progress; the relations of the principal classes among themselves, the necessity under which they found themselves of combating and yielding by turns; the variety of their interests and passions, the desire to conquer without the power to satisfy it; from all this has arisen perhaps the most energetic and fertile principle of the development of European civilization. The classes have incessantly struggled; they detested each other; an utter diversity of situation, of interests, and of manners, produced between them a profound moral hostility: and yet they have progressively approached nearer, come to an understanding, and assimilated; every European nation has seen the birth and development in its bosom of a certain universal spirit, a certain community of interests, ideas, and sentiments, which has triumphed over diversity and war. In France, for example, in the seventeenth and eighteenth centuries, the social and moral separation of the classes was still very profound; yet the fusion was advancing; still, without doubt, at that time there was a veritable French nation, not an exclusive class, but which embraced them all, and in which all were animated by a certain sentiment in common, having a common social existence, strongly impressed, in a word, with nationality. Thus, from the bosom of variety, enmity, and war, has arisen in modern Europe the national unity so striking in the present day, and which tends to develop and refine itself, from day to day, with still greater brilliancy.

Such are the great external, apparent, and social effects of the revolution which at present occupies us. Let us investigate its moral effects, what changes it brought about in the soul of the citizens themselves, what they became, what, in fact, they necessarily became morally in their new situation.

There is a fact by which it is impossible not to be struck while contemplating the relation of the burghers towards the state in general, the government of the state, and the general interests of the country, not only in the twelfth century, but also in subsequent ages; I mean the prodigious

timidity of the citizens, their humility, the excessive modesty of their pretensions as to the government of the country, and the facility with which
they contented themselves. Nothing is seen among them of the true political spirit, which aspires to influence, reform, and govern; nothing which
gives proof of boldness of thought, or grandeur of ambition: one might call
them sensible-minded, honest, freed men.

There are but two sources in the sphere of politics from which greatness of ambition or firmness of thought can arise. It is necessary to have
either the feeling of immense importance, of great power exercised upon
the destiny of others, and in a vast extent—or else it is necessary to bear
within oneself a feeling of complete individual independence, a confidence
in one's own liberty, a conviction of a destiny foreign to all will but that of
the man himself. To one or other of these two conditions seem to belong
boldness of thought, greatness of ambition, the desire of acting in an enlarged sphere, and of obtaining great results.[4]

Neither one nor the other of these conditions entered into the condition of the burghers of the middle ages. These, as you have just seen, were
only important to themselves; they exercised no sensible influence beyond
their own town, or upon the state in general. Nor could they have any great
sentiment of individual independence. It was in vain that they conquered,
in vain that they obtained a charter. The citizen of a town, in comparing
himself with the inferior lord who dwelt near him, and who had just been
conquered, was not the less sensible of his extreme inferiority; he was not
filled with the haughty sentiment of independence which animated the
proprietor of the fief; he held not his portion of liberty from himself alone,
but from his association with others; a difficult and precarious succour.
Hence that character of reserve, of timidity of spirit, of retiring modesty,

---

4. In effect, Guizot discriminates the sources of political independence available in
two types of society, aristocratic and democratic. In the first, political confidence and the
will to influence events derived from a superior social position or status; in the second, it
can only derive from *general* rights, rights which are not only civil but political in character,
opening the way to political participation by all, at least in principle. Guizot frequently
notices with regret that the timidity of the medieval burghers or townsmen in relation to
the government of society—their lack of a strong political will—continues to inhibit the
European bourgeoisie in their dealings with government.

and humility of language, even in conjunction with a firmness of conduct, which is so deeply imprinted in the life of the citizens, not only in the twelfth century, but even of their descendants. They had no taste for great enterprises; and when fate forced them among them, they were uneasy and embarrassed; the responsibility annoyed them; they felt that they were out of their sphere of action, and wished to return to it; they therefore treated on moderate terms. Thus one finds in the course of European history, especially of France, that the bourgeoisie has been esteemed, considered, flattered, and even respected, but rarely feared; it has rarely produced upon its adversaries an impression of a great and haughty power, of a truly political power. There is nothing to be surprised at in this weakness of the modern bourgeoisie; its principal cause lay in its very origin, and in the circumstances of its enfranchisement, which I have just placed before you. A high ambition, independent of social conditions, enlargement and firmness of political thought, the desire to participate in the affairs of the country, the full consciousness of the greatness of man as man, and of the power which belongs to him, if he is capable of exercising it, these are in Europe sentiments and dispositions entirely modern, the fruit of modern civilization, the fruit of that glorious and powerful universality which characterizes it, and which cannot fail of insuring to the public an influence and weight in the government of the country, which were always wanting, and necessarily so, to the burghers our ancestors.

On the other hand, they acquired and displayed, in the struggle of local interests which they had to maintain in their narrow stage, a degree of energy, devotedness, perseverance, and patience, which has never been surpassed. The difficulty of the enterprise was such, and such the perils which they had to strive against, that a display of unexampled courage was necessary. In the present day, a very false idea is formed of the life of the burghers in the twelfth and thirteenth centuries. You have read in one of the novels of Walter Scott, *Quentin Durward,* the representation he has given of the burgomaster of Liege; he has made of him a regular burgher in a comedy, fat, indolent, without experience or boldness, and wholly occupied in passing his life easily. Whereas, the burghers of this period always had a coat of mail upon their breast, a pike in their hand; their life was as tempestuous, as warlike, and as hardy, as that of the lords with whom they fought. It was in these continual perils, in struggling against all the difficulties of practical life, that they acquired that manly character, and that obstinate energy, which is, in a measure, lost in the soft activity of modern times.

None of these social or moral effects of the enfranchisement of the boroughs had attained their development in the twelfth century; it is in the following centuries that they distinctly appeared, and are easily discernible. It is certain, however, that the germ was laid in the original situation of the boroughs, in the manner of their enfranchisement, and the place then taken by the burghers in society. I was, therefore, right in placing them before you alone. Let us now investigate the interior of the borough of the twelfth century; let us see how it was governed, what principles and facts dominated in the relations of the citizens among themselves.

You will recollect that in speaking of the municipal system, bequeathed by the Roman empire to the modern world, I told you that the Roman empire was a great coalition of municipalities, formerly sovereign municipalities like Rome itself. Each of these towns had originally possessed the same existence as Rome, had once been a small independent republic, making peace and war, and governing itself as it thought proper. In proportion as they became incorporated with the Roman empire, the rights which constitute sovereignty, the right of peace and war, the right of legislation, the right of taxation, &c., left each town and centred in Rome. There remained but one sovereign municipality, Rome, reigning over a large number of municipalities which had now only a civil existence. The municipal system changed its character; and instead of being a political government and a system of sovereignty, it became a mode of administration.

This was the great revolution which was consummated under the Roman empire.[5] The municipal system became a mode of administration, was reduced to the government of local affairs, and the civic interests of the city. This was the condition in which the towns and their institutions were left at the fall of the Roman empire. In the midst of the chaos of barbarism, all ideas, as well as facts, were in utter confusion; all the attributes

　　5. Throughout his 1828 lectures Guizot relies upon an analogy between the growth of administrative despotism under the Roman Empire, with the municipalities losing political rights and an autonomous civic life, and the growth of a bureaucratic monarchy in early modern France, with the destruction of local autonomy.

of sovereignty and of administration were confounded. These distinctions were no longer attended to. Affairs were abandoned to the course of necessity. There was a sovereign, or an administrator, in each locality, according to circumstances. When the towns rose in insurrection, to recover some security, they took upon themselves the sovereignty. It was not, in any way, for the purpose of following out a political theory, nor from a feeling of their dignity; it was that they might have the means of resisting the lords against whom they rebelled that they appropriated to themselves the right of levying militia, of taxation for the purposes of war, of themselves nominating their chiefs and magistrates; in a word, of governing themselves. The government in the interior of the towns was the means of defence and security. Thus sovereignty re-entered the municipal system, from which it had been eradicated by the conquests of Rome. The boroughs again became sovereign. We have here the political character of their enfranchisement.

It does not follow that this sovereignty was complete. It always retained some trace of external sovereignty: sometimes the lord preserved to himself the right of sending a magistrate into the town, who took for his assessors the municipal magistrates; sometimes he possessed the right of receiving certain revenues; elsewhere, a tribute was secured to him. Sometimes the external sovereignty of the community lay in the hands of the king.

The boroughs themselves having entered within the frame of feudalism, had vassals, became suzerains, and by virtue of this title partly possessed themselves of the sovereignty which was inherent in the lord paramount. This caused a confusion between the rights which they had from their feudal position, and those which they had conquered by their insurrections; and under this double title the sovereignty belonged to them.

Thus we see, as far as can be judged from very deficient monuments, how government was administered, at least in the early ages, in the interior of a borough. The totality of the inhabitants formed the assembly of the borough; all those who had sworn the borough oath (and whoever lived within the walls was obliged to do so) were convoked by the ringing of a bell to the general assembly. It was there that they nominated the magistrates. The number and form of the magistracy were very various. The magistrates being once nominated, the assembly was dissolved, and the magistrates governed almost alone, somewhat arbitrarily, and without any other responsibility than that of the new elections, or popular riots, which were the chief mode of responsibility in those times.

You see that the internal organization of boroughs reduced itself to two very simple elements; the general assembly of the inhabitants, and a government invested with an almost arbitrary power, under the responsibility of insurrections and riots. It was impossible, principally from the state of manners, to establish a regular government, with veritable guarantees for order and duration. The greater portion of the population of the boroughs was in a state of ignorance, brutality, and ferocity, which it would have been very difficult to govern. After a short time, there was almost as little security in the interior of the borough as there had formerly been in the relations between the burgher and the lord. There was formed, however, very quickly a superior bourgeoisie. You easily comprehend the causes. The state of ideas and of social relations led to the establishment of industrial professions, legally constituted corporations. The system of privilege was introduced into the interior of boroughs, and from this a great inequality ensued. There was shortly everywhere a certain number of rich and important burghers, and a working population more or less numerous, which, in spite of its inferiority, had an important influence in the affairs of the borough. The boroughs were then divided into a high bourgeoisie, and a population subject to all the errors and vices of a populace. The superior bourgeoisie found itself pressed between the immense difficulty of governing the inferior population, and the incessant attempts of the ancient master of the borough, who sought to re-establish his power. Such was its situation, not only in France but in all Europe, down to the sixteenth century. This perhaps has been the chief means of preventing the corporations, in most European nations, and especially in France, from possessing all the important political influence which they might otherwise have had. Two principles carried on incessant warfare within them; in the inferior population, a blind, unbridled, and ferocious spirit of democracy; and, as a consequence, in the superior population, a spirit of timidity at making agreements, an excessive facility of conciliation, whether in regard to the king, the ancient lords, or in re-establishing some peace and order in the interior of the borough. Each of these principles could not but tend to deprive the corporation of any great influence in the state.

All these effects were not visible in the twelfth century; still, however, one might foresee them in the very character of the insurrection, in the manner of its commencement, and in the condition of the various elements of the communal population.

Such, if I mistake not, are the principal characteristics and the general results of the enfranchisement of the boroughs and of their internal government. I forewarn you, that these facts were neither so uniform nor so universal as I have broadly represented them. There is great diversity in the history of boroughs in Europe. For example, in Italy and in the south of France, the Roman municipal system dominated; there was not nearly so much diversity and inequality here as in the north, and the communal organization was much better, either by reason of the Roman traditions, or from the superior condition of the population. In the north, the feudal system prevailed in the communal existence; there, all was subordinate to the struggle against the lords. The boroughs of the south were more occupied with their internal organization, amelioration, and progress; they thought only of becoming independent republics. The destiny of the northern boroughs, in France particularly, showed themselves more and more incomplete, and destined for less fine developments. If we glance at the boroughs of Germany, Spain, and England, we shall find in them other differences. I shall not enter into these details; we shall remark some of them as we advance in the history of civilization. In their origin, all things are nearly confounded under one physiognomy; it is only by successive developments that variety shows itself. Then commences a new development which urges society towards free and high unity, the glorious end of all the efforts and wishes of the human race.

EIGHTH LECTURE

Object of the lecture—Glance at the general history of European civilization—Its distinctive and fundamental character—Epoch at which that character began to appear—State of Europe from the twelfth to the sixteenth century—Character of the crusades—Their moral and social causes—These causes no longer existed at the end of the thirteenth century—Effects of the crusades upon civilization.

I HAVE NOT AS YET explained to you the complete plan of my course. I commenced by indicating its object; I then passed in review European civilization without considering it as a whole, without indicating to you at one and the same time the point of departure, the route, and the port, the commencement, the middle, and the end. We have now, however, arrived at an epoch when this entire view, this general sketch of the region which we survey, has become necessary. The times which have hitherto occupied us in some measure explain themselves, or are explained by immediate and evident results. Those upon which we are about to enter would not be understood, nor would they excite any lively interest, unless they are connected with the even the most indirect and distant of their consequences.

In so extensive a study, moments occur when we can no longer consent to proceed, while all before us is unknown and dark; we wish not only to know whence we have come and where we are, but also to what point we tend. This is what we now feel. The epoch which we are approaching is not intelligible, nor can its importance be appreciated except by the relations which unite it to modern times. Its true meaning is not evident until a later period.

We are in possession of almost all the essential elements of European civilization. I say almost, because as yet I have not spoken to you of royalty. The decisive crisis of the development of royalty did not take place until the twelfth or even thirteenth century; it was not until then that the institution was really constituted, and that it began to occupy a definite place in modern society. I have, therefore, not treated of it earlier; it will form the subject of my next lecture. With this exception, I repeat, we have before us all the great elements of European civilization: you have beheld the birth of feudal aristocracy, of the church, the boroughs; you have seen the institutions which should correspond to these facts; and not only the institutions, but also the principles and ideas which these facts should raise up in the mind. Thus, while treating of feudalism, you were present at the cradle of the modern family, at the hearth of domestic life; you have comprehended, in all its energy, the sentiment of individual independence, and the place which it has held in our civilization. With regard to the church, you have seen the purely religious society rise up, its relations with the civil society, the theocratical principle, the separation of the spiritual and temporal powers, the first blows of persecutions, and the first cries of the liberty of conscience. The rising boroughs have shown you glimpses of an association founded upon altogether other principles than those of feudalism and the church, the diversity of the social classes, their struggles, the first and profound characteristics of modern burgher manners, timidity of spirit side by side with energy of soul, the demagogue spirit side by side with the legal spirit. In a word, all the elements which have contributed to the formation of European society, all that it has been, and, so to speak, all that it has suggested, have already met your view.

Let us now transport ourselves to the heart of modern Europe: I speak not of existing Europe, after the prodigious metamorphoses which we have witnessed, but of Europe in the seventeenth and eighteenth centuries. I ask you, do you recognize the society which we have just seen in the twelfth century? What a wonderful difference! I have already dwelt upon this difference as regards the boroughs: I afterwards tried to make you sensible of how little the third estate of the eighteenth century resembled that of the twelfth. If we make the same essay upon feudalism and the church, we shall be struck with the same metamorphosis. There was no more resemblance between the nobility of the court of Louis XV and the feudal aristocracy, or between the church of Cardinal de Bernis and that of the abbot Suger, than between the third estate of the eighteenth century and the bourgeoisie of the twelfth century. Between these two epochs, although already in possession of all its elements, society was entirely transformed.

I wish to establish clearly the general and essential character of this transformation. From the fifth to the twelfth century, society contained all that I have described. It possessed kings, a lay aristocracy, a clergy, burghers, labourers, religious and civil powers—in a word, the germs of everything which is necessary to form a nation and a government, and yet there was neither government nor nation. Throughout the epoch upon which we are occupied, there was nothing bearing a resemblance to a people, properly so called, nor to a veritable government, in the sense which the words have for us in the present day. We have encountered a multitude of particular forces, of special facts, and local institutions; but nothing general or public; no policy, properly so called, nor no true nationality.

Let us regard, on the contrary, the Europe of the seventeenth and eighteenth centuries; we shall everywhere see two leading figures present themselves upon the scene of the world, the government, and the people.[1] The action of a universal power upon the whole country, and the influence of the country upon the power which governs it, this is society, this is history: the relations of the two great forces, their alliance, or their struggle, this is what history discovers and relates. The nobility, the clergy, and the burghers, all these particular classes and forces, now only appear in a secondary rank, almost like shadows effaced by those two great bodies, the people and its government.

This, if I mistake not, is the essential feature which distinguishes modern from primitive Europe; this is the metamorphosis which was accomplished from the thirteenth to the sixteenth century.

It is, then, from the thirteenth to the sixteenth century, that is to say, in the period which we are about to enter upon, that the secret of this must be sought for; it is the distinctive character of this epoch that it was employed in converting primitive Europe into modern Europe; and hence its

1. Here Guizot's use of the categories of atomization and centralization, alias "the people" and "its government," emerging out of the different social elements or estates which had earlier constituted European society, is again evident.

historical importance and interest. If it is not considered from this point of view, and unless we everywhere seek what has arisen from it, not only will it not be understood, but we shall soon be weary of, and annoyed by it. Indeed, viewed in itself, and apart from its results, it is a period without character, a period when confusion continues to increase, without our being able to discover its causes, a period of movement without direction, and of agitation without result. Royalty, nobility, clergy, bourgeoisie, all the elements of social order seem to turn in the same circle, equally incapable of progress or repose. They make attempts of all kinds, but all fail; they attempt to settle governments, and to establish public liberties; they even attempt religious reforms, but nothing is accomplished—nothing perfected. If ever the human race has been abandoned to a destiny, agitated and yet stationary, to labour incessant, yet barren of effect, it was between the thirteenth and the fifteenth centuries that such was the physiognomy of its condition and its history.

I know of but one work in which this physiognomy is truly shown; the *Histoire des ducs de Bourgogne,* by M. de Barante. I do not speak of the truth which sparkles in the descriptions of manners, or in the detailed recital of facts, but of that universal truth which makes the entire book a faithful image, a sincere mirror of the whole epoch, of which it at the same time shows the movement and the monotony.

Considered, on the contrary, in its relation to that which follows, as the transition from the primitive to the modern Europe, this epoch brightens and becomes animated; we discover in it a totality, a direction, and a progress; its unity and interest consist in the slow and secret work which is accomplished in it.

The history of European civilization may then be summed up into three grand periods: 1st, A period which I shall call the period of origins, of formation—a time when the various elements of our society freed themselves from the chaos, took being, and showed themselves under their native forms with the principles which animated them. This period extended nearly to the twelfth century. 2nd, The second period is a time of essay, of trial, of groping; the various elements of the social order drew near each other, combined, and, as it were, felt each other, without the power to bring forth anything general, regular, or durable. This state was not ended,

properly speaking, till the sixteenth century. 3rd, The period of development, properly so called, when society in Europe took a definite form,
followed a determined tendency, and progressed rapidly and universally
towards a clear and precise end. This commenced at the sixteenth century,
and now pursues its course.

Such appears to me to be the spectacle of European civilization in its
whole, and such I shall endeavour to represent it to you. It is the second
period that we enter upon now. We have to seek in it the great crises and
determinative causes of the social transformation which has been the result of it.

The crusades constitute the first great event which presents itself to us,
which, as it were, opens the epoch of which we speak. They commenced
at the eleventh century, and extended over the twelfth and thirteenth. Of
a surety, a great event; for since it was completed, it has not ceased to occupy philosophic historians; even before reading the account of it, all have
foreseen that it was one of those events which change the condition of the
people, and which it is absolutely necessary to study in order to comprehend the general course of facts.

The first characteristic of the crusades is their universality; the whole of
Europe joined in them—they were the first European event. Previously to
the crusades, Europe had never been excited by one sentiment, or acted in
one cause; there was no Europe. The crusades revealed Christian Europe.
The French formed the vans of the first army of crusaders; but there were
also Germans, Italians, Spaniards, and English. Observe the second, the
third crusade; all the Christian nations engaged in it. Nothing like it had
yet been seen.[2]

This is not all: just as the crusades form an European event, so in each
country do they form a national event. All classes of society were animated
with the same impression, obeyed the same idea, abandoned themselves

---

2. This interpretation of the Crusades as the first event which brought Europe to a consciousness of itself as a geographical and cultural unity is parallel to Guizot's analysis of
the bourgeoisie becoming conscious of itself as a class. Until a common name or a shared
description becomes available such consciousness, on Guizot's analysis, is not possible.
Such names, and the consciousness they imply, he usually presents as emerging during a
struggle against some oppressor or threat.

to the same impulse. Kings, lords, priests, burghers, countrymen, all took the same part, the same interest in the crusades. The moral unity of nations was shown—a fact as novel as the European unity.

When such events happen in the infancy of a people, at a time when men act freely and spontaneously, without premeditation, without political intention or combination, one recognizes therein what history calls heroic events—the heroic age of nations. In fact, the crusades constitute the heroic event of modern Europe—a movement at once individual and general, national, and yet unregulated.

That such was really their primitive character is verified by all documents, proved by all facts. Who were the first crusaders that put themselves in motion? Crowds of the populace, who set out under the guidance of Peter the Hermit, without preparation, without guides, and without chiefs, followed rather than guided by a few obscure knights; they traversed Germany, the Greek empire, and dispersed or perished in Asia Minor.

The superior class, the feudal nobility, in their turn became eager in the cause of the crusade. Under the command of Godefroi de Bouillon, the lords and their followers set out full of ardour. When they had traversed Asia Minor, a fit of indifference and weariness seized the chiefs of the crusaders. They cared not to continue their route; they united to make conquests and establish themselves. The common people of the army rebelled; they wished to go to Jerusalem—the deliverance of Jerusalem was the aim of the crusade; it was not to gain principalities for Raimond de Toulouse, nor for Bohemond, nor for any other, that the crusaders came. The popular, national, and European impulsion was superior to all individual wishes; the chiefs had not sufficient ascendancy over the masses to subdue them to their interests. The sovereigns, who had remained strangers to the first crusade, were at last carried away by the movement, like the people. The great crusades of the twelfth century were commanded by kings.

I pass at once to the end of the thirteenth century. People still spoke in Europe of the crusades, they even preached them with ardour. The popes excited the sovereigns and the people—they held councils in recommendation of the Holy Land; but no one went there—it was no longer cared for. Something had passed into the European spirit and European society that put an end to the crusades. There were still some private expeditions. A few lords, a few bands, still set out for Jerusalem; but the general movement was evidently stopped; and yet it does not appear that either the necessity or the facility of continuing it had disappeared. The Muslims triumphed more and more in Asia. The Christian kingdom founded at Jerusalem had fallen into their hands. It was necessary to reconquer it; there were greater means of success than they had at the commencement of the crusades; a large number of Christians were established, and still powerful, in Asia Minor, Syria, and Palestine. They were better acquainted with the means of travelling and acting. Still nothing could revive the crusades. It was clear that the two great forces of society—the sovereigns on one side and the people on the other—were averse to it.

It has often been said that this was lassitude—that Europe was tired of thus falling upon Asia. We must come to an understanding upon this word *lassitude,* which is so often used upon similar occasions; it is strangely inexact. It is not possible that human generations can be weary with what they have never taken part in; weary of the fatigues undergone by their forefathers. Weariness is personal; it cannot be transmitted like an heritage. Men in the thirteenth century were not fatigued by the crusades of the twelfth: they were influenced by another cause. A great change had taken place in ideas, sentiments, and social conditions. There were no longer the same wants and desires. They no longer thought or wished the same things. It is these political or moral metamorphoses, and not weariness, which explain the different conduct of successive generations. The pretended lassitude which is attributed to them is a false metaphor.

Two great causes, one moral and the other social, threw Europe into the crusades. The moral cause, as you know, was the impulsion of religious sentiment and creeds. Since the end of the seventh century, Christianity had been struggling against Mahommedanism; it had conquered it in Europe after being dangerously menaced; it had succeeded in confining it to Spain. Thence also it still constantly strove to expel it. The crusades have been represented as a kind of accident, as an event unforeseen, unheard of, born solely of the recitals of pilgrims on their return from Jerusalem, and of the preachings of Peter the Hermit. It was nothing of the kind. The crusades were the continuation, the zenith of the grand struggle which had been going on for four centuries between Christianity and Mahommedanism. The theatre of this struggle had been hitherto in Europe; it was now transported into Asia. If I put any value upon those comparisons and parallels, into which some people delight at times to press, suitably, or not, historical facts, I might show you Christianity running precisely the same career in Asia, and undergoing the same destiny as Mahommedanism in Europe. Mahommedanism was established in Spain, and had there conquered and founded a kingdom and principalities. The Christians did the same in Asia. They there found themselves, with regard to Mahommedans, in the same situation as the latter in Spain with regard to the Christians. The kingdom of Jerusalem and the kingdom of Granada correspond to each other. But these similitudes are of little importance. The great fact is the struggle of the two social and religious systems; and of this the crusades was the chief crisis. In that lies their historical character, the connecting link which attaches them to the totality of facts.

There was another cause, the social state of Europe in the eleventh century, which no less contributed to their outburst. I have been careful to explain why, between the fifth and the eleventh centuries, nothing general could be established in Europe. I have attempted to show how everything had become local, how states, existences, minds, were confined within a very limited horizon. It was thus feudalism had prevailed. After some time, an horizon so restricted did not suffice; human thought and activity desired to pass beyond the circle in which they had been confined. The wandering life had ceased, but not the inclination for its excitement and adventures. The people rushed into the crusades as into a new existence, more enlarged and varied, which at one time recalled the ancient liberty of barbarism, at others opened out the perspective of a vast future.

Such, I believe, were the two determining causes of the crusades of the twelfth century. At the end of the thirteenth century, neither of these causes existed. Men and society were so much changed, that neither the moral impulsion nor the social need which had precipitated Europe upon Asia, was any longer felt. I do not know if many of you have read the original historians of the crusades, or whether it has ever occurred to you to compare the contemporaneous chroniclers of the first crusades, with those at the end of the twelfth and thirteenth centuries; for example, Albert d'Aix, Robert the Monk, and Raymond d'Agiles, who took part in the first crusade, with William of Tyre and James de Vitry. When we compare these two classes of writers, it is impossible not to be struck by the distance which separates them. The first are animated chroniclers, full of vivid imagination, who recount the events of the crusades with passion. But they are, at the same time, men of very narrow minds, without an idea beyond the little sphere in which they have lived; strangers to all science, full of prejudices, and incapable of forming any judgment whatever upon what passes around them, or upon the events which they relate. Open, on the contrary, the history of the crusades by William of Tyre: you will be surprised to find almost an historian of modern times, a mind developed, extensive and free, a rare political understanding of events, completeness of views, a judgment bearing upon causes and effects. James de Vitry affords an example of a different kind of development; he is a scholar, who not only concerns himself with what has reference to the crusades, but also occupies himself with manners, geography, ethnography, natural history; who observes and describes the country. In a word, between the chroniclers of the first crusades and the historians of the last, there is an immense interval, which indicates a veritable revolution in mind.

This revolution is above all seen in the manner in which each speaks of the Mahommedans. To the first chroniclers, and consequently to the first crusaders, of whom the first chroniclers are but the expression, the Mahommedans are only an object of hatred. It is evident that they knew nothing of them, that they weighed them not, considered them not, except under the point of view of the religious hostility which existed between them; we discover no trace of any social relation; they detested and fought them, and that was all. William of Tyre, James de Vitry, and Bernard the Treasurer, speak quite differently of the Mussulmans: one feels that, although fighting them, they do not look upon them as mere monsters; that to a certain point they have entered into their ideas; that they have lived with them, that there is a sort of relation, and even a kind of sympathy established between them. William of Tyre warmly eulogizes Noureddin—Bernard the Treasurer, Saladin. They even go so far as to compare the manners and conduct of the Mussulmans with those of the Christians; they take advantage of the Mussulmans to satirize the Christians, as Tacitus painted the manners of the Germans in contrast with the manners of the Romans. You see how enormous the change between the two epochs must have been, when you find in the last, with regard to the enemies of the Christians, to those against whom the crusades were directed, a liberty and impartiality of spirit which would have filled the first crusaders with surprise and indignation.

This, then, was the first and principal effect of the crusades, a great step towards the enfranchisement of mind, a great progress towards more extensive and liberal ideas. Commenced in the name and under the influence of religious creeds, the crusades removed from religious ideas, I will not say their legitimate influence, but the exclusive and despotic possession of the human mind. This result, doubtless altogether unforeseen, was born of many causes. The first is evidently the novelty, extension, and variety of the spectacle which was opened to the view of the crusaders. It happened with them as with travellers. It is a common saying that the mind of travellers becomes enlarged; that the habit of observing various nations and manners, and different opinions, extends the ideas, and frees the judgment from old prejudices. The same fact was accomplished among these travelling nations who were called crusaders: their minds were opened and elevated, by seeing a multitude of different things, and by observing other manners than their own. They also found themselves in juxtaposition with two civilizations, not only different from their own, but more advanced; the Greek on the one hand, and the Mahommedan on the other. There can be no doubt that the Greek society, although enervated, perverted, and falling into decay, had upon the crusaders the effect of a more advanced, polished, and enlightened society than their own. The Mahommedan society afforded them a spectacle of the same nature. It is curious to observe in the old chronicles the impression which the crusaders made upon the Mussulmans; these latter regarded them at first as barbarians, as the rudest, most ferocious, and most stupid class of men they had ever seen. The crusaders, on their part, were struck with the riches and elegance of manners of the Mussulmans. To this first impression succeeded frequent relations between the two people. These extended and became much more important than is generally supposed. Not only had the Christians of the east habitual relations with the Mussulmans, but the west and the east became acquainted, visited and mixed with each other. It is not long since that one of those scholars who honour France in the eyes of Europe, M. Abel Remusat, discovered the existence of relations between the Mongol emperors and the Christian kings. Mongol ambassadors were sent to the Frank kings, to Saint Louis among others, to treat for an alliance with them, and to recommence the crusades in the common interest of the Mongols and the Christians against the Turks. And not only were diplomatic and official relations thus established between the sovereigns; frequent and various national relations were formed. I quote the words of M. Abel Remusat.*

"Many Italian, French, and Flemish monks, were charged with diplomatic missions to the Great Khan. Mongols of distinction came to Rome, Barcelona, Valentia, Lyons, Paris, London, Northampton; and a Franciscan of the kingdom of Naples was archbishop of Pekin. His successor was a professor of theology of the faculty of Paris. But how many others, less known, were drawn after these, either as slaves, or attracted by the desire for gain, or guided by curiosity into countries till then unknown! Chance has preserved the names of some: the first who came to visit the king of Hungary, on the part of the Tartars, was an Englishman, banished from his country for certain crimes, and who, after wandering all over Asia, ended by taking service among the Mongols. A Flemish shoemaker met in the depths of Tartary a woman from Metz, named Paquette, who had been carried off from Hungary; a Parisian goldsmith, whose brother was established at Paris, upon the great bridge; and a young man from the environs of Rouen, who had been at the taking of Belgrade. He saw, also, Russians, Hungarians, and Flemings. A chorister, named Robert, after having travelled over Eastern Asia, returned to finish his days in the cathedral of Chartres. A Tartar was purveyor of helmets in the army of Philip the Handsome; John de Plancarpin found near Gayouk a Russian gentleman, whom he calls Temer, who was serving as an interpreter; many merchants of Breslaw, Poland, and Austria, accompanied him in his journey to Tartary. Others returned with him by way of Russia; these were Genoese, Pisans, and Venetians. Two merchants, whom chance had led to Bokhara,

---

* *Mémoires sur les Relations Politiques des Princes Chrétiens avec les Empereurs Mongols. Deuxième Mémoire*, pp. 154–7.

consented to follow a Mongol ambassador sent by Koulagou to Khoubilai. They sojourned several years both in China and Tartary, returned with letters from the Great Khan to the pope; again returned to the Great Khan, taking with them the son of one of them, the celebrated Marco Polo, and again quitted the court of Khoubilai to return to Venice. Travels of this kind were not less frequent in the following century. Among the number are those of Sir John Mandeville, an English physician, of Oderic of Friuli, of Pegoletti, of William de Bouldeselle, and several others; and we may suppose, that those whose memorials are preserved, form but the least part of what were undertaken, and that there were at this period more persons capable of executing long journeys than of writing an account of them. Many of these adventurers remained and died in the countries which they visited. Others returned to their country as obscure as when they left it; but with an imagination filled with what they had seen, relating it to their family, exaggerating, no doubt, but leaving around them, amidst absurd fables, useful remembrances and traditions capable of bearing fruit. Thus in Germany, Italy, and France, in the monasteries, in the castles of the lords, and even down to the lowest ranks of society, were deposited precious seeds destined before long to germinate. All these unknown travellers carried the arts of their native land into the most distant countries, brought back other knowledge no less precious, and thus made, without being aware of it, more advantageous exchanges than all those of commerce. By these means, not only the trade in silk, porcelain, and Indian commodities was extended and facilitated—new routes opened to commercial industry and activity—but, what was of much more importance, foreign manners, unknown nations, extraordinary productions, offered themselves in crowds to the minds of the Europeans, confined, since the fall of the Roman empire, within too narrow a circle. They began to know the value of the most beautiful, the most populous, and the most anciently civilized of the four quarters of the globe. They began to study the arts, creeds, and idioms of its inhabitants, and there was even talk of establishing a professorship of the Tartar language in the university of Paris. Romantic narrative, when duly discussed and investigated, spread on all sides more just and varied notions. The world seemed to open on the side of the east; geography took a great stride, and the desire for discovery became the new form which clothed the adventurous spirit of the Europeans. The idea of another hemisphere ceased to present itself as a paradox void of all probability, when our own became better known; and it was in searching for the Zipangri of Marco Polo that Christopher Columbus discovered the New World."

You see, by the facts which led to the impulsion of the crusades, what, at the thirteenth and fourteenth centuries, was the new and vast world which was thrown open to the European mind. There can be no doubt but that this was one of the most powerful causes of development, and of the freedom of mind which shone forth at the end of this great event.

There is another cause which merits observation. Down to the time of the crusades, the court of Rome, the centre of the church, had never been in communication with the laity, except through the medium of ecclesiastics, whether legates sent from the court of Rome, or the bishops and the entire clergy. There had always been some laymen in direct relation with Rome; but, taken all together, it was through the ecclesiastics that she communicated with the people. During the crusades, on the contrary, Rome became a place of passage to the greater part of the crusaders, both in going and in returning. Numbers of the laity viewed her policy and manners, and could see how much of personal interest influenced religious controversy. Doubtless this new knowledge inspired many minds with a hardihood till then unknown.

When we consider the state of minds in general, at the end of the crusades, and particularly in ecclesiastical matters, it is impossible not to be struck by one singular fact: religious ideas experienced no change; they had not been replaced by contrary or even different opinions. Yet minds were infinitely more free; religious creeds were no longer the only sphere in which it was brought into play; without abandoning them, it began to separate itself from them, and carry itself elsewhere. Thus, at the end of the thirteenth century, the moral cause which had determined the crusades, which at least was its most energetic principle, had vanished; the moral state of Europe was profoundly modified.

The social state had undergone an analogous change. Much investigation has been expended upon what was the influence of the crusades in this respect; it has been shown how they reduced a large number of fief-holders to the necessity of selling them to their sovereigns, or of selling charters to the boroughs in order to procure the means of following the crusade. It has been shown that by their mere absence, many of the lords must have lost the greater portion of their power. Without entering into the details of this inquiry, we may, I think, resolve into a few general facts, the influence of the crusades upon the social state.

They greatly diminished the number of petty fiefs and small domains, of inferior fief-holders; and they concentred property and power in a smaller number of hands. It is with the commencement of the crusades that we see the formation and augmentation of large fiefs, and great feudal existences.

I have often regretted that there is no map of France divided into fiefs, as there is of its division into departments, arrondissements, cantons, and parishes, in which all the fiefs should be marked, with their extent and successive relations and changes. If we were to compare, with the aid of such a map, the state of France before and after the crusades, we should see how many fiefs had vanished, and to what a degree the great and middle fiefs had increased. This was one of the most important facts to which the crusades led.[3]

Even where the petty proprietors preserved their fiefs, they no longer lived as isolated as formerly. The great fief-holders became so many centres, around which the smaller ones converged, and near to which they passed their lives. It had become necessary, during the crusades, for them to put themselves in the train of the richest and most powerful, to receive succour from him; they had lived with him, partaken of his fortune, gone through the same adventures. When the crusaders returned home, this sociability, this habit of living near to the superior lord, remained fixed in their manners. Thus as we see the augmentation of the great fiefs after the crusades, so we see the possessors of those fiefs holding a much more

3. There is a certain similarity between Guizot's analysis of the concentration of feudal properties in ever fewer hands—with the decline of smaller fiefs during the Crusades and growth of great feudatories—and Marx's later prediction that as capitalism developed it would also involve an ever-increasing concentration of property, with many of the intermediate groups between capitalist and proletariat classes sinking into the latter condition. In effect, Guizot extends the concept of centralization to economic and social relations, drawing on Adam Smith's argument about the increasing social division of labour, but placing even more emphasis on the distribution of property.

considerable court in the interior of their castles, having near them a larger number of gentlemen who still preserved their small domains, but did not shut themselves up within them.

The extension of the great fiefs and the creation of a certain number of centres of society, in place of the dispersion which formerly existed, are the two principal effects brought about by the crusades in the heart of feudalism.

As to the burghers, a result of the same nature is easily perceptible. The crusades created the great boroughs. Petty commerce and industry did not suffice to create boroughs such as the great towns of Italy and Flanders were. It was commerce on a great scale, maritime commerce, and especially that of the east, which gave rise to them; it was the crusades which gave to maritime commerce the most powerful impulsion it had ever received.

Upon the whole, when we regard the state of society at the end of the crusades, we find that this movement of dissolution, of the dispersion of existences and influences, this movement of universal localization, if such a phrase be permitted, which had preceded this epoch, had ceased, by a movement with an exactly contrary tendency, by a movement of centralization. All now tended to approximation. The lesser existences were either absorbed in the greater, or were grouped around them. It was in this direction that society advanced, that all its progress was made.

You now see, why, towards the end of the thirteenth and fourteenth centuries, neither people nor sovereigns any longer desired the crusades; they had no longer either the need or desire for them; they had been cast into them by the impulsion of the religious spirit, and by the exclusive domination of religious ideas upon the whole existence; this domination had lost its energy. They had sought, too, in the crusades a new life, more extensive and more varied; they now began to find it in Europe itself, in the progress of social relations. It was at this epoch the career of political aggrandizement opened itself to kings. Wherefore seek kingdoms in Asia, when they had them to conquer at their own doors? Philip Augustus went to the crusades against his will: what could be more natural? He had to make himself king of France. It was the same with the people. The career of riches opened before their eyes; they renounced adventures for work. For the sovereigns, the place of adventures was supplied by policy; for the people, by work on a great scale. One single class of society still had a taste for adventure: this was that portion of feudal nobility who, not being in a condition to think of political aggrandizement, and not liking work, preserved their ancient condition and manners. They therefore continued to rush to the crusades, and attempted their revival.

Such, in my opinion, are the great and true effects of the crusades: on one side, the extension of ideas, the enfranchisement of mind; on the other, the aggrandizement of existences, and a large sphere opened to activity of all kind: they produced at once a greater degree of individual liberty, and of political unity. They aided the independence of man and the centralization of society. Much has been asked as to the means of civilization which they directly imported from the east; it has been said that the chief portion of the great discoveries which, in the fourteenth and fifteenth centuries, called forth the development of European civilization—the compass, printing, gunpowder—were known in the east, and that the crusaders may have brought them thence. This, to a certain point, is true. But some of these assertions are disputable. That which is not disputable is this influence, this general effect of the crusades upon the mind on one hand, and upon society on the other hand; they drew European society from a very straightened track, and led it into new and infinitely more extensive paths; they commenced that transformation of the various elements of European society into governments and peoples, which is the character of modern civilization. About the same time, royalty, one of those institutions which have most powerfully contributed to this great result, developed itself. Its history, from the birth of modern states down to the thirteenth century, will form the subject of my next lecture.

NINTH LECTURE

Object of the lecture—Important part taken by royalty in the history
of Europe, and in the history of the world—True causes of this
importance—Two-fold point of view under which the institution of
royalty should be considered—1st. Its true and permanent nature—It
is the personification of the sovereignty of right—With what limits—
2nd. Its flexibility and diversity—European royalty seems to be the
result of various kinds of royalty—Of barbarian royalty—
Of imperial royalty—Of religious royalty—Of feudal royalty—
Of modern royalty, properly so called, and of its true character.

IN OUR LAST LECTURE, I attempted to determine the essential and distinctive character of modern European society, as compared with primitive European society; I believe that we discovered in this fact, that all the elements of the social state, at first numerous and various, reduce themselves to two: on one hand the government, and on the other, the people. Instead of encountering the feudal nobility, the clergy, the kings, burghers, and serfs, as the dominant powers and chief actors in history, we find in modern Europe but two great figures which alone occupy the historic scene, the government and the country.

If such is the fact in which European civilization terminates, such also is the end to which we should tend, and to which our researches should conduct us. It is necessary that we should see this grand result take birth, and progressively develop and strengthen itself. We are entered upon the epoch in which we may arrive at its origin: it was, as you have seen, between the twelfth and the sixteenth centuries that the slow and concealed work operated in Europe which has led our society to this new form and definitive state. We have likewise studied the first great event, which, in my opinion, evidently and powerfully impelled Europe in this direction, that is, the crusades.

About the same epoch, almost at the moment that the crusades broke out, that institution commenced its aggrandizement, which has, perhaps, contributed more than anything to the formation of modern society, and to that fusion of all the social elements into two powers, the government and the people: royalty.

It is evident that royalty has played a prodigious part in the history of European civilization; a single glance at facts suffices to convince one of it; we see the development of royalty marching with the same step, so to speak, at least for a long period, as that of society itself; the progress is mutual.

And not only is the progress mutual, but whenever society advances towards its modern and definitive character, royalty seems to extend and prosper; so that when the work is consummated, when there is no longer any, or scarcely any other important or decisive influence in the great states of Europe, than that of the government and the public, royalty is the government.

And it has thus happened, not only in France, where the fact is evident, but also in the greater portion of European countries: a little earlier or a little later, under somewhat different forms, the same result is offered us in the history of society in England, Spain, and Germany. In England, for example, it was under the Tudors, that the ancient, peculiar, and local elements of English society were perverted and dissolved, and gave place to the system of public powers; this also was the time of the greatest influence of royalty. It was the same in Germany, Spain, and all the great European states.

If we leave Europe, and if we turn our view upon the rest of the world, we shall be struck by an analogous fact; we shall everywhere find royalty occupying an important position, appearing as, perhaps, the most general and permanent of institutions, the most difficult to prevent, where it did not formerly exist, and the most difficult to root out where it had existed. From time immemorial it has possessed Asia. At the discovery of America, all the great states there were found with different combinations, subject to the monarchical system. When we penetrate into the interior of Africa, wherever we meet with nations in any way extensive, this is the prevailing system. And not only has royalty penetrated everywhere, but it has accommodated itself to the most diverse situations, to civilization and to barbarism, to manners the most pacific, as in China, for example, and to those in which war, in which the military spirit dominate. It has alike established itself in the heart of the system of castes, in the most rigorously classified societies, and in the midst of a system of equality, in societies which are utter strangers to all legal and permanent classification. Here despotic and oppressive, there favourable to civilization and even to liberty, it seems like a head which may be placed upon a multitude of different bodies, a fruit that will spring from the most dissimilar germs.

In this fact, we may discover many curious and important consequences. I will take only two. The first is, that it is impossible such a result should be the fruit of mere chance, of force or usurpation alone; it is impossible but that there should be a profound and powerful analogy between the nature of royalty, considered as an institution, and the nature, whether of individual man, or of human society. Doubtless, force is intermixed with the origin of the institution; doubtless, force has taken an important part in its progress; but when we meet with such a result as this, when we see a great event developing and reproducing itself during the course of many centuries, and in the midst of such different situations, we cannot attribute it to force. Force plays a great part, and an incessant one, in human affairs; but it is not their principle, their *primum mobile;* above force and the part which it plays, there hovers a moral cause which decides the totality of things. It is with force in the history of societies, as with the body in the history of man. The body surely holds a high place in the life of man, but still it is not the principle of life. Life circulates within it, but it does not emanate from it. So it is with human societies; whatever part force takes therein is not force which governs them, and which presides supremely over their destinies; it is ideas and moral influences, which conceal themselves under the accidents of force, and regulate the course of the society. It is a cause of this kind, and not force, which gave success to royalty.

A second fact, and one which is no less worthy of remark, is the flexibility of the institution, its faculty of modifying, and adapting itself to a multitude of different circumstances. Mark the contrast: its form is unique, permanent, and simple; it does not offer that prodigious variety of combinations which we see in other institutions, and yet it applies itself to societies which the least resemble it. It must evidently allow of great diversity, and must attach itself, whether in man himself or in society, to many different elements and principles.

It is from not having considered the institution of royalty in its whole extent; from not having on the one hand penetrated to its peculiar and fixed principle, which, whatever may be the circumstances to which it applies itself, is its very essence and being—and on the other, from not having estimated all the varieties to which it lends itself, and all the principles with which it may enter into alliance; it is, I say, from not having considered royalty under this vast and two-fold point of view, that the part taken by it in the history of the world has not been always comprehended, that its nature and effects have often been misconstrued.

This is the work which I wish to go through with you, and in such a manner as to take an exact and complete estimate of the effects of this institution in modern Europe, whether they have flowed from its own peculiar principles or the modifications which it has undergone.

There can be no doubt that the force of royalty, that moral power which is its true principle, does not reside in the sole and personal will of the man momentarily king; there can be no doubt that the people, in accepting it as an institution, philosophers in maintaining it as a system, have not intended or consented to accept the empire of the will of a man, essentially narrow, arbitrary, capricious, and ignorant.

Royalty is quite a distinct thing from the will of a man, although it presents itself in that form; it is the personification of the sovereignty of right, of that will, essentially reasonable, enlightened, just, and impartial, foreign and superior to all individual wills, and which in virtue of this title has a right to govern them. Such is the meaning of royalty in the minds of nations, such the motive for their adhesion.

Is it true that there is a sovereignty of right, a will which possesses the right of governing men?[1] It is quite certain that they believe so; because

1. Here Guizot puts forward his normative political theory more carefully than anywhere else in the 1828 lectures. It is a theory developed out of the political writings of Rousseau and Kant, but modified by Guizot in important respects. Formulated in terms of a will which is just—"a will which possesses the right of governing men"—Guizot makes it clearer than Rousseau had done in *The Social Contract,* that such a will can never entirely be embodied in any human institution. In that sense, the "sovereignty of right" remains

they seek, and constantly have sought, and indeed cannot but seek, to place themselves under its empire. Conceive to yourselves the smallest assembly of men, I will not say a people: conceive that assembly under the submission to a sovereign who is only so *de facto,* under a force which has no right except that of force, which governs neither according to reason, justice, nor truth; human nature revolts at such a supposition—it must have right to believe in. It is the supremacy of right which it seeks, that is the only power to which man consents to submit. What is history but the demonstration of this universal fact? What are the greater portion of the struggles which take place in the life of nations, but an ardent effort towards the sovereignty of right, so that they may place themselves under its empire? And not only nations but philosophers believe in its existence, and incessantly seek it. What are all the systems of political philosophy, but the search for the sovereign of right? What is it that they treat of, but the question of knowing who has a right to govern society? Take the theocratical, monarchical, aristocratical, or democratical systems, all of them boast of having discovered wherein the sovereignty of right resides; all promise to society that they will place it under the rule of its legitimate master. I repeat, this is the end alike of all the works of philosophers, of all efforts of nations.

How should they but believe in the sovereignty of right? How should they but be constantly in search of it? Take the most simple suppositions; let there be something to accomplish, some influence to exercise, whether upon society in its whole, or upon a number of its members, or upon a single individual; there is evidently always a rule for this action, a legitimate will to follow and apply. Whether you penetrate into the smallest details of social life, or whether you elevate yourselves to the greatest

---

a moral criterion which ought to preside over the construction and operation of a political system. Any claims of monarchy, aristocracy or even democracy to represent the sovereignty of right entirely are thus rejected (though Guizot suggests that the almost universal role of monarchy is due to its prefiguring the idea of a unified and just will, that is, the sovereignty of right). Because the sovereignty of right can never be fully embodied by any institution, Guizot argues for the separation and balancing of powers, as a necessary precaution in view of human fallibility. However, by insisting on the importance of local autonomy as well, he goes beyond Montesquieu's earlier doctrine. Guizot had worked out these ideas earlier in the Restoration, both in pamphlets and in his *History of Representative Government in Europe.*

events, you will everywhere encounter a truth to be proved, or a just and reasonable idea to be passed into reality. This is the sovereign of right, towards which philosophers and nations have never ceased and never can cease to aspire.

Up to what point can the sovereignty of right be represented in a general and permanent manner by a terrestrial force or by a human will? How far is such a supposition necessarily false and dangerous? What should be thought in particular of the personification of the sovereignty of right under the image of royalty? Upon what conditions, within what limits is this personification admissible? Great questions, which I can not treat properly here, but which I can not resist pointing out, and upon which I shall say a word in passing.

I affirm, and the merest commonsense will acknowledge, that the sovereignty of right completely and permanently can appertain to no one; that all attribution of the sovereignty of right to any human power whatsoever, is radically false and dangerous. Hence arises the necessity for the limitation of all powers, whatever their names or forms may be; hence the radical illegitimacy of all absolute power, whether its origin be from conquest, inheritance, or election. People may differ as to the best means of seeking the sovereign of right; they may vary as to place and times; but in no place, no time, can any legitimate power be the independent possessor of this sovereignty.

This principle being laid down, it is no less certain that royalty, in whatever system it is considered, presents itself as the personification of the sovereign of right. Listen to the theocratical system: it will tell you that kings are the image of God upon earth; this is only saying that they are the personification of sovereign justice, truth, and goodness. Address yourself to the jurisconsults: they will tell you that the king is the living law; that is to say, the king is the personification of the sovereign of right, the just law, which has the right of governing society. Ask royalty itself, in the system of pure monarchy: it will tell you that it is the personification of the state, of the general interest. In whatever alliance and in whatever situation you consider it, you will always find it summing itself up in the pretension of representing and reproducing the sovereign of right, alone capable of legitimately governing society.

There is no occasion for astonishment in all this. What are the characteristics of the sovereign of right, the characteristics derivable from his very nature? In the first place he is unique; since there is but one truth, one justice, there can be but one sovereign of right. He is permanent, always the same; truth never changes. He is placed in a superior situation, a stranger to all the vicissitudes and changes of this world; his part in the world is, as it were, that of a spectator and judge. Well! it is royalty which externally reproduces, under the most simple form, that which appears its most faithful image, these rational and natural characteristics of the sovereign of right. Open the work in which M. Benjamin Constant has so ingeniously represented royalty as a neutral and moderating power, raised above the accidents and struggles of social life, and only interfering at great crises. Is not this, so to speak, the attitude of the sovereign of right in the government of human things? There must be something in this idea well calculated to impress the mind, for it has passed with singular rapidity from books to facts. One sovereign made it in the constitution of Brazil the very foundation of his throne; there royalty is represented as a moderating power, raised above all active powers, as a spectator and judge.

Under whatever point of view you regard this institution, as compared with the sovereign of right, you will find that there is a great external resemblance, and that it is natural for it to have struck the minds of men. Accordingly, whenever their reflection or imagination turned with preference towards the contemplation or study of the nature of the sovereign of right, and his essential characteristics, they have inclined towards royalty. As, in the time of the preponderance of religious ideas, the habitual contemplation of the nature of God led mankind towards the monarchical system, so when the jurisconsults dominated in society, the habit of studying, under the name of the law, the nature of the sovereign of right, was favourable to the dogma of his personification in royalty. The attentive application of the human mind to the contemplation of the nature of the sovereignty of right when no other causes have interfered to destroy the effect, has always given force and credit to royalty, which presents its image.

Moreover, there are times peculiarly favourable to this personification: these are the times when individual powers display themselves in the world with all their risks and caprices; times when egotism dominates in individuals, whether from ignorance and brutality, or from corruption. Then society, abandoned to the contests of personal wills, and unable to raise itself by their free concurrence to a common and universal will, passionately longs for a sovereign to whom all individuals may be forced to submit; and the moment any institution, bearing any one of the characteristics of the sovereignty of right, presented itself, and promised its empire to society, society rallied round it with eager earnestness, like outlaws taking refuge in the asylum of a church. This is what has been seen in the disorderly youth of nations, such as we have surveyed. Royalty is admirably adapted to epochs of vigorous and fruitful anarchy, so to speak, when society desires to form and regulate itself, without knowing how to do so by the free concord of individual wills. There are other times when, from directly opposite causes, it has the same recommendation. Why did the Roman empire, so nearly in a state of dissolution at the end of the republic, subsist for nearly fifteen centuries afterwards, under the name of that empire, which, after all, was but a continual decay, a lengthened agony? Royalty alone could produce such an effect; that alone could hold together a society which selfishness incessantly tended to destroy. The imperial power struggled for fifteen centuries against the ruin of the Roman world.

Thus there are times when royalty alone can retard the dissolution of society, and times when it alone accelerates its formation. And in both these cases, it is because it represents more clearly and powerfully than any other form the sovereignty of right, that it exercises this power upon events.

From whatever point of view you may consider this institution, and at whatever epoch, you will acknowledge then that its essential characteristic, its moral principle, its true and inmost meaning is the image, the personification, the presumed interpreter of this unique, superior, and essentially legitimate will, which alone has the right of governing society.

Let us now regard royalty from the second point of view, that is to say, in its flexibility, in the variety of parts which it has played, and the effects which it has produced; it is necessary that we should give the reason of these features, and determine their causes.

Here we have an advantage; we can immediately enter upon history, and upon our own history. By a concourse of singular circumstances, it has happened, that in modern Europe royalty has assumed every character under which it has shown itself in the history of the world. If I may be allowed to use an arithmetical expression, European royalty is the sum total of all possible species of royalty. I will run over its history from the fifth to the twelfth century; you will see how various are the aspects under which it presents itself, and to what an extent we shall everywhere find this character of variety, complication, and conflict which belongs to all European civilization.

In the fifth century, at the time of the great German invasion, two royalties are present; the barbarian and the imperial royalty, that of Clovis and that of Constantine; both differing essentially in principles and effects. Barbaric royalty is essentially elective; the German kings were elected, although their election did not take place with the same forms which we are accustomed to attach to the idea; they were military chiefs, who were bound to make their power freely acceptable to a large number of companions who obeyed them as being the most brave and the most able among them. Election is the true source of barbaric royalty, its primitive and essential characteristic.

Not that this characteristic in the fifth century was not already a little modified, or that different elements had not been introduced into royalty. The various tribes had had their chiefs for a certain time; some families had raised themselves to more trust, consideration, and riches than others. Hence a commencement of inheritance; the chief was now mostly elected out of these families. This was the first differing principle which became associated with the dominant principle of election.

Another idea, another element, had also already penetrated into barbaric royalty: this was the religious element. We find among some of the barbarous nations, among the Goths, for example, that the families of their kings descended from the families of their gods, or from those heroes of whom they had made gods, such as Odin. This is the situation of the kings of Homer, who sprang from gods or demi-gods, and by reason of this title were the objects of a kind of religious veneration, despite their limited power.

Such, in the fifth century, was barbaric royalty, already varying and fluctuating, although its primitive principle still dominated.

I take imperial, Roman royalty; this is a totally different thing; it is the personification of the state, the heir of the sovereignty and majesty of the

Roman people. Consider the royalty of Augustus and Tiberius; the emperor is the representative of the senate, the comitia, and the whole republic; he succeeded them, and they are summed up in his person. Who would not recognize this in the modesty of language of the first emperors; of those, at least, who were men of sense, and understood their situation? They felt themselves in the presence of the late sovereign people who had abdicated in their favour; they addressed them as their representatives and ministers. But, in fact, they exercised the whole power of the people, and that with the most formidable intensity. It is easy for us to understand such a transformation; we have ourselves witnessed it; we have seen the sovereignty pass from the people to a man; that is the history of Napoleon. He also was the personification of the sovereign people; he unceasingly repeated to it, "Who like me has been elected by eighteen millions of men? Who like me is the representative of the people *Republique Française?*" And when upon one side of his coinage we read, *The French Republic,* and upon the other, *Napoleon, Empereur,* what does this mean, if not the fact which I have described, the people become king?

Such was the fundamental character of imperial royalty, which it preserved for the three first centuries of the empire: it was not till Diocletian that it took its definitive and complete form. It was then, however, upon the point of undergoing a great change; a new royalty had almost appeared. Christianity laboured for three centuries to introduce the religious element into society. It was under Constantine that it met with success, not in making it the prevalent fact, but in making it play an important part. Here royalty presents itself under a different aspect; its origin is not earthly; the prince is not the representative of the public sovereignty; he is the image of God, his representative and delegate. Power came down to him from above, while in imperial royalty it came from below. These are two utterly different situations, and have entirely different results. The rights of liberty, political guarantees are difficult to combine with the principle of religious royalty; but the principle itself is elevated, moral, and salutary. Let us see the idea which was formed of the prince in the seventh century, in the system of religious royalty. I take it from the canons of the councils of Toledo.

"The king is called king (*rex*), because he governs justly (*rectè*). If he act with justice (*recte*), he legitimately possesses the name of king; if he act with injustice, he miserably loses it. Our fathers, therefore, said, with good reason: *Rex ejus, eris si recta facis, si autem non facis, non eris.* The two principal royal virtues are justice and truth (science of the reason).

"The royal power is bound, like the people, to respect the laws. . . . Obedience to the will of Heaven, gives to us and to our subjects wise laws, which our greatness and that of our successors is bound to obey, as well as the whole population of our kingdom. . . .

"God, the creator of all things, in disposing the structure of the human body, has raised the head on high, and has willed that the nerves of all the members should proceed therefrom. And he has placed in the head the torch of the eyes, to the end that from thence may be viewed all things that might be prejudicial. He has established the power of intellect, charging it to govern all the members, and wisely to regulate their action. . . . It is first necessary, then, to regulate what relates to princes, to watch over their safety, and to protect their life, and then to order what relates to the people; so that in guaranteeing, as is fitting, the safety of kings, they at the same time guarantee, and more effectually, that of the people."*

But, in the system of religious royalty, another element, quite different from that of royalty itself, almost always introduced itself. A new power took its place by the side of it, a power nearer to God, to the source whence royalty emanates, than royalty itself: this was the clergy, the ecclesiastical power which interposed itself between God and kings, and between kings and the people; so that royalty, the image of divinity, ran a chance of falling to the rank of an instrument of the human interpreters of the divine will. This was a new cause of diversity in the destinies and effects of the institution.

Here, then, we see, what in the fifth century were the various royalties which manifested themselves upon the ruins of the Roman empire: the barbaric royalty, the imperial royalty, and the rising religious royalty. Their fortunes were as various as their principles.

In France, under the first race, barbaric royalty prevailed; there were many attempts of the clergy to impress upon it the imperial or religious character; but election in the royal family, with some mixture of inheritance

---

* *Forum Judicum*, i. lib. 2; tit. i. 1. 2, 1. 4.

and religious ideas, remained dominant. In Italy, among the Ostrogoths, imperial royalty superseded the barbarian customs. Theodoric asserted himself the successor of the emperors. You need only read Cassiodorus, to acknowledge this character of his government.

In Spain, royalty appeared more religious than elsewhere; as the councils of Toledo were, I will not say the masters, but the most influential power, the religious character dominated, if not in the government, properly so called, of the Visigoth kings, at least, in the laws with which the clergy inspired them, and the language which it made them speak.

In England, among the Saxons, barbarian manners subsisted almost entire. The kingdoms of the heptarchy were merely the domains of various bands, having each its chief. The military election is more evident there than elsewhere. Anglo-Saxon royalty is the most perfect type of barbaric royalty.

Thus from the fifth to the seventh century, three kinds of royalty manifested themselves at the same time, in general facts; one or other of them prevailed, according to circumstances, in each of the different states of Europe.

The chaos was such at this epoch, that nothing universal or permanent could be established; and, from one vicissitude to another, we arrive at the eighth century, without royalty having anywhere taken a definitive character. Towards the middle of the eighth century, with the triumph of the second race of the Frank kings, events generalized themselves and became clearer; as they were accomplished upon a greater scale, they were better understood, and led to more results. You will shortly see the different royalties distinctly succeed and combine with each other.

At the time when the Carlovingians replace the Merovingians, a return of barbaric royalty is visible; election again appears. Pepin causes himself to be elected at Soissons. When the first Carlovingians give the kingdoms to their sons they take care to have them accepted by the chief persons in the states assigned them; when they make a partition, they wish it to be sanctioned in the national assemblies. In a word, the elective principle, under the form of public acceptation, re-assumes some reality. You bear in mind, that this change of dynasty was like a new invasion of the Germans in the west of Europe, and brought back some shadow of their ancient institutions and manners.

At the same time we see the religious principle introduced more clearly into royalty, and playing therein a more important part. Pepin was acknowledged and crowned by the pope. He had need of religious sanction; it had already a great power, and he courted it. Charlemagne took the same precaution; religious royalty was developing. Still under Charlemagne this character did not dominate; imperial royalty was evidently what he attempted to resuscitate. Although he closely allied himself to the clergy, and made use of them, he was not their instrument. The idea of a great state, of a great political unity, the resurrection of the Roman empire, was the favourite idea, the dream of Charlemagne's reign. He died, and was succeeded by Louis le Debonnaire. Everyone knows what character the royal power instantly assumed; the king fell into the hands of the clergy, who censured, deposed, re-established, and governed him; religious royalty, late subordinate, seemed on the point of being established.

Thus, from the middle of the eighth to the middle of the ninth century, the diversity of three kinds of royalty manifested itself in important, closely connected, and palpable events.

After the death of Louis le Debonnaire, in the dissolution into which Europe fell, the three species of royalty disappeared almost simultaneously; all became confusion. After some time, when the feudal system prevailed, a fourth royalty presented itself, different from any that we have yet seen; this was feudal royalty. This is confused, and very difficult to define. It has been said that the king in the feudal system was sovereign of sovereigns, lord of lords, that he held by sure ties, from one class to another, the entire society; that in calling around him his vassals, then the vassals of his vassals, he called the whole nation, and truly showed himself a king. I do not deny that this was the theory of feudal royalty; but it is a mere theory, which has never governed facts. That general influence of the king by the means of an hierarchical organization, those ties which united royalty to the entire feudal society, are the dreams of publicists. In fact, the greater part of the feudal lords were at this epoch entirely independent of royalty; a large number scarcely knew the name, and had little or no connexion with it. All the sovereignties were local and independent: the title of king, borne by one of the feudal lords, expressed rather a remembrance than a fact.

This was the state of royalty during the course of the tenth and eleventh centuries. In the twelfth, with the reign of Louis le Gros, the aspect of things began to change. We more often find the king spoken of; his influence penetrated into places where hitherto he had never made way; his part in society became more active. If we seek by what title, we shall recognize none of the titles of which royalty had hitherto been accustomed to avail itself. It was not as the heir of the emperors, or by the title of imperial royalty, that it aggrandized itself and assumed more coherence; nor was it in virtue of election, nor as the emanation of divine power. All trace of election had disappeared, the hereditary principle of succession had become definitively established; and although religion sanctioned the accession of kings, the minds of men did not appear at all engrossed with the religious character of the royalty of Louis le Gros. A new element, a character hitherto unknown, produced itself in royalty; a new royalty commenced.

I need not repeat that society was at this epoch in a prodigious disorder, a prey to unceasing violence. Society had in itself no means of striving against this deplorable state, of regaining any regularity or unity. The feudal institutions, those parliaments of barons, those seigneurial courts, all those forms under which, in modern times, feudalism has been represented as a systematic and organized regime, all this was devoid of reality, of power; there was nothing there which could re-establish order or justice; so that, amidst this social desolation, none knew to whom to have recourse for the reparation of any great injustice, or to remedy any great evil, or in any way to constitute anything resembling a state. The name of king remained; a lord bore it, and some few addressed themselves to him. The various titles under which royalty had hitherto presented itself, although they did not exercise any great control, were still present to many minds, and on some occasions were recognized. It sometimes happened that they had recourse to the king to repress any scandalous violence, or to re-establish something like order in any place near to his residence, or to terminate any difference which had long existed; he was sometimes called upon to interfere in matters not strictly within his jurisdiction; he interfered as the protector of public order, as arbitrator and redresser of wrongs. The moral authority which remained attached to his name, by degrees attracted to him this power.

Such is the character which royalty began to take under Louis le Gros, and under the administration of Suger. Then, for the first time, we see in the minds of men the idea, although very incomplete, confused, and weak, of a public power, foreign to the powers which possessed society, called to render justice to those who were unable to obtain it by ordinary means, capable of establishing, or, at least, of commanding order; the idea of a great magistrate, whose essential character was that of maintaining or re-establishing peace, of protecting the weak, and of ending differences which none others could decide. This is the entirely new character under which, dating from the twelfth century, royalty presented itself in Europe, and especially in France. It was neither as a barbarous royalty, a religious royalty, nor as an imperial royalty, that it exercised its empire; it possessed only a limited, incomplete, and accidental power, the power, as it were (I know of no expression more exact) of a great justice of peace for the whole nation.

This is the true origin of modern royalty; this, so to speak, is its vital principle; that which has been developed in the course of its career, and which, I do not hesitate in saying, has brought about its success. At the different epochs of history, we see the different characters of royalty re-appear; we see the various royalties which I have described attempting by turns to regain the preponderance. Thus the clergy has always preached religious royalty; jurisconsults laboured to resuscitate imperial royalty; and the nobles have sometimes wished to revive elective royalty, or the feudal. And not only have the clergy, jurisconsults, and nobility, striven to make dominant in royalty such or such a character; it has itself made them all subservient to the aggrandizement of its power; kings have sometimes represented themselves as the delegates of God, sometimes as the successors of the emperors, according to the need or inclination of the moment; they have illegitimately availed themselves of these various titles, but none of them has been the veritable title of modern royalty, or the source of its preponderating influence. It is, I repeat, as the depositary and protector of public order, of universal justice, and common interest—it is under the aspect of a great magistracy, the centre and union of society—that it has shown itself to the eyes of the people, and has appropriated their strength by obtaining their adhesion.

You will see, as we advance, this characteristic of modern European royalty, which commenced at the twelfth century, under the reign of Louis le Gros, strengthen and develop itself, and became, so to speak, its political physiognomy. It is through it that royalty has contributed to the great result which characterizes European societies in the present day, namely, the reduction of all social elements into two, the government and the country.

Thus, at the termination of the crusades, Europe entered the path which was to conduct it to its present state; and royalty took its appropriate part in the great transformation. In our next lecture we shall study the different attempts made at political organization, from the twelfth to the sixteenth century, with a view to maintain, by regulating it, the order, then almost in ruin. We shall consider the efforts of feudalism, of the church, and even of the boroughs, to constitute society after its ancient principles, and under its primitive forms, and thus defend themselves against the general metamorphosis which was in preparation.

TENTH LECTURE

*Object of the lecture—Attempts to reconcile the various social
elements of modern Europe, and to make them live and act in
common, in one society, and under one central power—1st. Attempt
at theocratical organization—Why it failed—Four principal
obstacles—Faults of Gregory VII—Reaction against the domination
of the church—On the part of the people—On the part of the
sovereigns—2nd. Attempt at republican organization—Italian
republics—Their defects—Towns in the south of France—Crusade
of the Albigenses—Swiss confederation—Boroughs of Flanders
and the Rhine—Hanseatic league—Struggle between the feudal
nobility and the boroughs—3rd. Attempt at a mixed organization—
States-general of France—Cortes of Spain and Portugal—English
parliament—Peculiar state of Germany—Ill success of all their
attempts—From what causes—General tendency of Europe.*

I WISH TO DETERMINE CORRECTLY, and at the outset, the object of this lecture.

You will recollect, that one of the first facts which struck us in the elements of ancient European society, was their diversity, separation, and independence. The feudal nobility, clergy, and boroughs had a situation, laws, and manners, all entirely different; they were so many societies which governed themselves, each upon its own account, and by its own rules and power. They stood in relation and came in contact, but there was no true union; they did not form, properly speaking, a nation, a State.

The fusion of all these societies into one has been accomplished; it is precisely, as you have seen, the distinctive fact, the essential character of modern society. The ancient social elements are reduced to two, the government and the people; that is to say, the diversity has ceased, that similitude has led to union. But before this result was consummated, and even with a view to its prevention, many efforts were tried to make all particular societies live and act in common, without destroying their diversity or independence. It was not wished to strike a blow in any way prejudicial to their situation, privileges, or special nature, and yet to unite them in a single state, to form of them one nation, to rally them under one and the same government.

All these attempts failed. The result which I have just mentioned, the unity of modern society, proves their ill success. Even in those European countries with some traces of the ancient diversity of social elements, in Germany, for example, where there is still a true feudal nobility and a bourgeoisie; in England, where a national church is in possession of special revenues and a particular jurisdiction, it is clear that this pretended distinct existence is but an appearance, an illusion; that these special societies are politically confounded with the general society, absorbed in the state, governed by the public powers, in subjection to the same system, and carried away in the current of the same ideas, and the same manners. I repeat that, where even the form of it still subsists, the independence of the ancient social elements has no reality.

Still these attempts to make them co-ordinate without transforming them, to attach them to a national unity without abolishing their diversity, have held an important place in the history of Europe; they partly fill the epoch which now occupies our attention, that epoch which separates primitive from modern Europe, and in which the metamorphosis of European society was accomplished. And not only has it occupied an important place therein, but it has also greatly influenced posterior events, and the manner in which the reduction of all social elements into two, the government and the public, has been brought about. It is, therefore, of consequence to properly estimate and thoroughly understand all the essays at political organization which were made from the twelfth to the sixteenth century, to create nations and governments, without destroying the diversity of the secondary societies placed side by side. Such will be our business in this lecture.

It is a difficult and even a painful task. These attempts at political organization have not all been conceived and directed with a good intention; many of them have had no other views but those of selfishness and tyranny.

More than one, however, has been pure and disinterested; more than one has really had for its object the moral and social good of mankind. The state of incoherence, violence, and iniquity in which society was then placed, shocked great minds and elevated souls, and they incessantly sought the means of escaping from it. Still, even the best of these noble essays have failed; and so much courage and virtue, so many sacrifices and efforts, have been lost: is it not a heart-rending spectacle? There is even one thing still more painful, the source of a sadness still more bitter: not only have these attempts at social amelioration failed, but an enormous mass of error and evil has been mixed up therein. Despite the good intention, the greater part were absurd, and indicated a profound ignorance of reason, justice, the rights of humanity, and the foundations of the social state; so that not only has success been wanting to mankind, but they have merited their failures. We here, then, have the spectacle, not only of the hard destiny of humanity, but also of its weakness. One may here see how the merest instalment of truth suffices so to occupy the greatest minds, that they entirely forget all the rest, and become blind to everything which does not come within the straightened horizon of their ideas; how a mere glimpse of justice in a cause suffices to make them lose sight of all the injustice which it involves and permits. This outburst of the vices and imperfection of man, is, in my opinion, a contemplation even more melancholy than the misery of his condition; his faults weigh more heavily upon me than his sufferings. The attempts which I have to describe, exhibit each of these spectacles. It is necessary to go through with them, and to be just towards those men, those ages, who have so often gone astray, and have so cruelly failed, and who, notwithstanding, have displayed such high virtues, made such noble efforts, merited so much glory!

The attempts at political organization formed from the twelfth to the sixteenth century, are of two kinds: the object of the one was to bring about the predominance of a particular social element, whether the clergy, the feudal nobility, or the boroughs; to make all the others subordinate to this, and on these terms to establish unity. The other proposed to itself to reconcile all the particular societies, and make them act in common, leaving to each its liberty, and guaranteeing its share of influence. The first class of these attempts is much more liable to the suspicion of selfishness and tyranny than the second. They have, in fact, oftener been tainted with these vices; they are indeed, by their very nature, essentially tyrannical in their means of action. Some of them, however, may have been—in fact, have been— conceived with pure views for the good and progress of humanity.

The first which presents itself is the attempt at a theocratical organization—that is to say, the design of subduing the various classes of society to the principles and empire of the ecclesiastical society. You will call to mind what I have said concerning the history of the church. I have endeavoured to show what principles have been developed within it, what was the share of legitimacy of each, how they were born of the natural course of events, what services they have rendered, and what evil they have brought about. I have characterized the various states into which the church passed from the eighth to the twelfth century; I have shown the state of the imperial church, the barbarian, the feudal, and lastly, the theocratical church. I suppose these recollections to be present to your minds; I shall now endeavour to indicate what the clergy did to dominate in Europe, and why they failed.

The attempt at theocratical organization appeared at a very early period, whether in the acts of the court of Rome, or in those of the clergy in general; it naturally resulted from the political and moral superiority of the church, but we shall find that it encountered, from the first, obstacles which, even in its greatest vigour, it did not succeed in removing.

The first was the very nature of Christianity. Wholly different in this respect from the greater number of religious creeds, Christianity was established by persuasion alone, by simply moral means; it was never, from the time of its birth, armed with force.[1] In the early ages, it conquered by the Word alone, and it only conquered souls. Hence it happened, that even after its triumph, when the church was in possession of great riches and consideration, we never find her invested with the direct government of society. Her origin, purely moral, and merely by means of persuasion, was

---

1. This argument about what distinguishes Christianity from other religions, its reliance on "moral means," on argument rather than force for its expansion, had played an important part in Guizot's *Society for Christian Morality* in the mid-1820s. Clearly the argument prepared the way for what Guizot considered to be the heart of representative government, its reliance on persuasion and public argument rather than coercion as the dominant instrument of government.

found impressed in her condition. She had much influence, but she had no power. She insinuated herself into the municipal magistracies, she acted powerfully upon the emperors and their agents, but she had not the positive administration of public affairs, the government, properly so called. Now a system of government—the theocratical, or any other—cannot be established in an indirect manner by mere force of influence; it is necessary to administer, command, receive taxes, dispose of revenues, govern, in a word, actually to take possession of society. When nations and governments are acted upon by persuasion, much may be effected, and a great empire exercised; but there would be no government, no system would be founded, the future could not be provided for. Such has been, from its very origin, the situation of the Christian church; she has always been at the side of the government of society, but she has never removed it, and taken its place: a great obstacle which the attempt at theocratical organization could not surmount.

She met, at a very early period, with a second obstacle. The Roman empire once fallen, and the barbarian states founded, the church found herself among the conquered. The first thing necessary was to escape this situation; the work she had to commence by converting the conquerors, and thus raising herself to their rank. When this task was accomplished, and the church aspired to domination, she encountered the pride and resistance of the feudal nobility. This was a great service rendered to Europe by the feudal laity: in the eleventh century, nations were almost entirely subjected to the church—sovereigns were scarce able to defend themselves; the feudal nobility alone never received the yoke of the clergy, never humbled themselves before it. One need only recall the general physiognomy of the middle ages to be struck by the singular mixture of haughtiness and submission, of blind credulity and freedom of mind, in the relations between the lay lords and the priests: we there see some wreck of their primitive condition. You will call to mind how I endeavoured to represent to you the origin of feudalism, its first elements, and the manner in which the elementary feudal society was formed around the habitation of the fiefholder. I remarked how, in that society, the priest was below the lord. Well, there always remained in the heart of the feudal nobility a recollection and feeling of this situation; it always regarded itself, not only as independent of the church, but as superior to it, as alone called to possess and really govern the country; it was always willing to live in concord with the clergy, but so as to guard its own interests, and not to give in to those of the clergy. During many centuries, it was the lay aristocracy which maintained the independence of society with regard to the church—that haughtily defended it when kings and people were subdued. It was the first to oppose, and perhaps contributed more than any other power to the failure of the attempt at, a theocratical organization of society.

A third obstacle was likewise opposed, of which, in general, but little account has been held, and often even its effects been misconstrued.

Wherever a clergy has seized upon society, and subjected it to a theocratical organization, it is upon a married clergy that this empire has devolved, upon a body of priests recruiting themselves from their own bosom, and bringing up their children from their very birth in and for the same situation. Examine history: look at Asia, Egypt; all the great theocracies are the work of a clergy which is a complete society in itself, which suffices for its own wants, and borrows nothing from without.

By the celibacy of priests, the Christian clergy was in an entirely different position; it was obliged, in order to perpetuate itself, to have continual recourse to the laity; to seek from abroad, in all social positions and professions, the means of duration. In vain did the *esprit-de-corps* labour afterwards to assimilate these foreign elements; something of the origin of the newcomers always remained; burghers or nobles, they always preserved some trace of their ancient spirit, their former condition. Doubtless celibacy, in placing the Catholic clergy in an entirely special situation, foreign to the interests and common life of mankind, has been to it a chief cause of isolation; but it has thus unceasingly forced it into connexion with lay society, in order to recruit and renew itself therefrom, to receive and undergo some part of the moral revolutions which were accomplished in it; and I do not hesitate to say that this necessity, constantly renewing, has been much more prejudicial to the success of the attempt at theocratical organization, than the *esprit-de-corps*, strongly maintained by celibacy, has been able to promote it.

The church finally encountered, within her own bosom, powerful adversaries to this attempt. Much has been said concerning the unity of the church; and it is true she has constantly aspired to it, and in some respects has happily attained it. But let us not be deceived by the pomp of words, nor by that of partial facts. What society has presented more civil dissensions, or undergone more dismemberment than the clergy? What nation has been more divided, more disordered, more unfixed than the ecclesiastical nation? The national churches of the majority of European countries almost incessantly struggled against the court of Rome; councils struggled against popes; heresies have been innumerable and constantly renewing, schism always in readiness; nowhere has there been such diversity of opinions, such fury in contest, such parcelling out of power. The internal life of the church, the divisions which have broken out in it, the revolutions which have agitated it, have, perhaps, been the greatest obstacles to the triumph of that organization which she has attempted to impose upon society.

All these obstacles were in action and visible in the very cradle of the great attempt which we have in review. They did not, however, prevent its following its course, nor its being in progress for many centuries. Its most glorious time, its day of crisis, so to speak, was in the reign of Gregory VII, at the end of the eleventh century. You have already seen that the dominant idea of Gregory VII was to subjugate the world to the clergy, the clergy to the papal power, and Europe to a vast and regular theocracy. In this design, as far as it may be permitted us to judge of events at such a distance, this great man committed, in my opinion, two great faults; one the fault of a theorist, the other of a revolutionist. The first was that of ostentatiously displaying his plan, of systematically proclaiming his principles on the nature and rights of spiritual power, of drawing from them beforehand, like an intractable logician, the most distant consequences. He thus menaced and attacked all the lay sovereignties of Europe, before being assured of the means of conquering them. Success in human affairs is neither obtained by such absolute proceedings, nor in the name of philosophical argument. Moreover, Gregory VII fell into the common error of revolutionists, that of attempting more than they can execute, and not taking the possible as the measure and limit of their efforts. In order to hasten the domination of his ideas, he engaged in contest with the Empire, with all the sovereigns, and with the clergy itself. He hesitated at no consequence, nor cared for any interest, but haughtily proclaimed that he willed to reign over all kingdoms as well as over all minds, and thus raised against him, on one side, all the temporal powers, who saw themselves in pressing danger, and on the other, the free-thinkers, who began to appear, and who already dreaded the tyranny over thought. Upon the whole, Gregory perhaps compromised more than he advanced the cause he wished to serve.

It, however, continued to prosper during the whole of the twelfth and down to the middle of the thirteenth century. This is the time of the greatest power and brilliancy of the church, though I do not think it can be strictly said that she made any great progress in that epoch. Down to the end of the reign of Innocent III she rather cultivated than extended her glory and power. It was at the moment of her greatest apparent success that a popular reaction declared itself against her, in a large portion of Europe. In the south of France, the heresy of the Albigenses broke forth, which took possession of an entire, numerous, and powerful community. Almost at the same time, in the north, in Flanders, ideas and desires of the same nature appeared. A little later, in England, Wycliffe attacked with talent the power of the church, and founded a sect which will never perish. Sovereigns did not long delay entering the same path as the people. It was at the commencement of the thirteenth century that the most powerful and the ablest sovereigns of Europe, the emperors of the house of Hohenstaufen, succumbed in their struggle with the papacy. During this century, Saint Louis, the most pious of kings, proclaimed the independence of the temporal power, and published the first Pragmatic Sanction, which has been the basis of all others. At the commencement of the fourteenth century, the quarrel broke out between Philip le Bel and Boniface VIII; the king of England, Edward I was not more docile towards Rome. At this epoch, it is clear, the attempt at a theocratical organization has failed; the church, henceforth, will be on the defensive; she will no longer undertake to impose her system upon Europe; her only thought will be to preserve what she has conquered. It is from the end of the thirteenth century that the emancipation of the European lay society really dates; it was then that the church ceased to pretend to the possession of it.

She had long before renounced this claim, in the very sphere in which she seemed to have had the best chance of success. Long since, upon the very threshold of the church, around her very throne in Italy, theocracy had completely failed, and given place to an entirely different system—to that attempt at a democratic organization, of which the Italian republics are the type, and which, from the eleventh to the sixteenth century, played so brilliant a part in Europe.

You recollect what I have already related of the history of the boroughs, and the manner in which they were formed. In Italy, their destiny was more precocious and powerful than anywhere else; the towns there were much more numerous and wealthy than in Gaul, Britain, or Spain; the Roman municipal system remained more full of life and regular there.

The country parts of Italy, also, were much less fit to become the habitation of their new masters, than those of the rest of Europe. They had everywhere been cleared, drained, and cultivated; they were not clothed with forests; here the barbarians were unable to follow the hazards of the chase, or to lead an analogous life to that of Germany. Moreover, one part of this territory did not belong to them. The south of Italy, the Campagna di Roma, and Ravenna, continued to depend upon the Greek emperors. Favoured by its distance from the sovereign and the vicissitudes of war, the republican system, at an early period, gained strength and developed itself in this part of the country. And not only the whole of Italy was not in the power of the barbarians, but even where the barbarians did conquer it, they did not remain in tranquil and definitive possession. The Ostrogoths were destroyed and driven out by Belisarius and Narses. The kingdom of the Lombards succeeded no better in establishing itself. The Franks destroyed it; and, without destroying the Lombard population, Pepin and Charlemagne judged it expedient to form an alliance with the ancient Italian population, in order to struggle against the recently conquered Lombards. The barbarians, then, were not in Italy, as elsewhere, the exclusive and undisturbed masters of the land and of society. Hence it was, that beyond the Alps, only a very weak, thin, and scattered feudalism was established. The preponderance, instead of passing into the inhabitants of the country parts, as had happened in Gaul, for example, continued to appertain to the towns. When this result became evident, a large portion of the fief-holders, either from free-will or necessity, ceased to inhabit the country, and settled in the cities. Barbarian nobles became burghers. You may imagine what power and superiority this single fact gave the Italian towns as compared with the other boroughs of Europe.[2] What we have remarked in these latter, was the inferiority and timidity of the population. The burghers appeared to us like courageous freed men painfully struggling against a master who was always at their gates. The burghers of Italy were very different; the conquering and the conquered population mixed within the same walls; the towns had not to defend themselves from a neighbouring master; their inhabitants were citizens, from all time free, at least the majority of them, who defended their independence and their rights against distant and foreign sovereigns, at one time against the Frank kings, at another against the emperors of Germany. Hence, the immense and early superiority of the towns of Italy: while elsewhere even the poorest boroughs were formed with infinite trouble, here we see republics, states arise.

Thus is explained the success of the attempt at republican organization in this part of Europe. It subdued feudalism at a very early period, and became the dominant form of society. But it was little calculated to spread or perpetuate itself; it contained but few germs of amelioration, the necessary condition to extension and duration.

When we examine the history of the republics of Italy, from the eleventh to the fifteenth century, we are struck with two apparently contradictory yet incontestable facts. We find an admirable development of courage, activity, and genius, and in consequence great prosperity; there is there a movement and liberty which is wanting to the rest of Europe. Let us ask, what was the real condition of the inhabitants, how their life was passed, what was their share of happiness? Here the aspect changes; no history can be more melancholy and gloomy. There is, perhaps, no epoch or country in which the position of man appears to have been more agitated, subject to more deplorable mischances, or where we meet with more dissensions, crimes, and misfortunes. Another fact is manifest at the same time; in the political system of the greater part of the republics liberty continually

---

2. The fact that Italy never fully developed feudalism and that noble families in Italy took up residence in the cities, becoming "burghers" after a fashion, makes it possible for Guizot to argue that Italian cities acquired a political ambition and will which contrasted sharply with the timid, less ambitious communes of northern Europe.

diminished. The want of security was such, that the factions were inevitably forced to seek refuge in a system less tempestuous though less popular than that with which the state had commenced. Take the history of Florence, Venice, Genoa, Milan, Pisa; you will everywhere see that the general course of events, instead of developing liberty, and enlarging the circle of institutions, tends to contract it, and to concentre the power within the hands of a small number of men. In a word, in these republics, so energetic, brilliant, and wealthy, two things were wanting: security of life, the first condition of a social state, and the progress of institutions.

Thence a new evil, which did not allow of the extension of the attempt at republican organization. It was from without, from foreign sovereigns, that the greatest danger was threatened to Italy. Yet this danger had never the effect of reconciling these republics and making them act in concert; they would never resist in common a common enemy. Many of the most enlightened Italians, accordingly, the best patriots of our time, deplore the republican system of Italy in the middle ages as the real cause of its never having become a nation. It was parcelled out, they say, into a multitude of petty people, too much under the control of their passions to allow of their confederating, or constituting themselves a state. They regret that their country, like the rest of Europe, has not passed through a despotic centralization, which would have formed it into a nation, and have rendered it independent of foreigners. It seems, then, that the republican organization, even under the most favourable circumstances, did not contain within itself, at this epoch, the principle of progress, of duration, extension—that it had no future.[3] Up to a certain point, one may compare the organization of Italy in the middle ages to that of ancient Greece. Greece also was a country full of petty republics, always rivals and often enemies, and sometimes rallying towards a common end. The advantage in this comparison is entirely with Greece. There can be no doubt that, although history gives us many instances of iniquity in them, too, there was more order, security, and

3. In explaining the failure of Italy to become a nation-state, Guizot draws attention not only to the limitations of the republican organization of the Italian cities in the later Middle Ages, but also to the frequent need for a phase of "despotic centralization" to prepare the ground for national unity—something which Madame de Staël had argued in her *Considerations on the Revolution in France,* first published in 1818.

justice, in the interior of Athens, Lacedaemon, Thebes, than in the Italian republics. Yet how short was the political existence of Greece! What a principle of weakness existed in that parcelling out of power and territory! When Greece came in contact with great neighbouring states, with Macedonia and Rome, she at once succumbed. These small republics, so glorious and still so flourishing, could not form a coalition for defence. How much stronger was the reason for the same result happening in Italy, where society and human reason had been so much less developed and less firm than among the Greeks.

If the attempt at republican organization had so little chance of duration in Italy, where it had triumphed, where the feudal system had been vanquished, you may easily conceive that it would much sooner succumb in the other parts of Europe.

I will rapidly place its destinies before you.

There was one portion of Europe which bore a great resemblance to Italy; this was the south of France and the neighbouring Spanish provinces, Catalonia, Navarre, and Biscay. There likewise the towns had gained great development, importance, and wealth. Many of the petty lords were allied with the burghers; a portion of the clergy had likewise embraced their cause; in a word, the country was in a situation remarkably analogous to that of Italy. Accordingly, in the course of the eleventh century, and at the commencement of the twelfth, the towns of Provence, Languedoc, and Aquitaine, aimed at a political flight, at forming themselves into independent republics, just like those beyond the Alps. But the south of France was in contact with a very strong feudalism, that of the north. At this time occurred the heresy of the Albigenses, and war broke out between feudal and municipal France.[4] You know the history of the crusade against the Albigenses, under Simon de Montfort. This was the contest of the feudalism of the north against the attempt at democratical organization of the south. Despite the southern patriotism, the north carried the day; political

---

4. Guizot's family background in Nîmes, and his pride in the survival of Roman municipal forms in the south of France into the Middle Ages, contributed to his interpretation of the Albigensian Crusade of the thirteenth century as a struggle between feudal (northern) France and municipal (southern) France.

unity was wanting in the south, and civilization was not sufficiently advanced for men to supply its place by concert. The attempt at republican organization was put down, and the crusade re-established the feudal system in the south of France.

At a later period, the republican attempt met with better success in the mountains of Switzerland. There the theatre was very straitened: they had only to struggle against a foreign sovereign, who, although of a superior force to the Swiss, was by no means among the most formidable sovereigns of Europe. The struggle was courageously sustained. The Swiss feudal nobility allied themselves in a great measure with the towns; a powerful succour, which, however, altered the nature of the revolution which it aided, and imprinted upon it a more aristocratic and less progressive character than it seemed at first intended to bear.

I now pass to the north of France, to the boroughs of Flanders, the banks of the Rhine, and the Hanseatic league. There the democratical organization triumphed fully in the interior of the towns; yet we perceive, from its outset, that it was not destined to extend itself, or to take entire possession of society. The boroughs of the north were surrounded and oppressed by feudalism, by lords and sovereigns, so that they were constantly on the defensive. It is clear that all they did was to defend themselves as well as they could, they essayed no conquests. They preserved their privileges, but remained shut up within their own walls. There the democratical organization was confined and stopped short; if we go elsewhere, into the country, we do not find it.

You see what was the state of the republican attempt; triumphant in Italy, but with little chance of success or progress; vanquished in the south of Gaul; victorious on a small scale, in the mountains of Switzerland; in the north, in the boroughs of Flanders, the Rhine, and the Hanseatic league, condemned never to pass beyond the town walls. Still, in this position, evidently inferior in force to the other elements of society, it inspired the feudal nobility with a prodigious terror. The lords were jealous of the wealth of the boroughs, and feared their power; the democratical spirit penetrated into the rural districts; the insurrections of the peasants became more frequent and obstinate. A great coalition was formed among the feudal nobility against the boroughs, almost throughout Europe. The party was unequal;

the boroughs were isolated; there was no understanding or communication between them; all was local. There existed, indeed, a certain sympathy between the burghers of various countries; the successes or reverses of the towns in Flanders in the struggles with the dukes of Burgundy, certainly excited a lively emotion in the French towns; but this emotion was transitory and without result; no tie, no real union, was established; nor did the boroughs lend strength to one another. Feudalism, then, had immense advantages over them. But, itself divided and incoherent, it did not succeed in destroying them. When the struggle had lasted a certain time, when they had acquired the conviction that a complete victory was impossible, it became necessary to acknowledge the petty republican burghers, to treat with them, and to receive them as members of the state. Then a new order commenced, a new attempt at political organization, that of mixed organization, the object of which was to reconcile all the elements of society, the feudal nobility, the boroughs, clergy, and sovereigns, and to make them live and act together, in spite of their profound hostility.[5]

All of you know what are the States-general in France, the Cortes in Spain and Portugal, the Parliament in England, and the Diets in Germany. You know, likewise, what were the elements of these various assemblies; the feudal nobility, the clergy, and the boroughs, collected at them with a view to unite themselves into a single society, into one state, under one law and one power. They all, under various names, have the same tendency and design.

I shall take, as the type of this attempt, the fact which is the most interesting and the best known to us, namely, the states-general in France. I say the best known to us; yet I am convinced that the name of states-general awakens in your minds only vague and incomplete ideas. None of you can say what there was fixed or regular in the states-general of France, what was the number of their members, what the subjects of deliberation, or what the periods of convocation and the duration of sessions; nothing is known

---

5. This analysis of the failure on the part of theocratic, municipal and feudal forms to impose themselves completely on European society and become the basis for a viable "mixed" or aristocratic organization of society, paves the way for the next stage of Guizot's analysis of political and social development, the emergence of a democratic society through the process of despotic centralization.

of these things; it is impossible to draw from history any clear, general, or universal results as to this subject. When we examine closely the character of these assemblies in the history of France, they look like mere accidents, political last resource alike for people and kings; as a last resource for kings when they had no money, and knew not how to escape from their embarrassments; and as a last resource for the people when the evil became so great that they knew not what remedy to apply. The nobility were present in the states-general; the clergy likewise took part in them; but they came full of indifference, for they knew that this was not their great means of action, that they could not promote by it the real part they took in the government. The burghers themselves were scarcely more eager about it; it was not a right which they took an interest in exercising, but a necessity which they tolerated. Thus may be seen the character of the political activity of these assemblies. They were sometimes utterly insignificant, and sometimes terrible. If the king was the strongest, their humility and docility were carried to an extreme; if the situation of the crown was unfortunate, if it had absolute need of the states, they fell into faction, and became the instruments of some aristocratical intrigue, or some ambitious leaders. In a word, they were sometimes mere assemblies of notables, sometimes regular conventions. Thus their works almost always died with them; they promised and attempted much, and did nothing. None of the great measures which have really acted upon society in France, no important reform in the government, the legislation, or the administration, has emanated from the states-general. It must not, however, be supposed that they were without utility or effect; they have had a moral effect, of which too little account is generally taken; they have been, from one epoch to another, a protest against political servitude, a violent proclamation of certain tutelary principles; for example, that the country has the right to impose taxes, to interfere in its own affairs, and to impose a responsibility upon the agents of power.

That these maxims have never perished in France, is to be attributed to the states-general, and it is no small service to render to a people, to maintain in its manners, and renew in its thoughts, the remembrances and rights of liberty. The states-general have possessed this virtue, but they have never been a means of government; they have never entered into the political organization; they have never attained the end for which they were formed, that is to say, the fusion into a single body of the various societies which divided the country.

The Cortes of Spain and Portugal offer us the same result. In a thousand circumstances, however, they are different. The importance of the Cortes varies according to place and time; in Aragon, and Biscay, amidst the debates concerning the succession to the crown, or the struggles against the Moors, they were more frequently convoked and more powerful. In certain Cortes, for example, in those of Castile, in 1370 and 1373, the nobles and the clergy were not called. There is a crowd of details which it is necessary should be taken into account, if we look closely into events. But in the general view to which I am obliged to confine myself, it may be said of the Cortes, as of the states-general of France, that they have been an accident in history, and never a system, political organization, or a regular means of government.

The destiny of England was different. I shall not now enter upon this subject in detail. I propose to devote one lecture especially to the political life of England; I shall now merely say a few words upon the causes which have imparted to it a direction entirely different from that of the continent.

And first, there were no great vassals in England, no subject in a condition to strive personally against royalty. The English barons and great lords were obliged to coalesce in order to resist in common. Thus have prevailed, in the high aristocracy, the principle of association and true political manners. Moreover, English feudalism, the petty fief-holders, have been gradually led, by a series of events which I cannot enumerate at present, to unite themselves with the burghers, to sit with them in the House of Commons, which thus possessed a power superior to that of the continental assemblies, a force truly capable of influencing the government of the country.[6] Let us see what was the state of the British parliament in the fourteenth century. The House of Lords was the great council of the king,

---

6. England remained an alternative pattern of development because the feudal system had been far more centralized in England after the Norman Conquest than it had been on the continent. The consequences were a different pattern of class alliance and the claim of Parliament to share sovereignty with the Crown—which became, as we have seen, a *leitmotif* of Doctrinaire social and political argument in the 1820s.

a council actively associated in the exercise of power. The House of Commons, composed of the deputies of the petty fief-holders, and of burghers, took scarcely any part in the government, properly so called, but it established rights, and very energetically defended private and local interests. The parliament, considered as a whole, did not yet govern, but it was already a regular institution, a means of government adopted in principle, and often, in fact, indispensable. Thus the attempt at junction and alliance between the various elements of society, with a view to form of them a single political body, a regular state, was successful in England, while it had failed everywhere on the continent.

I shall say but a few words as to Germany, and those only to indicate the dominant character of its history. There, the attempts at fusion, unity, and general political organization, were followed with little ardour. The various social elements remained much more distinct and independent than in the rest of Europe. If a proof is wanted, one may be found in modern times. Germany is the only country in which the feudal election long took part in the creation of royalty. I do not speak of Poland, nor the Sclavonian nations, which entered at so late an age into the system of European civilization. Germany is likewise the only country of Europe where ecclesiastical sovereigns remained; which preserved free towns, having a true political existence and sovereignty. It is clear that the attempt to combine in a single society the elements of primitive European society, has there had much less activity and effect than elsewhere.

I have now placed before you the great essays at political organization in Europe down to the end of the fourteenth century and the beginning of the fifteenth. You have seen them all fail. I have endeavoured to indicate in passing, the causes of this ill success; indeed, truly speaking, they are reducible to one. Society was not sufficiently advanced for unity; everything was as yet too local, too special, too narrow, too various in existence, and in men's minds. There were neither general interests nor general opinions capable of controlling particular interests and opinions. The most elevated and vigorous minds had no idea of administration, nor of true political justice. It was evidently necessary that a more active and vigorous civilization should first mix, assimilate, and, so to speak, grind together all these incoherent elements; it was first necessary that a powerful centralization of interest, laws, manners, and ideas, should be brought about; in a word, it was necessary that a public power and public opinion should arise. We have arrived at the epoch when this great work was consummated. Its first symptoms, the state of mind and manners during the course of the fifteenth century, the tendency towards the formation of a central government, and a public opinion, will form the subject of our next lecture.

ELEVENTH LECTURE

Object of the lecture—Special character of the fifteenth century—
Progressive centralization of nations and governments—1st. Of
France—Formation of the national French spirit—Government of
Louis XI—2nd. Of Spain—3rd. Of Germany—4th. Of England—
5th. Of Italy—Origin of the external relations of states and of
diplomacy—Movement in religious ideas—Attempt at aristocratical
reform—Council of Constance and Basle—Attempt at popular
reform—John Huss—Regeneration of literature—Admiration for
antiquity—Classical school, or free-thinkers—General activity—
Voyages, discoveries, inventions—Conclusion.

WE TOUCH THE THRESHOLD of modern history, properly so called—the threshold of that society which is our own, of which the institutions, opinions, and manners were, forty years ago, those of France, are still those of Europe, and still exercise so powerful an influence upon us, despite the metamorphosis brought about by our revolution. It was with the sixteenth century, as I have already said, that modern society really commenced. Before entering upon it, recall to your minds, I pray you, the roads over which we have passed. We have discovered, amidst the ruins of the Roman empire, all the essential elements of the Europe of the present day; we have seen them distinguish and aggrandize themselves, each on its own account, and independently. We recognized, during the first epoch of history, the constant tendency of these elements to separation, isolation, and a local and special existence. Scarcely was this end obtained—scarcely had feudalism, the boroughs, and the clergy each taken its distinct form and place, than we see them tending to approach each other, to reunite, and form themselves into a general society, into a nation and a government. In order to arrive at this result, the various countries of Europe addressed themselves to all the different systems which co-existed in its bosom; they demanded the principle of social unity, the political and moral tie, from theocracy, aristocracy, democracy, and royalty. Hitherto, all these attempts had failed; no system or influence had known how to seize upon society, and by its empire to insure it a truly public destiny. We have found the cause of this ill success in the absence of universal interests and ideas. We have seen that all was, as yet, too special, individual, and local; that a long and powerful labour of centralization was necessary to enable society to extend and cement itself at the same time, to become at once great and regular—an end to which it necessarily aspired. This was the state in which we left Europe at the end of the fourteenth century.

She was far from understanding her position, such as I have endeavoured to place it before you. She did not know distinctly what she wanted or what she sought; still she applied herself to the search, as if she knew. The fourteenth century closed. Europe entered naturally, and, as it were, instinctively, the path which led to centralization. It is the characteristic of the fifteenth century to have constantly tended to this result; to have laboured to create universal interests and ideas, to make the spirit of speciality and locality disappear, to reunite and elevate existences and minds; in fine, to create, what had hitherto never existed on a large scale, nations and governments. The emergence of this fact belongs to the sixteenth and seventeenth centuries; it was in the fifteenth that it was preparing. It is this preparation which we have to investigate at present—this silent and concealed work of centralization, whether in social relations or ideas, a work accomplished by the natural course of events, without premeditation or design.[1]

Thus man advances in the execution of a plan which he has not himself conceived, or which, perhaps, he does not even understand. He is the intelligent and free artificer of a work which does not belong to him. He does not recognize or comprehend it until a later period, when it manifests itself outwardly and in realities; and even then he understands it but very

1. Another passage illustrating the way Guizot uses the concept of centralization more broadly than his predecessors, applying it to economic interests and ideas, to the increasing social division of labour as well as the growth of despotic monarchies.

incompletely. Yet it is by him, it is by the development of his intellect and his liberty that it is accomplished. Conceive a great machine, of which the idea resides in a single mind, and of which the different pieces are confided to different workmen, who are scattered, and are strangers to one another; none of them knowing the work as a whole, or the definitive and general result to which it concurs, yet each executing with intelligence and liberty, by rational and voluntary acts, that of which he has the charge. So is the plan of Providence upon the world executed by the hand of mankind; thus do the two facts which manifest themselves in the history of civilization co-exist; on the one hand, its fatality, that which escapes science and the human will—and on the other, the part played therein by the liberty and intellect of man, that which he infuses of his own will by his own thought and inclination.

In order properly to comprehend the fifteenth century—to obtain a clear and exact idea of this prelude, as it were, of modern society—we will distinguish the different classes of facts. We will first examine the political facts, the changes which have tended to form both nations and governments. Thence we will pass to moral facts; we will observe the changes which have been produced in ideas and manners, and we will thence deduce what general opinions were in preparation. As regards political facts, in order to proceed simply and quickly, I will run over all the great countries of Europe, and show you what the fifteenth century made of them—in what state it found and left them.

I shall commence with France. The last half of the fourteenth century and the first half of the fifteenth were, as you know, the times of great national wars—the wars against the English. It was the epoch of the struggle for the independence of France and the French name against a foreign dominion. A glance at history will show with what ardour, despite a multitude of dissensions and treasons, all classes of society in France concurred in this struggle; what patriotism took possession of the feudal nobility, the burghers, and even the peasants. If there were nothing else to show the popular character of the event than the history of Joan of Arc, it would be more than sufficient proof. Joan of Arc sprang from the people. It was by the sentiments, creed, and passions of the people that she was inspired and sustained. She was looked upon with distrust, scorn, and even enmity, by the people of the court and the chiefs of the army; but she had the soldiers and the people ever on her side. It was the peasants of Lorraine who sent her to the succour of the burghers of Orleans. No event has more strikingly shown the popular character of this war, and the feeling with which the whole country regarded it.

Thus began the formation of French nationality. Up to the reign of the Valois, it was the feudal character which dominated in France; the French nation, the French mind, French patriotism, did not as yet exist. With the Valois commenced France, properly so called. It was in the course of their wars, through the phases of their destiny, that the nobility, the burghers, and the peasants, were for the first time united by a moral tie, by the tie of a common name, a common honour, and a common desire to conquer the enemy. But expect not to find there as yet any true political spirit, nor any great purpose of unity in the government and institutions, such as we conceive them in the present day. Unity, in the France of this epoch, resided in its name, its national honour, and in the existence of a national royalty, whatever it might be, provided the foreigner did not appear therein. It is in this way that the struggle against the English powerfully contributed to the formation of the French nation, to impel it towards unity. At the same time that France was thus morally forming herself, and the national spirit was being developed, she was also forming herself materially, so to speak—that is to say, her territory was being regulated, extended, strengthened. This was the period of the incorporation of the greater part of the provinces which have become *France*. Under Charles VII, after the expulsion of the English, almost all the provinces which they had occupied, Normandy, Angoumois, Touraine, Poitou, Saintonge, &c., became definitively French. Under Louis XI, ten provinces, three of which were afterwards lost and regained, were united to France; namely, Roussillon and Cerdagne, Burgundy, Franche-Comté, Picardy, Artois, Provence, Maine, Anjou, and Perche. Under Charles VIII and Louis XII, the successive marriages of Anne with these two kings brought us Brittany. Thus, at the same epoch, and during the course of the same events, the national territory and mind were forming together; moral and material France conjointly acquired strength and unity.

Let us pass from the nation to the government; we shall see the accomplishment of similar facts, shall move towards the same result. Never had the French government been more devoid of unity, connexion, and strength, than under the reign of Charles VI and during the first part of that of Charles VII. At the end of this latter reign, the aspect of all things changed. There was evidently a strengthening, extending, and organizing of power; all the great means of government—taxes, military force, law— were created upon a great scale, and with some uniformity. This was the time of the formation of standing armies—free companies, cavalry—and free archers, infantry. By these companies Charles VII re-established some order in those provinces which had been desolated by the disorders and exactions of the soldiery, even after war had ceased. All contemporary historians speak with astonishment of the marvellous effects of the free companies. It was at the same epoch that the poll-tax, one of the principal revenues of the kingdom, became perpetual; a serious blow to the liberty of the people, but which powerfully contributed to the regularity and strength of the government. At this time, too, the great instrument of power, the administration of justice, was extended and organized; parliaments multiplied. There were five new parliaments constituted within a very short period of time; under Louis XI, the parliament of Grenoble (in 1451), of Bordeaux (in 1462), and of Dijon (1477); under Louis XII, the parliaments of Rouen (in 1499) and of Aix (in 1501). The parliament of Paris, also, at this time greatly increased in importance and firmness, both as regards the administration of justice, and as charged with the policy of its jurisdiction.

Thus, as regards military force, taxation, and justice, that is, in what constitutes its very essence, government in France, in the fifteenth century, acquired a character of permanence and regularity hitherto unknown; public power definitively took the place of the feudal powers.

At the same time another and far different change was brought about; a change which was less visible, and which has less impressed itself upon historians, but which was perhaps of still more importance—namely, the change which Louis XI effected in the manner of governing.

Much has been said concerning the struggle of Louis XI against the high nobles of the kingdom, of their abasement, and of his favour towards the burghers and the lower classes. There is truth in this, although much of it is exaggerated; it is also true, that the conduct of Louis XI towards the different classes oftener troubled than served the state. But he did something much more important. Up to this time, the government had proceeded almost entirely by force and by material means. Persuasion, address, the managing of men's minds, and leading them to particular views, in a word, policy—policy, doubtless, of falsehood and imposition, but also of management and prudence, had hitherto been but little attended to. Louis XI substituted in the government intellectual in place of material means, artifice instead of force, the Italian policy in place of the feudal. Look at the two men whose rivalry occupies this epoch of our history, Charles le Téméraire and Louis XI. Charles was the representative of the ancient form of governing; he proceeded by violence alone, he appealed incessantly to war, he was incapable of exercising patience, or of addressing himself to the minds of men in order to make them instruments to his success. It was, on the contrary, the pleasure of Louis XI to avoid the use of force, and take possession of men individually by conversation, and the skilful handling of interests and minds. He changed neither the institutions nor the external system, but only the secret proceedings, the tactics of power. It was left for modern times to attempt a still greater revolution, by labouring to introduce, alike into political means as into political ends, justice instead of selfishness, and publicity in place of lying fraud. It is not less true, however, that there was great indication of progress in renouncing the continual employment of force, in invoking chiefly intellectual superiority, in governing through mind, and not by the ruin of existences. It was this that Louis XI commenced, by force of his high intellect alone, amidst all his crimes and faults, despite his bad nature.

From France I pass to Spain; there I find events of the same nature; it was thus that the national unity of Spain was formed in the fifteenth century; at that time, by the conquest of the kingdom of Granada, the lengthened struggle between the Christians and the Arabs was put an end to. Then, also, the country was centralized; by the marriage of Ferdinand the Catholic and Isabella, the two principal kingdoms of Castile and Aragon were united under one power. As in France, royalty was here extended and strengthened; sterner institutions, and which bore a more mournful name, served as its fulcrum; instead of parliament, the inquisition arose. It contained in germ what it was to be, but it was not then the same as in its maturer age. It was at first rather political than religious, and intended rather to maintain order, than to defend the faith. The analogy extends beyond institutions; it is found even in the persons. With less artifice, mental movement, and restless and busy activity, the character and government of Ferdinand the Catholic resemble that of Louis XI. I hold as unimportant all arbitrary comparisons and fanciful parallels; but here the analogy is profound, and visible alike in general facts and in details.

We find the same in Germany. It was in the middle of the fifteenth century, in 1438, that the house of Austria returned to the Empire, and with it the imperial power acquired a permanence which it had never possessed before; election afterwards did little more than consecrate the hereditary successor. At the end of the fifteenth century, Maximilian I definitively founded the preponderance of his house, and the regular exercise of central authority; Charles VII first created in France a standing army, for the maintenance of order; Maximilian was also the first, in his hereditary states, to attain the same end by the same means. Louis XI established the post-office in France; and Maximilian introduced it into Germany. Everywhere the same progressions of civilization were similarly cultivated for the good of central power.

The history of England in the fifteenth century consists of two great events; without, the struggle against the French, and within, that of the two Roses, the foreign and the civil war. These two so dissimilar wars led to the same result. The struggle against the French was sustained by the English people with an ardour which profited only royalty. This nation, already more skilful and firm than any other in keeping back its forces and supplies, at this epoch abandoned them to its kings without foresight or limit. It was under the reign of Henry V that a considerable tax, the customs, was granted to the king from the commencement of his reign, until his death. When the foreign war was ended, or almost so, the civil war, which had at first been associated with it, continued alone; the houses of York and Lancaster disputed for the throne. When they came to the end of their bloody contests, the high English aristocracy found itself ruined, decimated, and incapable of preserving the power which it had hitherto exercised. The coalition of the great barons could no longer influence the throne. The Tudors ascended it, and with Henry VII in 1485, commenced the epoch of political centralization, and the triumph of royalty.

Royalty was not established in Italy, at least not under that name; but this matters little as regards the result. It was in the fifteenth century that the republics fell; even where the name remained, the power was concentrated in the hands of one or more families; republican life was extinct. In the north of Italy, almost all the Lombard republics were absorbed in the duchy of Milan. In 1434, Florence fell under the domination of the Medicis; in 1464, Genoa became subject to the Milanese. The greater portion of the republics, great and small, gave place to sovereign houses. The pretensions of foreign sovereigns were soon put forth upon the north and south of Italy, upon the Milanese on one side, and on the kingdom of Naples on the other.

Upon whatever country of Europe we turn our eyes, and whatever portion of its history we may consider, whether it has reference to the nations themselves, or to their governments, to the institutions or the countries, we shall everywhere see the ancient elements and forms of society on the point of disappearing. The traditional liberties perish, and new and more concentrated and regular powers arise. There is something profoundly sad in the fall of the old European liberties; at the time, it inspired the bitterest feelings.[2] In France, Germany, and, above all, in Italy, the patriots of the fifteenth century contested with ardour, and deplored with despair, this revolution, which, on all sides, was bringing about what might justly be called despotism. One cannot help admiring their courage and commiserating their sorrow; but, at the same time, it must be understood that this revolution was not only inevitable, but beneficial also. The primitive system of Europe, the old feudal and communal liberties, had failed in the organization of society. What constitutes social life is security and progress.

2. One reason why Guizot expresses sadness at the spectacle of the ruin of the "old European liberties" in the fifteenth century was of course because such liberties had guaranteed the dispersal of power, even if the price paid was an hierarchical or aristocratic—and hence unjust—organization of society. Madame de Staël had also shown herself sad at the destruction of what she called "aristocratic liberty."

Any system which does not procure present order and future progress, is vicious, and soon abandoned. Such was the fate of the ancient political forms, the old European liberties, in the fifteenth century. They could give to society neither security nor progress. These were sought elsewhere, from other principles and other means. This is the meaning of all the facts which I have just placed before you.

From the same epoch dates another fact, which has held an important place in the political history of Europe. It was in the fifteenth century that the relations of governments between themselves began to be frequent, regular, permanent. It was then, for the first time, that those great alliances were formed, whether for peace or war, which at a later period produced the system of equilibrium. Diplomacy in Europe dates from the fifteenth century. Towards the end of this century you see the principal powers of continental Europe, the popes, the dukes of Milan, the Venetians, the emperors of Germany, and the kings of Spain and of France, form connexions, negotiate, unite, balance each other. Thus, at the time that Charles VII formed his expedition to conquer the kingdom of Naples, a great league was formed against him, between Spain, the pope, and the Venetians. The league of Cambrai was formed some years later (in 1508), against the Venetians. The holy league, directed against Louis XII, succeeded in 1511 to the league of Cambrai. All these alliances arose from Italian policy, from the desire of various sovereigns to possess Italy, and from the fear that some one of them, by seizing it exclusively, should acquire an overpowering preponderance. This new order of facts was highly favourable to the development of royalty. On the one hand, from the nature of the external relations of states, they can only be conducted by a single person or a small number of persons, and exact a certain secrecy; on the other, the people had so little foresight, that the consequences of an alliance of this kind escaped them; it was not, for them, of any internal or direct interest; they cared little about it, and left such matters to the discretion of the central power. Thus diplomacy, at its birth, fell into the hands of the kings, and the idea that it belonged exclusively to them, that the country, although free, and having the right of voting its taxes and interfering in its affairs, was not called upon to mix itself in external matters—this idea, I say, was established in almost all European minds, as an accepted principle, a maxim of common law. Open

English history at the sixteenth and seventeenth centuries, you will see what power this idea exercised, and what obstacles it opposed to English liberties under the reigns of Elizabeth, James I, and Charles I. It was always under the name of this principle that peace and war, commercial relations, and all external affairs, appertained to the royal prerogative; and it was by this that absolute power defended itself against the rights of the country. Nations have been excessively timid in contesting this part of prerogative; and this timidity has cost them the more dear, since, from the epoch upon which we are now entering, that is to say, the sixteenth century, the history of Europe is essentially diplomatic. External relations, during nearly three centuries, are the important fact of history. Within, nations became regulated, the internal government, upon the continent, at least, led to no more violent agitations, nor absorbed public activity. It is external relations, wars, negotiations, and alliances, which attract attention, and fill the pages of history, so that the greater portion of the destiny of nations has been abandoned to the royal prerogative and to central power.

Indeed, it was hardly possible it should be otherwise. A very great progress in civilization, and a great development of intellect and political skill are necessary, before the public can interfere with any success in affairs of this kind. From the sixteenth to the eighteenth century, the people were very far from being thus qualified. See what took place under James I in England, at the commencement of the seventeenth century: his son-in-law, the elector-palatine, elected king of Bohemia, lost his crown; he was even robbed of his hereditary states, the palatinate. The whole of protestantism was interested in his cause, and for that reason, England testified a lively interest towards him. There was a powerful ebullition of public opinion to force King James to take the part of his son-in-law, and regain for him the palatinate. Parliament furiously demanded war, promising all the means for carrying it on. James was unwilling; he eluded the matter, made some attempts at negotiation, sent some troops to Germany, and then came to tell parliament that £900,000 sterling were necessary to maintain the contest with any chance of success. It is not said, nor indeed does it appear to have been the case, that his calculation was exaggerated. But the parliament recoiled with surprise and terror at the prospect of such a charge, and it unwillingly voted £70,000 sterling to re-establish a prince, and reconquer a country three hundred leagues from England. Such was the political ignorance and incapacity of the public in matters of this kind; it acted without knowledge of facts, and without troubling itself with any responsibility. It was not, then, in a condition to interfere in a regular or efficacious manner. This is the principal cause of the external relations falling into the hands of the central power; that alone was in a condition to direct them, I do not say for the public interest, for it was far from being always consulted, but with any continuity or good sense.

You see, under whatever point of view the political history of Europe at this epoch is presented to us, whether we turn our eyes upon the internal state of nations, or upon the relations of nations with each other, whether we consider the administration of war, justice, or taxation, we everywhere find the same character; everywhere we see the same tendency to the centralization, unity, formation, and preponderance of general interests and public powers. This was the secret work of the fifteenth century, a work which did not as yet lead to any very prominent result, nor any revolution, properly so called, in society, but which prepared the way for all of them. I shall immediately place before you facts of another nature, moral facts, facts which relate to the development of the human mind and universal ideas. There also we shall acknowledge the same phenomenon, and arrive at the same result.

I shall commence with a class of facts which has often occupied us, and which, under the most various forms, has always held an important place in the history of Europe, namely, facts relative to the church. Down to the fifteenth century we have seen in Europe no universal and powerful ideas acting truly upon the masses, except those of a religious nature. We have seen the church alone invested with the power of regulating, promulgating, and prescribing them. Often, it is true, attempts at independence, even separation, were formed, and the church had much to do to overcome them. But hitherto she had conquered them; creeds repudiated by the church had taken no general and permanent possession of the minds of the people; the Albigenses themselves were crushed. Dissension and contest were of incessant occurrence in the heart of the church, but without any decisive or eminent result. At the beginning of the fifteenth century, an entirely different fact announced itself; new ideas, a public and avowed want of change and reform, agitated the church herself. The end of the fourteenth and commencement of the fifteenth century were marked by the great schism of the west, the result of the translation of the holy see to Avignon, and of the creation of two popes, one at Avignon, the other at Rome. The struggle between these two papacies is what is called the great schism of the west. It commenced in 1378. In 1409, the council of Pisa wishing to end it, deposed both popes, and nominated a third, Alexander V. So far from being appeased, the schism became warmer; there were three popes instead of two. The disorder and abuses continued to increase. In 1414, the council of Constance assembled, at the summons of the emperor Sigismond. It proposed to itself a work very different from nominating a new pope; it undertook the reform of the church. It first proclaimed the indissolubility of the general council, and its superiority over the papal power; it undertook to make these principles prevalent in the church, and to reform the abuses which had crept into it, above all the exactions by which the court of Rome had procured supplies. For the attainment of this end, the council nominated what we will call a commission of inquiry, that is to say, a *college of reform,* composed of deputies of the council taken from different nations; it was the duty of this college to seek what were the abuses which disgraced the church, and how they might best be remedied, and to make a report to the council, which would consult upon the means of execution. But while the council was occupied in this work, the question was mooted as to whether they could proceed in the reformation of abuses, without the visible participation of the chief of the church, without the sanction of the pope. The negative was passed by the influence of the Romanist party, supported by honest, but timid men; the council elected a new pope, Martin V, in 1417. The pope was desired to present on his part a plan of reform in the church. This plan was not approved, and the council separated. In 1431 a new council assembled at Basle with the same view. It resumed and continued the work of reform of the council of Constance, and met with no better success. Schism broke out in the interior of the assembly, the same as in Christianity. The pope transferred the council of Basle to Ferrara, and afterwards to Florence. Part of the prelates refused to obey the pope, and remained at Basle; and as formerly there had been two popes, so there were now two councils. That of Basle continued its projects of reform, and nominated its pope, Felix V. After a certain time, it transported itself to Lausanne; and in 1449 dissolved itself, without having effected anything.

Thus papacy carried the day, and remained in possession of the field of battle and the government of the church. The council could not accomplish what it had undertaken; but it effected things which it had not undertaken, and which survived it. At the time that the council of Basle failed in its attempts at reform, sovereigns seized upon the ideas which it proclaimed, and the institutions which it suggested. In France, upon the foundation of the decrees of the council of Basle, Charles V formed the Pragmatic Sanction, which he issued at Bourges in 1438; it enunciated the election of bishops, the suppression of first fruits, and the reform of the principal abuses which had been introduced into the church. The Pragmatic Sanction was declared in France the law of the state. In Germany, the diet of Mayence adopted it in 1439, and likewise made it a law of the German empire. What the spiritual power had unsuccessfully attempted, the temporal power seemed destined to accomplish.

New reverses sprang up for the projects of reform. As the council had failed, so did the Pragmatic Sanction. In Germany it perished very abruptly. The diet abandoned it in 1448, in consequence of a negotiation with Nicholas V. In 1516, Francis I likewise abandoned it, and in its place substituted his Concordat with Leo X. The princes' reform did not succeed any better than that of the clergy. But it must not be supposed that it entirely perished. As the council effected things which survived it, so also the Pragmatic Sanction had consequences which it left behind, and which played an important part in modern history. The principles of the council of Basle were powerful and fertile. Superior men, and men of energetic character, have adopted and supported them. John of Paris, D'Ailly, Gerson, and many distinguished men of the fifteenth century, devoted themselves to their defence. In vain was the council dissolved; in vain was the Pragmatic Sanction abandoned; its general doctrines upon the government of the church, and upon the reforms necessary to be carried out, had taken root in France; they were perpetuated; they passed into the parliaments, and became a powerful opinion. They gave rise first to the Jansenists, and afterwards to the Gallicans. All this series of maxims and efforts tending to reform the church, which commenced with the council of Constance, and terminated with the four propositions of Bossuet, emanated from the same source, and were directed towards the same end; it was the same fact successively transformed. It was in vain that the attempt at legal reform in the fifteenth century failed; not the less has it taken its place in the course of civilization—not the less has it indirectly exercised an enormous influence.

The councils were right in pursuing a legal reform, for that alone could prevent a revolution. Almost at the moment when the council of Pisa undertook to bring the great schism of the west to a termination, and the council of Constance to reform the church, the first essays at popular religious reform violently burst forth in Bohemia. The predictions and progress of John Huss date from 1404, at which period he began to teach at Prague. Here, then, are two reforms marching side by side; the one in the very heart of the church, attempted by the ecclesiastical aristocracy itself—a wise, but embarrassed and timid reform; the other, outside and against the church, violent and passionate. A contest arose between these two powers and designs. The council summoned John Huss and Jerome of Prague to Constance, and condemned them as heretics and revolutionists. These events are perfectly intelligible to us at the present day. We can very well understand this simultaneousness of separate reforms—enterprises undertaken, one by the governments, the other by the people, opposed to one another, and yet emanating from the same cause and tending to the same end, and, in fine, although at war with each other, still concurring to the same result. This is what occurred in the fifteenth century. The popular reform of John Huss was for the instant stifled; the war of the Hussites broke forth three or four years after the death of their master. It lasted long, and was violent, but the Empire finally triumphed. But as the reform of the councils had failed, as the end which they pursued had not been attained, the popular reform ceased not to ferment. It watched the first opportunity, and found it at the commencement of the sixteenth century. If the reform undertaken by the councils had been well carried out, the Reformation might have been prevented. But one or the other must have succeeded; their coincidence shows a necessity.

This, then, is the state in which Europe was left by the fifteenth century with regard to religious matters—an aristocratical reform unsuccessfully attempted, and a popular reform commenced, stifled, and always ready to re-appear. But it was not to the sphere of religious creeds that the fermentation of the human mind at this epoch was confined. It was in the course of the fourteenth century, as you all know, that Greek and Roman antiquity were, so to speak, restored in Europe. You know with what eagerness Dante, Petrarch, Boccaccio, and all their contemporaries sought for the Greek and Latin manuscripts, and published and promulgated them, and what noise and transports the least discovery of this kind excited.

In the midst of this excitement, a school was commenced in Europe which has played a very much more important part in the development of the human mind than has generally been attributed to it: this was the classical school. Let me warn you from attaching the same sense to this word which we give to it in the present day; it was then a very different thing from a literary system or contest. The classical school of that period was inflamed with admiration, not only for the writings of the ancients, for Virgil and Homer, but for the whole of ancient society, for its institutions, opinions, and philosophy, as well as for its literature. It must be confessed that antiquity, under the heads of politics, philosophy, and literature, was far superior to the Europe of the fourteenth and fifteenth centuries. It cannot therefore be wondered at that it should exercise so great a sway, or that for the most part elevated, active, refined, and fastidious minds, should take a disgust at the coarse manners, confused ideas, and barbarous forms of their own times, and that they should devote themselves with enthusiasm to the study, and almost to the worship of a society at once more regular and developed. Thus was formed that school of free-thinkers which appeared at the commencement of the fifteenth century, and in which prelates, jurisconsults, and scholars, met together.

Amidst this excitement happened the taking of Constantinople by the Turks, the fall of the Eastern empire, and the flight into Italy of the Greek fugitives. They brought with them a higher knowledge of antiquity, numerous manuscripts, and a thousand new means of studying ancient civilization. The redoubled admiration and ardour with which the classical school was animated may easily be imagined. This was the time of the most brilliant development of the high clergy, particularly in Italy, not as regards political power, properly speaking, but in point of luxury and wealth; they abandoned themselves with pride to all the pleasures of a voluptuous, indolent, elegant, and licentious civilization—to the taste for letters and arts, and for social and material enjoyments. Look at the kind of life led by the men who played a great political and literary part at this epoch—by Cardinal Bembo, for instance; you will be surprised at the mixture of sybaritism and intellectual development, of effeminate manners and hardihood of mind. One would think, indeed, when we glance over this epoch, when we are present at the spectacle of its ideas and the state of its moral relations, one would think we were living in France in the midst of the eighteenth century. There is the same taste for intellectual excitement, for new ideas, for an easy, agreeable life; the same effeminateness and licentiousness; the same deficiency in political energy and moral faith, with a singular sincerity and activity of mind. The literati of the fifteenth century were, with regard to the prelates of the high church, in the same relation as men of letters and philosophers of the eighteenth century with the high aristocracy; they all had the same opinions and the same manners, lived harmoniously together, and did not trouble themselves about the commotions that were in preparation around them. The prelates of the fifteenth century, commencing with Cardinal Bembo, most certainly no more foresaw Luther and Calvin than the people of the court foresaw the French revolution. The position, however, was analogous.

Three great facts, then, present themselves at this epoch in the moral order: first, an ecclesiastical reform attempted by the church herself; secondly, a popular religious reform; and finally an intellectual reform, which gave rise to a school of free-thinkers. And all these metamorphoses were in preparation amidst the greatest political change which had taken place in Europe, amidst the work of centralization of people and governments.

This was not all. This also was the time of the greatest external activity of mankind; it was a period of voyages, enterprises, discoveries, and inventions of all kinds. This was the time of the great expeditions of the Portuguese along the coast of Africa, of the discovery of the passage of the Cape of Good Hope by Vasco da Gama, of the discovery of America by Christopher Columbus, and of the wonderful extension of European commerce.

A thousand new inventions came forth; others already known, but only within a narrow sphere, became popular and of common use. Gunpowder changed the system of war; the compass changed the system of navigation. The art of oil painting developed itself, and covered Europe with masterpieces of art: engraving on copper, invented in 1460, multiplied and promulgated them. Linen paper became common; and lastly, from 1436 to 1452, printing was invented; printing, the theme of so much declamation and so many common-places, but the merit and effects of which no common-place nor any declamation can ever exhaust.

You see what was the greatness and activity of this century—a greatness still only partially apparent, an activity, the results of which have not yet been fully developed. Violent reforms seem unsuccessful, governments strengthened, and nations pacified. It might be thought that society was preparing to enjoy a better order of things, amidst a more rapid progress. But the powerful revolutions of the sixteenth century were impending: the fifteenth had been preparing them. They will be the subject of my next lecture.

TWELFTH LECTURE

*Object of the lecture—Difficulty of distinguishing general facts in
modern history—Picture of Europe in the sixteenth century—
Danger of precipitate generalization—Various causes assigned to
the Reformation—Its dominant character was the insurrection
of the human mind against absolute power in the intellectual
order—Evidences of this fact—Fate of the Reformation in different
countries—Weak side of the Reformation—The Jesuits—Analogy
between the revolutions of religious society and those of civil society.*

W E HAVE OFTEN DEPLORED the disorder and chaos of
European society; we have complained of the difficulty of understanding and describing a society thus scattered, incoherent, and broken up; we have longed for, and patiently invoked, the epoch
of general interests, order, and social unity. We have now arrived at it; we
are entering upon the epoch when all is general facts and general ideas,
the epoch of order and unity. We shall here encounter a difficulty of another kind. Hitherto we have had much trouble in connecting facts with
one another, in making them co-ordinate, in perceiving whatever they may
possess in common, and distinguishing some completeness. Everything
reverses itself in modern Europe; all the elements and incidents of social
life modify themselves, and act and re-act on one another; the relations of
men among themselves become much more numerous and complicated.
It is the same in their relations with the government of the state, the same
in the relations of the states among themselves, the same in ideas and in
the works of the human mind. In the times which we have gone through,
a large number of facts passed away isolated, foreign to one another, and
without reciprocal influence. We shall now no longer find this isolation;
all things touch, commingle, and modify as they meet. Is there anything

more difficult than to seize the true unity amid such diversity, to determine the direction of a movement so extended and complex, to recapitulate this prodigious number of various elements so clearly connected with one another; in fine, to ascertain the general dominant fact, which sums up a long series of facts, which characterizes an epoch, and is the faithful expression of its influence and its share in the history of civilization? You will measure with a glance this difficulty, in the great event which now occupies our attention. We encountered, in the twelfth century, an event which was religious in its origin if not in its nature, I mean the crusades. Despite the greatness of this event, despite its long duration and the variety of incidents to which it led, we found it difficult enough to distinguish its general character, and to determine with any precision its unity and its influence. We have now to consider the religious revolution of the sixteenth century, usually called the Reformation. Permit me to say, in passing, that I shall use the word *reformation* as a simple and understood term, as synonymous with *religious revolution,* and without implying any judgment of it. You see, at the very commencement, how difficult it is to recognize the true character of this great crisis, to say in a general manner what it was and what it effected.

It is between the commencement of the sixteenth and the middle of the seventeenth centuries that we must look for the Reformation; for that period comprises, so to speak, the life of the event, its origin and end. All historical events have, so to speak, a limited career; their consequences are prolonged to infinity; they have a hold upon all the past and all the future; but it is not the less true that they have a particular and limited existence, that they are born, that they increase, that they fill with their development a certain duration of time, and then decrease and retire from the scene in order to make room for some new event.

The precise date assigned to the origin of the Reformation is of little importance; we may take the year 1520, when Luther publicly burnt, at Wittenberg, the bull of Leo X which condemned him, and thus formally separated himself from the Roman church. It was between this epoch and the middle of the seventeenth century, the year 1648, the date of the treaty of Westphalia, that the life of the Reformation was comprised. Here is the proof of it. The first and greatest effect of the religious revolution was to create in Europe two classes of states, the Catholic states and the Protestant states, to place them opposite each other, and open the contest between them. With many vicissitudes, this struggle lasted from the commencement of the sixteenth century down to the middle of the seventeenth. It was by the treaty of Westphalia, in 1648, that the Catholic and Protestant states at last acknowledged one another; agreed to, then, a mutual existence, and promised to live in society and peace, independently of the diversity of religion. Dating from 1648, diversity in religion ceased to be the dominant principle of the classification of states, of their external policy, their relations, and alliances. Up to this epoch, in spite of great variations, Europe was essentially divided into a Catholic and a Protestant league. After the treaty of Westphalia, this distinction vanished; states were either allied or divided upon other considerations than religious creeds. At that point, then, the preponderance, that is to say, the career, of the Reformation stopped, although its consequences did not then cease to develop themselves. Let us now glance hastily over this career; and without doing more than naming events and men, let us indicate what it contains. You will see by this mere indication, by this dry and incomplete nomenclature, what must be the difficulty of recapitulating a series of facts so varied and so complex—of recapitulating them, I say, in one general fact; of determining what was the true character of the religious revolution of the sixteenth century, and of assigning its part in the history of our civilization. At the moment when the Reformation broke forth, it fell, so to speak, into the midst of a great political event, the struggle between Francis I and Charles V, between France and Spain; a contest, first for the possession of Italy, afterwards for that of the empire of Germany, and, lastly, for the preponderance in Europe. It was then the house of Austria elevated itself, and became dominant in Europe. It was then, also, that England, under Henry VIII, interfered in continental politics with more regularity, permanence, and to a greater extent than she had hitherto done.

Let us follow the course of the sixteenth century in France. It was filled by the great religious wars of the Protestants and Catholics, the means and the occasion of a new attempt of the great lords to regain the power they had lost. This is the political purport of our religious wars, of the League, of the struggle of the Guises against the Valois, a struggle which ended by the accession of Henry IV.

In Spain, during the reign of Philip II, the revolution of the United Provinces broke out. The inquisition and civil and religious liberty waged war under the names of the duke of Alva and the prince of Orange. While liberty triumphed in Holland by force of perseverance and good sense, she perished in the interior of Spain, where absolute power prevailed, both lay and ecclesiastical.

In England, during this period, Mary and Elizabeth reigned; there was the contest of Elizabeth, the head of protestantism, against Philip II. The accession of James Stuart to the throne of England saw commencement of the great quarrels between royalty and the English people.

About the same time, new powers were created in the north. Sweden was reinstated by Gustavus Vasa, in 1523. Prussia was created by the secularizing of the Teutonic order. The powers of the north then took in European politics a place which they had never hitherto occupied, the importance of which was soon to be shown in the thirty years war.

I return to France. The reign of Louis XIII; Cardinal Richelieu changed the internal administration of France, entered into relations with Germany, and lent aid to the Protestant party. In Germany, during the last part of the sixteenth century, the contest took place against the Turks; and at the commencement of the seventeenth century the thirty years war, the greatest event of modern Eastern Europe. At this time flourished Gustavus Adolphus, Wallenstein, Tilly, the duke of Brunswick, and the duke of Weimar, the greatest names that Germany has yet to pronounce.

At the same epoch, in France, Louis XIV ascended the throne; the Fronde commenced. In England, the revolution which dethroned Charles I, broke out.

I only take the leading events of history, events whose name everyone knows; you see their number, variety, and importance. If we seek events of another nature, events which are less apparent, and which are less summed up in names, we shall find this epoch equally full. This is the period of the greatest changes in the political institutions of almost all nations, the time when pure monarchy prevailed in the majority of great states, whilst in Holland the most powerful republic in Europe was created, and in England constitutional monarchy triumphed definitively, or nearly so. In the church, this was the period when the ancient monastic orders lost almost all political power, and were replaced by a new order of another character, and the importance of which, perhaps erroneously, is held as far superior to theirs, the Jesuits. At this epoch, the council of Trent effaced what might still remain of the influence of the councils of Constance and Basle, and secured the definitive triumph of the court of Rome in the ecclesiastical order. Let us leave the church, and cast a glance upon philosophy, upon the free career of the human mind; two men present themselves, Bacon and Descartes, the authors of the greatest philosophical revolution which the modern world has undergone, the chiefs of the two schools which disputed its empire. This also was the period of the brilliancy of Italian literature, and of the commencement of French and of English literature. And lastly, it was the time of the foundation of great colonies and the most active developments of the commercial system. Thus, under whatever point of view you consider this epoch, its political, ecclesiastical, philosophical, and literary events are in greater number, and more varied and important, than in any century preceding it. The activity of the human mind manifested itself in every way, in the relations of men between themselves, in their relations with power, in the relations of states, and in purely intellectual labours; in a word, it was a time for great men and for great things. And in the midst of this period, the religious revolution which occupies our attention is the greatest event of all; it is the dominant fact of this epoch, the fact which gives to it its name, and determines its character. Among so many powerful causes which have played so important a part, the Reformation is the most powerful, that in which all the others ended, which modified them all, or was by them modified. So that what we have to do at present is to truly characterize and accurately sum up the event which in a period of the greatest events dominated over all, the cause which effected more than all others in a time of the most influential causes.

You will easily comprehend the difficulty of reducing facts so various, so important, and so closely united, to a true historical unity. It is, however, necessary to do this. When events are once consummated, when they have become history, what are most important, and what man seeks above all things, are general facts, the connexion of causes and effects. These, so to speak, are the immortal part of history, that to which all generations must refer in order to understand the past, and to understand themselves.

The necessity for generalization and rational result, is the most powerful and the most glorious of all intellectual wants; but we should be careful not to be contented with incomplete and precipitate generalizations. Nothing can be more tempting than to give way to the pleasure of assigning immediately and at the first view, the general character and permanent results of an epoch or event. The human mind is like the will, always urgent for action, impatient of obstacles, and eager for liberty and conclusions; it willingly forgets facts which impede and cramp it; but in forgetting, it does not destroy them; they subsist to condemn it some day and convict it of error. There is but one means for the human mind to escape this danger; that is, courageously and patiently to exhaust the study of facts before generalizing and concluding. Facts are to the mind what rules of morality are to the will. It is bound to know them and to bear their weight; and it is only when it has fulfilled this duty, when it has viewed and measured their whole extent, it is then only that it is permitted to unfold its wings, and take flight to the high region where it will see all things in their totality and their results. If it attempt to mount too quickly, and without having gained a knowledge of all the territory which it will have to contemplate from thence, the chance of error and failure is very great. It is the same as in an arithmetical calculation, where one error leads to others, *ad infinitum*. So in history, if in the first labour we do not attend to all the facts, if we give ourselves up to the taste for precipitate generalization, it is impossible to say to what mistakes we may be led.

I am warning you in a measure against myself. I have only made, and, indeed, could only make, attempts at generalization, general recapitulations of facts which we have not studied closely and at large. But having arrived at an epoch when this undertaking is much more difficult than at any other, and when the chances of error are much greater, I have thought it a duty thus to warn you. That done, I shall now proceed and attempt as to the Reformation what I have done as to other events; I shall endeavour to distinguish its dominant fact, to describe its general character, to say, in a word, what is the place and the share of this great event in European civilization.

You will call to mind how we left Europe at the end of the fifteenth century. We have seen, in its course, two great attempts at religious revolution and reform: an attempt at legal reform by the councils, and an attempt at revolutionary reform in Bohemia by the Hussites; we have seen them stifled and failing one after the other; but still we have seen that it was impossible the event should be prevented, that it must be reproduced under one form or another; that what the fifteenth century had attempted, the sixteenth would inevitably accomplish. I shall not recount in any way the details of the religious revolution of the sixteenth century: I take it for granted that they are almost universally known. I attend only to its general influence upon the destinies of the human race.

When the causes which determined this great event have been investigated, the adversaries of the Reformation have imputed it to accidents, to misfortunes in the course of civilization; for example, to the sale of indulgences having been confided to the Dominicans, which made the Augustines jealous: Luther was an Augustin, and, therefore, was the determining cause of the Reformation. Others have attributed it to the ambition of sovereigns, to their rivalry with the ecclesiastical power, and to the cupidity of the lay nobles, who wished to seize upon the property of the church. They have thus sought to explain the religious revolution merely from the ill side of men and human affairs, by suggestions of private interests and personal passions.

On the other hand, the partisans and friends of the Reformation have endeavoured to explain it merely by the necessity for reform in the existing abuses of the church; they have represented it as a redressing of religious grievances, as an attempt conceived and executed with the sole design of reconstituting a pure and primitive church. Neither of these explanations seems to me sound. The second has more truth in it than the first; at least it is more noble, more in unison with the extent and importance of the event; still I do not think it correct. In my opinion, the Reformation was neither an accident, the result of some great chance, of personal interest, nor a mere aim at religious amelioration, the fruit of an Utopia of humanity and truth. It had a far more powerful cause than all this, and which dominates over all particular causes. It was a great movement of the liberty of the human mind, a new necessity for freely thinking and judging, on its own account, and with its own powers, of facts and ideas which hitherto Europe had received, or was held bound to receive, from the hands of authority. It was a grand attempt at the enfranchisement of the human mind;

and, to call things by their proper names, an insurrection of the human mind against absolute power in the spiritual order. Such I believe to be the true, general, and dominant character of the Reformation.

When we consider the state, at this epoch, of the human mind on the one hand, and on the other, that of the church which governed the human mind, we are struck by this two-fold fact: on the part of the human mind there was much more activity, and much more thirst for development and empire than it had ever felt. This new activity was the result of various causes, but which had been accumulating for ages. For example, there had been ages when heresies took birth, occupied some space of time, fell, and were replaced by others; and ages when philosophical opinions had run the same course as the heresies. The labour of the human mind, whether in the religious or in the philosophical sphere, had accumulated from the eleventh to the sixteenth century: and at last the moment had arrived when it was necessary that the result should appear. Moreover, all the means of instruction, created or encouraged in the very bosom of the church, bore their fruits. Schools had been instituted: from these schools had issued men with some knowledge, and their number was daily augmented. These men wished at last to think for themselves, and on their own account, for they felt stronger than they had ever yet done. Finally arrived that renewal and regeneration of the human mind by the restoration of antiquity, the progress and effects of which I have described to you.

The union of all these causes at the commencement of the sixteenth century, impressed upon the mind a highly energetic movement, an imperative necessity for progress.

The situation of the government of the human mind, the spiritual power, was quite different; it, on the contrary, had fallen into a state of indolence and immobility. The political credit of the church, of the court of Rome, had very much diminished; European society no longer belonged to it; it had passed into the dominion of lay governments. Still the spiritual power preserved all its pretensions, all its splendour and external importance. It happened with it, as it has more than once done with old governments. The greater part of the complaints urged against it no longer applied. It is not true that the court of Rome in the sixteenth century was very tyrannical; nor is it true that its abuses, properly so called, were more numerous, or more crying than they had been in other times. On the contrary, perhaps ecclesiastical government had never been more easy and tolerant, more disposed to let all things take their course, provided they did not put itself in question, provided it was so far acknowledged as to be left in the enjoyment of the rights which it had hitherto possessed, that it was secured the same existence, and paid the same tributes. It would willingly have left the human mind in tranquillity, if the human mind would have done the same towards it. But it is precisely when governments are least held in consideration, when they are the least powerful, and do the least evil, that they are attacked, because then they can be attacked, and formerly they could not be.[1]

It is evident, then, by the mere examination of the state of the human mind, and that of its government at this epoch, that the character of the Reformation must have been a new impulse of liberty, a great insurrection of the human intellect. Do not doubt but this was the dominant cause, the cause which rose above all the others—a cause superior to all interests, whether of nations or sovereigns—superior also to any mere necessity for reform, or the necessity for redressing of grievances which were then complained of.

I will suppose that after the first years of the Reformation, when it had displayed all its pretensions, set forth all its grievances, the spiritual power had suddenly fallen in with its views, and had said—"Well, so be it. I will reform everything; I will return to a more legal and religious order; I will suppress all vexations, arbitrariness, and tributes; even in doctrinal matters, I will modify, explain, and return to the primitive meaning. But when all grievances are thus redressed, I will preserve my position—I will be as formerly, the government of the human mind, with the same power and the same rights." Do you suppose that on these conditions the religious revolution would have been content, and would have stopped its progress? I do not think it. I firmly believe that it would have continued its career, and that after having demanded reformation, it would have demanded liberty. The crisis of the sixteenth century was not merely a reforming one, it was essentially revolutionary. It is impossible to take from it this character, its merits and its vices; it had all the effects of this character.

---

1. This argument that powers are usually attacked *not* when they are at their most tyrannical or arbitrary, but often when they are least so, was to be taken up and used again by Tocqueville with great effect, in *L'Ancien Régime and the Revolution* (1856).

Let us cast a glance upon the destinies of the Reformation; let us see, especially and before all, what it effected in the different countries where it was developed. Observe that it was developed in very various situations, and amidst very unequal chances. If we find that in spite of the diversity of situations, and the inequality of chances, it everywhere pursued a certain end, obtained a certain result, and preserved a certain character, it will be evident that this character, which surmounted all diversities of situation, and all inequalities of chances, must have been the fundamental character of the event—that this result must have been its essential aim.

Well, wherever the religious revolution of the sixteenth century prevailed, if it did not effect the entire enfranchisement of the human mind, it procured for it new and very great increase of liberty. It doubtless often left the mind to all the chances of the liberty or servitude of political institutions; but it abolished or disarmed the spiritual power, the systematic and formidable government of thought. This is the result which the Reformation attained amidst the most various combinations. In Germany, there was no political liberty; nor did the Reformation introduce it. It fortified rather than weakened the power of princes. It was more against the free institutions of the middle ages than favourable to their development. Nevertheless, it resuscitated and maintained in Germany a liberty of thought greater, perhaps, than anywhere else.

In Denmark, a country where absolute power dominated, where it penetrated into the municipal institutions, as well as into the general institutions of the state, there also, by the influence of the Reformation, thought was enfranchised and freely exercised in all directions.

In Holland, in the midst of a republic, and in England, under constitutional monarchy, and despite a religious tyranny of long duration, the emancipation of the human mind was likewise accomplished. And, lastly, in France, in a situation which seemed the least favourable to the effects of the religious revolution, in a country where it had been conquered, there even it was a principle of intellectual independence and liberty. Down to 1685, that is to say, until the revocation of the edict of Nantes, the Reformation had a legal existence in France. During this lengthened period it wrote and discussed, and provoked its adversaries to write and discuss with it. This single fact, this war of pamphlets and conferences between the old and new opinions, spread in France a liberty far more real and active than is commonly believed—a liberty which tended to the profit of science, the honour of the French clergy, as well as to the profit of thought in general. Take a glance at the conferences of Bossuet with Claude upon all the religious polemics of that period, and ask yourselves whether Louis XIV would have allowed a similar degree of liberty upon any other subject. It was between the Reformation and the opposite party that there existed the greatest degree of liberty in France during the seventeenth century. Religious thought was then far more bold, and treated questions with more freedom than the political spirit of Fénélon himself in *Telemachus*. This state of things did not cease until the revocation of the edict of Nantes. Now, from 1685 to the outburst of the human mind in the eighteenth century, there were not forty years; and the influence of the religious revolution in favour of intellectual liberty had scarcely ceased, when that of the philosophical revolution commenced.

You see that wherever the Reformation penetrated, wherever it played an important part, victorious or vanquished, it had as a general, dominant, and constant result, an immense progress in the activity and liberty of thought, and towards the emancipation of the human mind.

And not only had the Reformation this result, but with this it was satisfied; wherever it obtained that, it sought for nothing further, so much was it the foundation of the event, its primitive and fundamental character. Thus, in Germany it accepted, I will not say political servitude, but, at least, the absence of liberty. In England, it consented to the constitutional hierarchy of the clergy, and the presence of a church with quite as many abuses as there had ever been in the Romish church, and far more servile.

Why should the Reformation, so passionate and stubborn in some respects, show itself in this so easy and pliant? It was because it had obtained the general fact to which it tended, the abolition of spiritual power, the enfranchisement of the human mind. I repeat, that wherever it attained this end, it accommodated itself to all systems and all situations.

Let us now take the counter-proof of this inquiry; let us see what happened in countries into which the religious revolution had not penetrated, where it had been stifled in the beginning, where it had never been developed. History shows that there the human mind has not been enfranchised; two great countries, Spain and Italy, will prove this. Whilst in those European countries where the Reformation had taken an important place, the human mind, during the three last centuries, has gained an activity and a freedom before unknown, in those where it has not penetrated it has fallen, during the same period, into effeminacy and indolence; so that the proof and counter-proof have been made, so to speak, simultaneously, and given the same result.

Impulse of thought, and the abolition of absolute power in the spiritual order, are therefore the essential character of the Reformation, the most general result of its influence, and the dominant fact of its destiny.

I designedly say, the *fact*. The emancipation of the human mind was in reality, in the course of the Reformation, a fact rather than a principle, a result rather than an intention. In this respect, I think the Reformation executed more than it had undertaken; more perhaps than it had even desired. Contrary to most other revolutions, which have remained far behind their wishes, of which the event is far inferior to the thought, the consequences of this revolution surpassed its views; it is greater as an event than as a plan; what it effected it did not fully foresee, nor fully avow.

What were the reproaches with which its adversaries constantly upbraid the Reformation? Which of its results did they in a manner cast in its teeth to reduce it to silence?

Two principal ones. 1st. The multiplicity of sects, the prodigious licence allowed to mind, the dissolution of the religious society as a whole. 2nd. Tyranny and persecution. "You provoke licence," said they to the reformers; "you even produce it; and when you have created it, you wish to restrain and repress it. And how do you repress it? By the most severe and violent means. You yourselves persecute heresy, and by virtue of an illegitimate authority."

Survey and sum up all the great attacks directed against the Reformation, discarding the purely dogmatical questions; these are the two fundamental reproaches to which they always reduce themselves.

The reformed party was greatly embarrassed by them. When they imputed to it the multiplicity of sects, instead of avowing them, and maintaining the legitimacy of their development, it anathematized them, deplored their existence, and denied them. Taxed with persecution, it defended itself with the same embarrassment; it alleged the necessity; it had, it said, the right to repress and punish error, because it was in the possession of truth; its creed and institutions alone were legitimate; and if the Roman church had not the right to punish the reformers, it was because she was in the wrong as against them.

And when the reproach of persecution was addressed to the dominant party in the Reformation, not by its enemies, but by its own offspring, when the sects which it anathematized said to it, "We only do what you have done; we only separate ourselves, as you separated yourselves," it was still more embarrassed for an answer, and often only replied by redoubled rigour.

In fact, while labouring for the destruction of absolute power in the spiritual order, the revolution of the sixteenth century was ignorant of the true principles of intellectual liberty; it enfranchised the human mind, and yet pretended to govern it by the law; in practice it was giving prevalence to free inquiry, and in theory it was only substituting a legitimate in place of an illegitimate power. It did not elevate itself to the first cause, nor descend to the last consequences of its work. Thus it fell into a double fault; on the one hand, it neither knew nor respected all the rights of human thought; at the moment that it clamoured for them on its own account, it violated them with regard to others; on the other hand, it knew not how to measure the rights of authority in the intellectual order; I do not speak of coercive authority, which in such matters should possess none, but of purely moral authority, acting upon the mind alone, and simply by way of influence. Something is wanting in most of the reformed countries, to the good organization of the intellectual society, and to the regular action of ancient and general opinions. They could not reconcile the rights and wants of tradition with those of liberty; and the cause doubtless lay in this fact, that the Reformation did not fully comprehend and receive its own principles and effects.

Hence, also, it had a certain air of inconsistency and narrow-mindedness, which often gave a hold and advantage over it to its adversaries. These last knew perfectly well what they did, and what they wished to do; they went back to the principles of their conduct, and avowed all the consequences of it. There was never a government more consistent and systematic than that of the Roman church. In practice the court of Rome has greatly yielded and given way, much more so than the Reformation; in theory, it has much more completely adopted its peculiar system, and kept to a much more coherent conduct. This is a great power, this full knowledge of what one does and wishes, this complete and rational adoption of a doctrine and a design. The religious revolution of the sixteenth century presented in its course a striking example of it. Everyone knows that the chief power instituted to struggle against it was the order of Jesuits. Throw a glance upon their history; they have everywhere failed. Wherever they have interfered to any extent, they have carried misfortune into the cause with which they mixed. In England they ruined kings; in Spain, the people. The general course of events, the development of modern civilization, the liberty of the human mind, all these powers against which the Jesuits were called upon to contest, fought and conquered them. And not only have they failed, but call to mind the means they have been obliged to employ. No splendour or grandeur; they brought about no great events, nor put in motion powerful masses of men; they have acted only by underhanded, obscure, and subordinate means; by ways which are nothing suited to strike the imagination, to conciliate that public interest which attaches to great things, whatever may be their principle or end. The party against which it struggled, on the contrary, not only conquered, but conquered with splendour; it did great things, and by great means; it aroused the people, it gave to Europe great men, and changed, in the face of day, the fashion and form of states. In a word, everything was against the Jesuits, both fortune and appearances; neither good sense which desires success, nor imagination which requires splendour, were satisfied by their career. And yet nothing can be more certain than that they have had grandeur; that a great idea is attached to their name, their influence, and their history. How so?

It is because they knew what they were doing, and what they desired to do; because they had a full and clear acquaintance with the principles upon which they acted, and the aim to which they tended; that is to say, they had greatness of thought and greatness of will, and this saved them from the ridicule which attaches itself to constant reverses and contemptible means. Where, on the contrary, the event was greater than the thought, where the actors appeared to want a knowledge of the first principles and last results of their action, there remained something incomplete, inconsistent, and narrow, which placed the conquerors themselves in a sort of rational and philosophical inferiority, of which the influence has been sometimes felt in events. This was, I conceive, in the struggle of the old against the new spiritual order, the weak side of the Reformation, the circumstance which often embarrassed it, and hindered it from defending itself as it ought to have done.

We might consider the religious revolution of the sixteenth century under many other aspects. I have said nothing, and have nothing to say, concerning its dogmas, concerning its effect on religion, and in regard to the relations of the human soul with God and the eternal future; but I might exhibit it to you in the diversity of its relations with the social order, bringing on, in all directions, results of mighty importance. For instance, it awoke religion amidst the laity, and in the world of the faithful. Up to that time, religion had been, so to speak, the exclusive domain of the clergy, of the ecclesiastical order, who distributed the fruits, but disposed themselves of the tree, and had almost alone the right to speak of it. The Reformation caused a general circulation of religious creeds; it opened to believers the field of faith, which hitherto they had had no right to enter. It had, at the same time, a second result—it banished, or nearly banished, religion from politics; it restored the independence of the temporal power. At the very moment when, so to speak, religion came again to the possession of the faithful, it quitted the government of society. In the reformed countries, notwithstanding the diversity of ecclesiastical constitutions, even in England, where that constitution is nearer to the ancient order of things, the spiritual power no longer makes any serious pretensions to the direction of the temporal power.

I might enumerate many other consequences of the Reformation, but I must check myself, and rest content with having placed before you its principal character, the emancipation of the human mind, and the abolition of absolute power in the spiritual order—an abolition which, no doubt, was not complete, but nevertheless formed the greatest step that has, up to our days, been taken in this direction.

Before concluding, I must pray you to remark the striking similarity of destiny which, in the history of modern Europe, presents itself as existing between the civil and religious societies, in the revolutions to which they have been subject.

The Christian society, as we saw when I spoke of the church, began by being a perfectly free society, and formed solely in virtue of a common creed, without institutions or government, properly so called, and regulated only by moral powers, varying according to the necessity of the moment. Civil society commenced in like manner in Europe, or partially at least, with bands of barbarians; a society perfectly free, each one remaining in it because he thought proper, without laws or constituted powers. At the close of this state, which could not co-exist with any considerable development, religious society placed itself under an essentially aristocratic government; it was the body of the clergy, the bishops, councils, and ecclesiastical aristocracy, which governed it. A fact of the same kind happened in civil society at the termination of barbarism; it was the lay aristocracy, the lay feudal chiefs, by which it was governed. Religious society left the aristocratic form to assume that of pure monarchy; that is the meaning of the triumph of the court of Rome over the councils and over the European ecclesiastical aristocracy. The same revolution accomplished itself in civil society: it was by the destruction of aristocratical power that royalty prevailed and took possession of the European world. In the sixteenth century, in the bosom of religious society, an insurrection burst forth against the system of pure monarchy, against absolute power in the spiritual order. This revolution brought on, consecrated, and established free inquiry in Europe. In our own days we have seen the same event occurring in the civil order. Absolute temporal power was attacked and conquered. Thus you have seen that the two societies have undergone the same vicissitudes, have been subject to the same revolutions; only religious society has always been the foremost in this career.

We are now in possession of one of the great facts of modern society, namely, free inquiry, the liberty of the human mind. We have seen that, at the same time, political centralization almost everywhere prevailed. In my next lecture I shall treat of the English revolution; that is to say, of the event in which free inquiry and pure monarchy, both results of the progress of civilization, found themselves for the first time in conflict.

THIRTEENTH LECTURE

Object of the lecture—General character of the English revolution—
Its principal causes—It was more political than religious—The
three great parties in it: 1. The party of legal reform; 2. The party
of the political revolution; 3. The party of the social revolution—
They all fail—Cromwell—The restoration of the Stuarts—The
legal ministry—The profligate ministry—The revolution of 1688 in
England and Europe.

Y OU HAVE SEEN that during the sixteenth century all the elements and features that had belonged to former European society resolved themselves into two great facts, free inquiry, and the
centralization of power. The first prevailed among the clergy, the second
among the laity. There simultaneously triumphed in Europe the emancipation of the human mind, and the establishment of pure monarchy.

It was scarcely to be expected but that sooner or later a struggle should
arise between these two principles; for they were contradictory; the one
was the overthrow of absolute power in the spiritual order, the other was
its victory in the temporal; the first paved the way for the decay of the ancient ecclesiastical monarchy, the last perfected the ruin of the ancient feudal and communal liberties. The fact of their advent being simultaneous,
arose, as you have seen, from the revolution in religious society advancing
with a more rapid step than that in the civil society: the one occurred exactly at the time of the enfranchisement of the individual mind, the other
not until the moment of the centralization of universal power under one
head. The coincidence of these two facts, so far from springing out of their
similitude, did not prevent their inconsistency. They were each advances
in the course of civilization, but they were advances arising from dissimilar
situations, and of a different moral date, if I may be allowed the expression,

although cotemporary. That they should run against one another before they came to an understanding was inevitable.

Their first collision was in England. In the struggle of free inquiry, the fruit of the Reformation; against the ruin of political liberty, the fruit of the triumph of pure monarchy; and in the effort to abolish absolute power both in the temporal and spiritual orders, we have the purport of the English revolution, its share in the course of our civilization.

The question arises, why should this struggle take place in England sooner than elsewhere? wherefore should the revolutions in the political order have coincided more closely with those in the moral order, in that country, than on the continent?

Royalty in England has undergone the same vicissitudes as on the continent: under the Tudors, it attained to a concentration and energy which it has never known since. It does not follow that the despotism of the Tudors was more violent, or that it cost dearer to England than that of their predecessors. I believe that there were at least as many acts of tyranny and instances of vexation and injustice under the Plantagenets as under the Tudors, perhaps even more. And I believe, likewise, that at this era the government of pure monarchy was more harsh and arbitrary on the continent than in England. The new feature under the Tudors was, that absolute power became systematic; royalty assumed a primitive and independent sovereignty; it adopted a style hitherto unknown. The theoretical pretensions of Henry VIII, of Elizabeth, of James I, or of Charles I, are entirely different to those of Edward I or Edward III; though the power of these two last kings was neither less arbitrary nor less extensive. I repeat, that it was the principle, the rational system of monarchy, rather than its practical power, which experienced a mutation in England during the sixteenth century: royalty assumed absolute power, and pretended to be superior to all laws, to those even which it had declared should be respected.

Again, the religious revolution was not accomplished in England in the same manner as on the continent; here it was the work of the kings themselves. Not but that in this country, as elsewhere, there had long been the germs of, and even attempts at a popular reformation, which would probably, ere long, have been carried out. But Henry VIII took the initiative; power became revolutionary. The result was that, in its origin at least, as a redress of ecclesiastical tyranny and abuse, and as the emancipation of the human mind, the Reformation was far less complete in England than on the continent. It consulted, and very naturally, the interest of its authors. The king and the retained episcopacy shared the riches and power, the spoils of the preceding government, of the papacy. It was not long before the consequence was felt. It was said that the Reformation was finished; yet most of the motives which had made it necessary still existed. It reappeared under a popular form; it exclaimed against the bishops as it had done against the court of Rome; it accused them of being so many popes. As often as the general character of the religious reformation was compromised, whenever there was question of a struggle with the ancient church, all portions of the reformed party rallied, and made head against the common enemy; but the danger passed, the interior struggle recommenced; popular reform again attacked regal and aristocratical reform, denounced its abuses, complained of its tyranny, called upon it for a fulfilment of its promises, and not again to establish the power which it had dethroned.

There was, about the same time, a movement of enfranchisement manifested in civil society, a need for political freedom, till then unknown, or at least powerless. During the sixteenth century, the commercial prosperity of England increased with excessive rapidity; at the same time, territorial wealth, landed property, in a great measure changed hands. The division of land in England in the sixteenth century, consequent on the ruin of the feudal aristocracy and other causes, too many for present enumeration, is a fact deserving more attention than has yet been given to it. All documents show us the number of landed proprietors increasing to an immense extent, and the larger portion of the lands passing into the hands of the gentry, or inferior nobility, and the citizens. The upper house, the higher nobility, was not nearly so rich at the commencement of the seventeenth century as the House of Commons. There was then at the same time a great development of commercial wealth, and a great mutation in landed property. Amidst these two influences came a third—the new movement in the minds of men. The reign of Elizabeth is, perhaps, the greatest period of English history for literary and philosophical activity, the era of lofty and fertile imaginations; the puritans without hesitation followed out all the consequences of a vigorous although narrow doctrine; the opposite class of minds, less moral and more free, strangers to any principle or method, received with enthusiasm everything which promised to satisfy their curiosity or feed their excitement. Wherever the impulse of intelligence brings with it a lively pleasure, liberty will soon become a want, and will quickly pass from the public mind into the government.

There was on the continent, in some of those countries where the Reformation had gone forth, a manifestation of a similar feeling, a certain want for political liberty; but the means of satisfying it were wanting; they knew not where to look for it; no aid for it could be found either in the institutions or in manners; they remained vague and uncertain, seeking in vain to satisfy their want. In England, it was very different: there the spirit of political freedom, which reappeared in the sixteenth century, following the Reformation, found its fulcrum and the means of action in the ancient institutions and social conditions.

Everyone knows the origin of the free institutions of England; it is universally known how the union of the great barons in 1215, forced *Magna Charta* from King John. What is not so generally known is that the great charter was from time to time recalled and again confirmed by most of the succeeding kings. There were more than thirty confirmations of it between the thirteenth and the sixteenth centuries. And not only was the charter confirmed, but new statutes were introduced for the purpose of maintaining and developing it. It therefore lived, as it were, without interval or interruption. At the same time, the House of Commons was formed, and took its place among the supreme institutions of the country. It was under the Plantagenets that it truly struck root; not that it took any great part in the state during that period; the government did not, properly speaking, belong to it, even in the way of influence; it only interfered therein at the call of the king, and then always reluctantly and hesitatingly, as if it was more fearful of engaging and compromising itself than desirous of augmenting its power. But when the matter in hand was the defence of private rights, the families or fortune of the citizens, in a word, the liberties of the individual, the House of Commons acquitted itself of its duty with much energy and perseverance, and founded all those principles which have become the basis of the English constitution.

After the Plantagenets, and especially under the Tudors, the House of Commons, or rather the entire parliament, presented itself under a different aspect. It no longer defended the individual liberties, as under the Plantagenets. Arbitrary detentions, the violation of private rights, now become much more frequent, are often passed over in silence. On the other hand, the parliament took a much more active part in the general government of the state. In changing the religion and in regulating the order of succession, Henry VIII had need of some medium, some public instrument, and in this want he was supplied by the parliament, and especially by the House of Commons. Under the Plantagenets it had been an instrument of resistance, the guardian of private rights; under the Tudors it became an instrument of government and general policy; so that at the end of the sixteenth century, although it had undergone almost every species of tyranny, its importance was much augmented, its great power began, that power upon which the representative government depends.

When we glance at the state of the free institutions of England at the end of the sixteenth century, we find first, fundamental rules and principles of liberty, of which neither the country nor the legislature had ever lost sight; second, precedents, examples of liberty, a good deal mixed, it is true, with inconsistent examples and precedents, but sufficing to legalize and sustain the claims, and to support the defenders of liberty in any struggle against tyranny or despotism; third, special and local institutions, replete with germs of liberty; the jury, the right of assembling, and of being armed; the independence of municipal administrations and jurisdictions; fourth, and last, the parliament and its power, of which the crown had more need than ever, since it had lavished away the greater part of its independent revenues, domains, feudal rights, &c., and was dependent for its very support upon the national vote.

The political condition of England, therefore, in the sixteenth century was wholly different from that of the continent. In spite of the tyranny of the Tudors, and systematic triumph of pure monarchy, there was still a fixed fulcrum, a sure means of action for the new spirit of liberty.

There were, then, two national wants in England at this period: on one side was the need of religious revolution and liberty in the heart of the reformation already commenced; and on the other, was required political liberty in the heart of the pure monarchy then in progress; and in the course of their progress these two wants were able to invoke all that had already been done in either direction. They combined. The party who wished to pursue religious reformation, invoked political liberty to the assistance of its faith and conscience against the king and the bishops. The friends of political liberty again sought the aid of the popular reformation. The two parties united to struggle against absolute power in the temporal and in the spiritual orders, a power now concentrated in the hands of the king. This is the origin and purport of the English revolution.

It was thus essentially devoted to the defence or achievement of liberty. For the religious party it was a means, and for the political party an end; but with both, liberty was the question, and they were obliged to pursue it in common. There was no real religious quarrel between the episcopal and the puritan party; little dispute upon dogmas, or concerning faith; not but that there existed real differences of opinion between them, differences of great importance; but this was not the principal point. Practical liberty was what the puritans wished to force from the episcopal party: it was for this that they strove. There was also another religious party who had to found a system, to establish its dogmas, ecclesiastical constitution, and discipline; this was the presbyterian party: but although it worked to the utmost of its power, it did not in this point progress in proportion to its desire. Placed on the defensive, oppressed by the bishops, unable to act without the assent of the political reformers, its allies and chief supporters, its dominant aim was liberty, the general interest and common aim of all the parties, whatever their diversity, who concurred in the movement. Taking everything together, the English revolution was essentially political; it was brought about in the midst of a religious people and in a religious age; religious thoughts and passions were its instruments; but its chief design and definite aim were political, were devoted to liberty, and the abolition of all absolute power.

I shall now glance at the different phases of this revolution, and its great parties; I shall then connect it with the general course of European civilization; I shall mark its place and influence therein; and show you by a detail of the facts, as at the first view, that it was the first blow which had been struck in the cause of free inquiry against pure monarchy, the first manifestation of a struggle between these two great powers.

Three principal parties sprang up in this great crisis, three revolutions in a manner were comprised in it, and successively appeared upon the scene. In each party, and in each revolution, two parties are allied, and work conjointly, a political and a religious party; the first at the head, the second followed, but each necessary to the other; so that the two-fold character of the event is impressed upon all its phases.

The first party which appeared was the party of legal reform, under whose banner all the others at first ranged themselves. When the English revolution commenced, when the long parliament was assembled in 1640, it was universally said, and by many sincerely believed, that the legal reform would suffice for all things; that in the ancient laws and customs of the country, there was that which would remedy all abuses, and which would re-establish a system of government entirely conformable to the public wishes. This party loudly censured, and sincerely wished to prevent the illegal collecting of taxes, arbitrary imprisonments, in a word, all acts disallowed by the known laws of the country. At the root of its ideas was the belief in the king's sovereignty—that is, in absolute power. A secret instinct warned it, indeed, there was something false and dangerous therein; it wished, therefore, to say nothing of it; pushed to the extremity, however, and forced to explain itself, it admitted in royalty a power superior to all human origin, and above all control, and, when need was, defended it. It believed at the same time that this sovereignty, absolute in theory, was bound to observe certain forms and rules; that it could not extend beyond certain limits; and that these rules, forms, and limits, were sufficiently established and guaranteed in the great charter, in the confirmatory statutes, and in the ancient laws of the country. Such was its political idea. In religious matters, the legal party thought that the episcopal power was excessive; that the bishops had too much political power, that their jurisdiction was too extensive, and that it was necessary to overlook and restrain its exercise. Still it firmly supported the episcopacy, not only as an ecclesiastical institution, and as a system of church government, but as a necessary support for the royal prerogative, as a means of defending and maintaining the supremacy of the king in religious matters. The sovereignty of the king in the political order being exercised according to known forms, and within the limits of acknowledged rules, royalty in the religious order should be sustained by the episcopacy; such was the two-fold system of the legal party, of which the chiefs were Clarendon, Colepepper, Lord Capel, and Lord Falkland himself, although an ardent advocate of public liberty, and a man who numbered in his ranks almost all the high nobility who were not servilely devoted to the court.

Behind these followed a second party, which I shall call the party of the political revolution: these were of opinion that the ancient guarantees and legal barriers had been and still were insufficient; that a great change, a regular revolution was necessary, not in the forms, but in the realities of government: that it was necessary to withdraw from the king and his council the independence of their power, and to place the political preponderance in the House of Commons; that the government, properly so called, should belong to this assembly and its chiefs. This party did not give an account of their ideas and intentions as clearly and systematically as I have done; but this was the essence of its doctrines, of its political tendencies. Instead of the sovereignty of the king, pure monarchy, it believed in the sovereignty of the House of Commons as the representative of the country. Under this idea was hidden that of the sovereignty of the people, an idea, the bearing of which, and its consequences, the party was very far from contemplating, but which presented itself, and was received under the form of the sovereignty of the House of Commons.

A religious party, that of the presbyterians, was closely united with the party of the political revolution. The presbyterians wished to bring about in the church a revolution analogous to that meditated by their allies in the state. They wished to govern the church by assemblies, giving the religious power to an hierarchy of assemblages agreeing one with the other, as their allies had invested the House of Commons with the political power. But the presbyterian revolution was more vigorous and complete, for it tended to change the form as well as the principle of the government of the church, while the political party wished only to moderate the influences and preponderating power of institutions, and did not meditate an overthrow of the form of the institutions themselves.

But the chiefs of the political party were not all of them favourable to the presbyterian organization of the church. Many of them, as for instance, Hampden and Holles, would have preferred, it seems, a moderate episcopacy, confined to purely ecclesiastical duties, and more freedom of conscience. But they resigned themselves to it, being unable to do without their fanatical allies.

A third party was yet more exorbitant in its demands: this party asserted that an entire change was necessary, not only in the form of government, but in government itself; that the whole political constitution was bad. This party repudiated the past ages of England, renounced the national institutions and memories, with the intention of founding a new government, according to a pure theory, or what it supposed to be such. It was not a mere reform in the government, but a social revolution which this party wished to bring about. The party of which I just now spoke, that of the political revolution, wished to introduce important changes in the relations between the parliament and the crown; it wished to extend the power of parliament, particularly that of the House of Commons, giving them the nomination to high public offices, and the supreme direction in general affairs; but its projects of reform extended very little further than this. For instance, it had no idea of changing the electoral, judicial, or municipal and administrative systems of the country. The republican party meditated all these changes, and proclaimed their necessity; and, in a word, wished to reform, not only the public administration, but also the social relations and the distribution of private rights.

This party, like that which preceded it, was partly religious and partly political. The political portion included the republicans, properly so called, the theorists, Ludlow, Harrington, Milton, &c. On that side were ranged the republicans from interest, the chief officers of the army, Ireton, Cromwell, and Lambert, who, more or less sincere at the onset, were soon swayed and guided by interested views and the necessities of their situations. Around these collected the religious republican party, which included all those enthusiasts who acknowledged no legitimate power except that of Jesus Christ, and who, while waiting for his advent, wished to be governed by his elect. And, lastly, the party was followed by a large number of inferior free-thinkers, and fantastical dreamers, the one set in hope of licence, the others of equality of property and universal suffrage.

In 1653, after a struggle of twelve years, all these parties had successively failed; at least, they had reason to believe they had failed, and the public was convinced of their failure. The legal party, which quickly disappeared, had seen the ancient laws and constitution disdained and trodden under foot, and innovation visible upon every side. The party of political reform saw parliamentary forms perish under the new use which they wished to make of them; they saw the House of Commons, after a sway of twelve years, reduced, by the successive expulsion of the royalists and the presbyterians, to a very trifling number of members, and those looked upon by the public with contempt and detestation, and incapable of governing. The republican party seemed to have succeeded better: it remained, to all appearance, master of the field of battle, of power; the House of Commons reckoned no more than from fifty to sixty members, and all of these were republicans. They might fairly deem themselves and declare themselves masters of the country. But the country absolutely rejected them; they could nowhere carry their resolutions into effect; they exercised no practical influence either over the army or over the people. There no longer subsisted any social tie, any social security; justice was no longer administered, or, if it was, it was no longer justice, but the arbitrary rendering of decrees at the dictation of passion, prejudice, party. And not only was there an entire disappearance of security from the social relations of men, there was none whatever on the highways, which were covered with thieves and robbers; material anarchy as well as moral anarchy, manifested itself in every direction, and the House of Commons and the Republican Council were wholly incapable of repressing either the one or the other.

The three great parties of the revolution had thus been called successively to conduct it, to govern the country according to their knowledge and will, and they had not been able to do it; they had all three of them completely failed; they could do nothing more. "It was then," says Bossuet, "that a man was found who left nothing to fortune which he could take from it by council or foresight"; an expression full of error, and controverted by all history. Never did man leave more to fortune than Cromwell; never has man hazarded more, gone on with more temerity, without design or aim, but determined to go as far as fate should carry him. An unlimited ambition, an admirable faculty of extracting from every day and circumstance some new means of progress, the art of turning chance to profit, without pretending to rule it, all these were Cromwell's. It was with

Cromwell as perhaps it has been with no other man in his circumstances; he sufficed for all the most various phases of the revolution; he was a man for its first and latest epochs; first of all, he was the leader of insurrection, the abettor of anarchy, the most fiery of the English revolutionists; afterwards the man for the anti-revolutionary reaction, for the re-establishment of order, and for social organization; thus performing singly all the parts which, in the course of revolutions, are divided among the greatest actors. One can hardly say that Cromwell was a Mirabeau; he wanted eloquence, and although very active, did not make any show during the first years of the Long Parliament. But he was successively a Danton and a Buonaparte. He, more than any others, had contributed to the overthrow of power; and he raised it up again because none but he knew how to assume and manage it; some one must govern; all had failed, and he succeeded. That constituted his title. Once master of the government, this man, whose ambition had shown itself so bold and insatiable, who, in his progress, had always driven fortune before him, determined never to stop, now displayed a good sense, prudence, and knowledge of the possible, which dominated all his most violent passions. He had, no doubt, a great love for absolute power, and a strong desire to place the crown on his own head, and establish it in his family. He renounced this last design, the danger of which he saw in time; and as to the absolute power, although, in fact, he exercised it, he always knew that the tendency of his age was against it; that the revolution in which he had co-operated, and which he had followed through all its phases, had been directed against despotism, and that the imperishable desire of England was to be governed by a parliament, and in parliamentary forms. Therefore he himself, a despot by inclination and in fact, undertook to have a parliament and to govern in a parliamentary manner. He addressed himself unceasingly to all parties; he endeavoured to form a parliament of religious enthusiasts, of republicans, of presbyterians, of officers of the army. He attempted all means to constitute a parliament which could and would co-operate with him. He tried in vain: all parties, once seated in Westminster, wished to snatch from him the power which he exercised, and rule in their turn. I do not say that his own interest and personal passion were not first in his thoughts; but it is not therefore the less certain that, if he had abandoned power, he would have been obliged to take it up again the next day. Neither puritans nor royalists, republicans nor officers, none, besides Cromwell, was in condition to govern with any degree of order or justice. The proof had been shown. It was impossible to allow the parliament, that is to say, the parties sitting in parliament, to take the empire which they could not keep. Such, then, was the situation of Cromwell; he governed according to a system which he knew very well was not that of the country; he exercised a power acknowledged as necessary, but accepted by no one. No party regarded his dominion as a definitive government. The royalists, the presbyterians, the republicans, the army itself, the party which seemed most devoted to Cromwell, all were convinced that he was but a transitory master. At bottom, he never reigned over men's minds; he was never anything but a make-shift, a necessity of the moment. The protector, the absolute master of England, was all his life obliged to employ force in order to protect his power; no party could govern like him, but no party wished him for governor: he was constantly attacked by all parties at once.

At his death the republicans alone were in a condition to seize upon power; they did so, and succeeded no better than they had done before. This was not for want of confidence, at least as regards the fanatics of the party. A pamphlet of Milton, published at this period, and full of talent and enthusiasm, is entitled "A ready and easy way to establish a free commonwealth." You see what was the blindness of these men. They very soon fell again into that impossibility of governing which they had already experienced. Monk undertook the conduct of the event which all England looked for. The restoration was accomplished.

The restoration of the Stuarts in England was a deeply national event. It presented itself with the advantages at once of an ancient government, of a government which rests upon its traditions, upon the recollections of the country, and with the advantages of a new government, of which no recent trial has been made, and of which the faults and weight have not been experienced. The ancient monarchy was the only species of government which for the last twenty years had not been despised for its incapacity and ill-success in the administration of the country. These two causes rendered the restoration popular; it had nothing to oppose it but the remnants of violent parties; and the public rallied around it heartily. It was, in the opinion of the country, the only means of legal government; that is to say, of that which the country most ardently desired. This was also what the restoration promised, and it was careful to present itself under the aspect of a legal government.

The first royalist party which, at the return of Charles II, undertook the management of affairs was, in fact, the legal party, represented by its most able chief, the chancellor Clarendon. You are aware that, from 1660 to 1667, Clarendon was prime minister, and the truly predominating influence in England. Clarendon and his friends reappeared with their ancient system, the absolute sovereignty of the king, kept within legal limits, and restrained, in matters of taxation, by parliament, and in matters of private rights and individual liberties, by the tribunals; but possessing, as regards government properly so called, an almost complete independence, the most decisive preponderance, to the exclusion, or even against the wishes, of the majority in parliament, especially in the House of Commons. As to the rest, they had a due respect for legal order, a sufficient solicitude for the interests of the country, a noble sentiment of its dignity, and a grave and honourable moral tone: such was the character of Clarendon's administration of seven years.

But the fundamental ideas upon which this administration rested, the absolute sovereignty of the king, and the government placed beyond the influence of the preponderating opinion of parliament, these ideas, I say, were obsolete, impotent. In spite of the reaction of the first moments of the restoration, twenty years of parliamentary rule, in opposition to royalty, had irremediably ruined them. A new element soon burst forth in the centre of the royalist party: free-thinkers, rakes, and libertines, who participated in the ideas of the time, conceived that power was vested in the Commons, and, caring very little for legal order or the absolute sovereignty of the king, troubled themselves only for their own success, and sought it whenever they caught a glimpse of any means of influence or power. These formed a party which became allied with the national discontented party, and Clarendon was overthrown.

Thus arose a new system of government, namely, that of the portion of the royalist party which I have just described: profligates and libertines formed the ministry, which is called the ministry of the Cabal, and many other administrations which succeeded it. This was their character: no care for principles, laws, or rights; as little for justice and for truth; they sought upon each occasion to discover the means of succeeding: if success depended upon the influence of the Commons, they chimed in with their opinions; if it seemed expedient to flout the House of Commons, they did so, and begged its pardon on the morrow. Corruption was tried one day, flattery of the national spirit, another; there was no regard paid to the general interests of the country, to its dignity, or to its honour; in a word, their government was profoundly selfish and immoral, a stranger to all public doctrine or views; but, at bottom, and in the practical administration of affairs, very intelligent and liberal. Such was the character of the Cabal, of the ministry of the earl of Danby, and of the entire English government, from 1667 to 1679. Notwithstanding its immorality, notwithstanding its contempt of the principles and the true interests of the country, this government was less odious and less unpopular than the ministry of Clarendon had been: and why? because it was much better adapted to the times, and because it better understood the sentiments of the people, even in mocking them. It was not antiquated and foreign to them, like that of Clarendon; and though it did the country much more harm, the country found it more agreeable. Nevertheless, there came a moment when corruption, servility, and contempt of rights and public honour were pushed to such a point that the people could no longer remain resigned. There was a general rising against the government of the profligates. A national and patriotic party had formed itself in the bosom of the House of Commons. The king decided upon calling its chiefs to the council. Then came to the direction of affairs Lord Essex, the son of him who had commanded the first parliamentary armies during the civil war, Lord Russell, and a man who, without having any of their virtues, was far superior to them in political ability, Lord Shaftesbury. Brought thus to the management of affairs, the national party showed itself incompetent; it knew not how to possess itself of the moral force of the country; it knew not how to treat the interests either of the king, the court, or of any of those with whom it had to do. It gave to no one, neither to the people nor to the king, any great notion of its ability and energy. After remaining a short time in power, it failed. The virtue of its chiefs, their generous courage, the nobleness of their deaths, have exalted them in history, and have justly placed them in the highest rank; but their political capacity did not answer to their virtue, and they knew not how to wield the power which could not corrupt them, nor to secure the triumph of the cause for the sake of which they knew how to die.

This attempt having failed, you perceive the condition of the English restoration; it had, after a manner, and like the revolution, tried all parties and all ministries, the legal ministry, the corrupted ministry, and the national ministry; but none had succeeded. The country and the court found themselves in much the same situation as that of England in 1653, at the end of the revolutionary tempest. Recourse was had to the same expedient; what Cromwell had done for the good of the revolution, Charles II did for the good of his crown: he entered the career of absolute power.

James II succeeded his brother. Then a second question was added to that of absolute power; namely, the question of religion. James II desired to bring about the triumph of popery as well as that of despotism. Here, then, as at the beginning of the revolution, we have a religious and a political warfare, both directed against the government. It has often been asked, what would have happened had William III never existed, or had he not come with his Hollanders to put an end to the quarrel which had arisen between James II and the English nation? I firmly believe that the same event would have been accomplished. All England, except a very small party, had rallied, at this epoch, against James, and, under one form or another, it would have accomplished the revolution of 1688. But this crisis was produced by other and higher causes than the internal state of England. It was European as well as English. It is here that the English revolution connects itself by facts themselves, and independently of the influence which its example may have had, with the general course of European civilization.

While this struggle, which I have sketched in outline, this struggle of absolute power against civil and religious liberty, was taking place in England, a struggle of the same kind was going on upon the continent, very different, indeed, as regards the actors, forms, and theatre, but at bottom the same, and originated by the same cause. The pure monarchy of Louis XIV endeavoured to become an universal monarchy; at least it gave reason for the fear that such was the case; and in fact, Europe did fear that it was. A league was made in Europe, between various political parties, in order to resist this attempt, and the chief of this league was the chief of the party in favour of civil and religious liberty upon the continent, William, prince of Orange. The protestant republic of Holland, with William at its head, undertook to resist the pure monarchy represented and conducted by Louis XIV. It was not civil and religious liberty in the interior of the states, but their external independence which was apparently the question. Louis XIV and his adversaries did not imagine that, in fact, they were contesting between them the question which was being contested in England. This struggle went on, not between parties, but between states; it proceeded by war and diplomacy, not by political movements and by revolutions. But, at bottom, one and the same question was at issue.

When, therefore, James II resumed in England the contest between absolute power and liberty, this contest occurred just in the midst of the general struggle which was going on in Europe between Louis XIV and the prince of Orange, the representatives, severally, of the two great systems at war upon the banks of the Scheldt, as well as on those of the Thames. The league was so powerful against Louis XIV that, openly, or in a hidden but very real manner, sovereigns were seen to enter it, who were assuredly very far from being interested in favour of civil and religious liberty. The emperor of Germany and Pope Innocent XI supported William III against Louis XIV. William passed into England, less in order to serve the internal interests of the country than to draw it completely into the struggle against Louis XIV. He took this new kingdom as a new power of which he was in want, and of which his opponent had, up to that time, made use against him. While Charles II and James II reigned, England belonged to Louis XIV; he had directed its external relations, and had constantly opposed it to Holland. England was now snatched from the party of pure and universal monarchy, in order to become the instrument and strongest support of the party of religious liberty. This is the European aspect of the revolution of 1688; it was thus that it occupied a place in the total result of the events of Europe, independently of the part which it played by means of its example, and the influence which it exercised upon minds in the following century.

Thus you see that, as I told you in the beginning, the true meaning and essential character of this revolution was the attempt to abolish absolute power in temporal as well as spiritual things. This act discovers itself in all the phases of the revolution—in its first period up to the restoration, in the second up to the crisis of 1688—and whether we consider it in its internal development or in its relations with Europe in general.

It now remains for us to study the same great event upon the continent, the struggle of pure monarchy and free inquiry, or, at least, its causes and approaches. This will be the subject of our next lecture.

FOURTEENTH LECTURE

Object of the lecture—Difference and likeness between the progress
of civilization in England and on the Continent—Preponderance
of France in Europe in the seventeenth and eighteenth centuries—In
the seventeenth century by reason of the French government—In
the eighteenth by reason of the country itself—Of the government
of Louis XIV—Of his wars—Of his diplomacy—Of his
administration—Of his legislation—Causes of his rapid decline—
Of France in the eighteenth century—Essential characteristics of the
philosophical revolution—Conclusion of the course.

IN MY LAST LECTURE I endeavoured to determine the true character and political meaning of the English revolution. We have seen that
it was the first shock of the two great facts to which all the civilization
of primitive Europe reduced itself in the course of the sixteenth century,
namely, pure monarchy, on one hand, and free inquiry on the other; those
two powers came to strife for the first time in England. Attempts have been
made to infer from this fact the existence of a radical difference between
the social state of England and that of the continent; some have pretended
that no comparison was possible between countries of destinies so different; they have affirmed that the English people had existed in a kind of
moral isolation analogous to its material situation.

It is true that there had been an important difference between English civilization, and the civilization of the continental states—a difference which we are bound to calculate. You have already, in the course of
my lectures, been enabled to catch a glimpse of it. The development of
the different principles and elements of society occurred in England simultaneously, and, as it were, abreast; at least, far more so than upon the
continent. When I attempted to determine the peculiar physiognomy of

European civilization as compared with the ancient and Asiatic civilizations, I showed you the first varied, rich, and complex; that it never fell under the dominion of an exclusive principle; that therein the various elements of the social state were modified, combined, and struggled with each other, and had been constantly compelled to agree and live in common. This fact, the general characteristic of European civilization, has above all characterized the English civilization; it was in England that this character developed itself with the most continuity and obviousness; it was there that the civil and religious orders, aristocracy, democracy, royalty, local and central institutions, moral and political developments, progressed and increased together, pell-mell, so to speak, and if not with an equal rapidity, at least always within a short distance of each other. Under the reign of the Tudors, for instance, in the midst of the most brilliant progress of pure monarchy, we see the democratical principle, the popular power, arising and strengthening itself at the same time. The revolution of the seventeenth century burst forth; it was at the same time religious and political. The feudal aristocracy appeared here in a very weakened condition, and with all the symptoms of decline: nevertheless, it was ever in a position to preserve a place and play an important part therein, and to take its share in the results. It is the same with the entire course of English history: never has any ancient element completely perished; never has any new element wholly triumphed, or any special principle attained to an exclusive preponderance. There has always been a simultaneous development of different forces, a compromise between their pretensions and their interests.

Upon the continent, the progress of civilization has been much less complex and complete. The various elements of society—the religious and civil orders—monarchy, aristocracy, and democracy, have developed themselves, not together and abreast, but in succession. Each principle, each system has had, after a certain manner, its turn. Such a century belongs, I will not say exclusively, which would be saying too much, but with a very marked preponderance, to feudal aristocracy, for example; another belongs to the monarchical principle; a third to the democratical system.

Compare the French with the English middle ages, the eleventh, twelfth, and thirteenth centuries of our history with the corresponding centuries beyond the channel; you will find that at this period, in France, feudalism was almost absolutely sovereign, while royalty and the democratical principle were next to nullities. Look to England: it is, indeed, the feudal aristocracy which predominates; but royalty and democracy were nevertheless powerful and important.

Royalty triumphed in England under Elizabeth, as in France under Louis XIV; but how many precautions was it obliged to take; to how many restrictions—now from the aristocracy, now from the democracy, did it submit! In England, also, each system and each principle has had its day of power and success; but never so completely, so exclusively, as upon the continent; the conqueror has always been compelled to tolerate the presence of his rivals, and to allow each his share.

With the differences in the progress of the two civilizations, are connected advantages and disadvantages, which manifest themselves, in fact, in the history of the two countries. There can be no doubt, for instance, but that this simultaneous development of the different social elements greatly contributed to carry England, more rapidly than any other of the continental states, to the final aim of all society—namely, the establishment of a government at once regular and free. It is precisely the nature of a government to concern itself for all interests and all powers, to reconcile them, and to induce them to live and prosper in common; now, such, beforehand, by the concurrence of a multitude of causes, was the disposition and relation of the different elements of English society: a general and somewhat regular government had therefore less difficulty in becoming constituted there. So, the essence of liberty is the manifestation and simultaneous action of all interests, rights, powers, and social elements. England was therefore much nearer to its possession than the majority of other states. For the same reasons, national good sense, the comprehension of public affairs, necessarily formed themselves there more rapidly than elsewhere; political good sense consists in knowing how to estimate all facts, to appreciate them, and render to each its share of consideration; this, in England, was a necessity of the social state, a natural result of the course of civilization.

On the other hand, in the continental states, each system, each principle having had its turn, having predominated after a more complete and more exclusive manner, its development was wrought upon a larger scale, and with more grandeur and brilliancy. Royalty and feudal aristocracy, for instance, came upon the continental stage with far greater boldness, extension, and freedom. Our political experiments, so to speak, have been broader and more finished: the result of this has been that political ideas (I speak of general ideas, and not of good sense applied to the conduct of affairs) and political doctrines have risen higher, and displayed themselves with much more rational vigour. Each system having, in some measure, presented itself alone, and having remained a long time upon the stage, men have been enabled to consider it in its entirety, to mount up to its first principles, to follow it out into its last consequences, and fully to unfold its theory. Whoever attentively observes the English character, must be struck with a two-fold fact—on the one hand, with the soundness of its good sense and its practical ability; on the other, with its lack of general ideas, and its distrust of theoretical questions. Whether we open a work upon English history, upon jurisprudence, or any other subject, it is rarely that we find the grand reason of things, the fundamental reason. In all things, and especially in the political sciences, pure doctrine, philosophy, and science, properly so called, have prospered much better on the continent than in England; their flights have, at least, been far more powerful and bold; and we cannot doubt but that the different developments of civilization in the two countries have greatly contributed to this result.[1]

For the rest, whatever we may think of the advantages or disadvantages which this difference has entailed, it is a real and incontestable fact, the fact which most deeply distinguishes England from the continent. But it does not follow, because the different principles and social elements have been there developed more simultaneously, here more successively, that, at bottom, the path and the goal have not been one and the same. Considered in their entirety, the continent and England have traversed the same grand phases of civilization; events have, in either, followed the same course, and the same causes have led to the same effects. You have been enabled to convince yourselves of this fact from the picture which I have placed before you of civilization up to the sixteenth century, and you will

1. Guizot's sociological acumen emerges sharply here where he is able to show how the development of "English pluralism" shaped the development of the English mind, helping to give it a markedly practical character and a distrust for general or all-embracing ideas, for the abstractions beloved of the French.

equally recognize it in studying the seventeenth and eighteenth centuries. The development of free inquiry, and that of pure monarchy, almost simultaneous in England, accomplished themselves upon the continent at long intervals; but they did accomplish themselves, and the two powers, after having successively preponderated with splendour, came equally, at last, to blows. The general path of societies, considering all things, has thus been the same, and though the points of difference are real, those of resemblance are more deeply seated. A rapid sketch of modern times will leave you in no doubt upon this subject.

Glancing over the history of Europe in the seventeenth and eighteenth centuries, it is impossible not to perceive that France has advanced at the head of European civilization. At the beginning of this work I have already insisted upon this fact, and I have endeavoured to point out its cause. We shall now find it more striking than ever.

The principle of pure monarchy, of absolute royalty, predominated in Spain under Charles V and Philip II, before developing itself in France under Louis XIV. In the same manner the principle of free inquiry had reigned in England in the seventeenth century, before developing itself in France in the eighteenth. Nevertheless, pure monarchy and free inquiry came not from Spain and England to take possession of the world. The two principles, the two systems remained, in a manner, confined to the countries in which they had arisen. It was necessary that they should pass through France in order that they might extend their conquests; it was necessary that pure monarchy and free inquiry should become French in order to become European. This communicative character of French civilization, this social genius of France, which has displayed itself at all periods, was thus more than ever manifest at the period with which we now occupy ourselves. I will not further insist upon this fact; it has been developed to you with as much reason as brilliancy in other lectures wherein you have been called upon to observe the influence of French literature and philosophy in the eighteenth century.[2] You have seen that philosophic France possessed

2. Guizot refers here to the other celebrated lectures being given at the Old Sorbonne in that spring of 1828, after the fall of the ultra-royalist government. They were lectures on French literature by Villemain and on eighteenth-century philosophy by Victor Cousin.

more authority over Europe, in regard to liberty, than even free England. You have seen that French civilization showed itself far more active and contagious than that of any other country. I need not, therefore, pause upon the details of this fact, which I mention only in order to rest upon it my right to confine my picture of modern European civilization to France alone. Between the civilization of France and that of the other states of Europe at this period, there have, no doubt, been differences, which it would have been necessary to bear in mind, if my present purpose had been a full and faithful exposition of the history of those civilizations; but I must go on so rapidly that I am compelled to omit entire nations and ages, so to speak. I choose rather to concentrate your attention for a moment upon the course of French civilization, an image, though imperfect, of the general course of things in Europe.

The influence of France in Europe, during the seventeenth and eighteenth centuries, presents itself under very different aspects. In the former, it was French government that acted upon Europe, and advanced at the head of general civilization. In the latter it was no longer to the government, but France herself, that the preponderance belonged. In the first case, it was Louis XIV and his court, afterwards France and her opinion, that governed minds and attracted attention. In the seventeenth century there were peoples who, as peoples, appeared more prominently upon the scene, and took a greater part in events than the French people. Thus during the thirty years war, the German nation, in the English revolution, the English people, played, in their own destinies, a much greater part than was played, at this period, by the French in theirs. So, also, in the eighteenth century, there were governments stronger, of greater consideration, and more to be dreaded, than the French government. No doubt Frederick II, Catherine II, and Maria Theresa, had more influence and weight in Europe than Louis XV; nevertheless, at both periods, it was France that was at the head of European civilization, placed there, first, by its government, afterwards, by itself; now by the political action of its masters, now by its peculiar intellectual development.

In order to fully understand the predominant influence in the course of civilization in France, and therefore in Europe, we must study, in the seventeenth century, French government, in the eighteenth, French society.

We must change the plan and the drama according as time alters the stage and the actors.

When we occupy ourselves with the government of Louis XIV, when we endeavour to appreciate the causes of his power and influence in Europe, we scarcely think of anything but his renown, his conquests, his magnificence, and the literary glory of his time. It is to external causes that we apply ourselves, and attribute the European preponderance of the French government. But I conceive that this preponderance had deeper and more serious foundations. We must not believe that it was simply by means of victories, *fêtes,* or even master-works of genius, that Louis XIV and his government, at this epoch, played the part which it is impossible to deny them.

Many of you may remember, and all of you have heard speak of the effect which the consular government produced in France twenty-nine years ago, and of the condition in which it found our country. Without, was impending foreign invasion, and continual disasters were occurring in our armies; within, was an almost complete dissolution of power and of the people; there were no revenues, no public order; in a word, society was prostrate, humiliated, and disorganized: such was France on the advent of the consular government. Who does not recall the prodigious and felicitous activity of this government, that activity which, in a little time, secured the independence of the land, revived national honour, reorganized the administration, remodelled the legislation, and, after a manner, regenerated society under the hand of power?

Well, the government of Louis XIV, when it commenced, did something analogous to this for France; with great difference of times, proceedings, and forms, it pursued and attained nearly the same results.

Recall to your memory the state into which France was fallen after the government of Cardinal Richelieu, and during the minority of Louis XIV: the Spanish armies always on the frontiers, sometimes in the interior; continual danger of an invasion; internal dissensions urged to extremity, civil war, the government weak and discredited at home and abroad. Society was perhaps in a less violent, but still sufficiently analogous state to ours, prior to the eighteenth *Brumaire.* It was from this state that the government of Louis XIV extricated France. His first victories had the effect of the victory of Marengo: they secured the country, and retrieved the national honour. I am about to consider this government under its principal aspects—in its wars, in its external relations, in its administration, and in its legislation; and you will see, I imagine, that the comparison of which I speak, and to which I attach no puerile importance (for I think very little of the value of historical parallels), you will see, I say, that this comparison has a real foundation, and that I have a right to employ it.

First of all let us speak of the wars of Louis XIV. The wars of Europe have originated, as you know, and as I have often taken occasion to remind you, in great popular movements. Urged by necessity, caprice, or any other cause, entire populations, sometimes numerous, sometimes in simple bands, have transported themselves from one territory to another. This was the general character of European wars until after the crusades, at the end of the thirteenth century.

At that time began a species of wars scarcely less different from modern wars than the above. These were the distant wars, undertaken no longer by the people, but by governments, which went at the head of their armies to seek states and adventures afar off. They quitted their countries, abandoned their own territories, and plunged, some into Germany, others into Italy, and others into Africa, with no other motives than personal caprice. Almost all the wars of the fifteenth and even of a part of the sixteenth century were of this description. What interest—I speak not of a legitimate interest—but what possible motive had France that Charles VIII should possess the kingdom of Naples? This evidently was a war dictated by no political consideration: the king conceived that he had a personal right to the kingdom of Naples, and with a personal aim, and to satisfy his personal desire, he undertook the conquest of a distant country, which was in no way adapted for annexation to his kingdom; which, on the contrary, did nothing but compromise his power externally, and internally, his repose. It was the same with the expedition of Charles the Fifth to Africa. The latest war of this kind was the expedition of Charles XII against Russia. The wars of Louis XIV had no such character; they were the wars of a regular government, fixed in the centre of its states, and labouring to make conquests around it, to extend or consolidate its territory; in a word, they were political wars.

They may have been just or unjust; they may have cost France too dearly; there are a thousand reasons which might be adduced against their morality and their excess; but they bear a character incomparably more rational than the antecedent wars: they were no longer undertaken for whim or adventure; they were dictated by some serious motive; it was some natural limit that it seemed desirable to attain; some population speaking the same language that they aimed at annexing; some point of defence against a neighbouring power, which it was thought necessary to acquire. No doubt personal ambition had a share in these wars; but examine one after another of the wars of Louis XIV, particularly those of the first part of his reign, and you will find that they had truly political motives; and that they were conceived for the interest of France, for obtaining power, and for the country's safety.

The results are proofs of the fact. France of the present day is still, in many respects, what the wars of Louis XIV have made it. The provinces which he conquered, Franche-Comté, Flanders, and Alsace, remain yet incorporated with France. There are sensible as well as senseless conquests: those of Louis XIV were of the former species; his enterprises have not the unreasonable and capricious character which, up to his time, was so general; a skilful, if not always just and wise policy, presided over them.

Leaving the wars of Louis XIV, and passing to the consideration of his relations with foreign states, of his diplomacy, properly so called, I find an analogous result. I have insisted upon the occurrence of the birth of diplomacy in Europe at the end of the fifteenth century. I have endeavoured to show how the relations of governments and states between themselves up to that time accidental, rare, and transitory, became at this period more regular and enduring; how they took a character of great public interest; how, in a word, at the end of the fifteenth, and during the first half of the sixteenth century, diplomacy came to play an immense part in events. Nevertheless, up to the seventeenth century, it had not been, truly speaking, systematic; it had not led to long alliances, or to great, and above all, durable combinations, directed, according to fixed principles, towards a constant aim, with that spirit of continuity which is the true character of established governments. During the course of the religious revolution, the external relations of states were almost completely under the power of the religious interest; the Protestant and Catholic leagues divided Europe. It was in the seventeenth century, after the treaty of Westphalia, and under the influence of the government of Louis XIV, that diplomacy changed its character. It then escaped from the exclusive influences of the religious principle; alliances and political combinations were formed upon other considerations. At the same time it became much more systematic, regular, and constantly directed towards a certain aim, according to permanent principles. The regular origin of this system of balance in Europe belongs to this period. It was under the government of Louis XIV that the system, together with all the considerations attached to it, truly took possession of European policy. When we investigate what was the general idea in regard to this subject, what was the predominating principle of the policy of Louis XIV, I believe that the following is what we discover:

I have spoken of the great struggle between the pure monarchy of Louis XIV, aspiring to become universal monarchy, and civil and religious liberty, and the independence of states, under the direction of the prince of Orange, William III. You have seen that the great fact of this period was the division of the powers under these two banners. But this fact was not then estimated as we estimate it now; it was hidden and unknown even to those who accomplished it; the suppression of the system of pure monarchy and the consecration of civil and religious liberty was, at bottom, the necessary result of the resistance of Holland and its allies to Louis XIV; but the question was not thus openly enunciated between absolute power and liberty. It has been often said that the propagation of absolute power was the predominant principle of the diplomacy of Louis XIV; but I do not believe it. This consideration played no very great part in his policy, until latterly, in his old age. The power of France, its preponderance in Europe, the humbling of rival powers, in a word, the political interest and strength of the state, was the aim which Louis XIV constantly pursued, whether in fighting against Spain, the emperor of Germany, or England; he acted far less with a view to the propagation of absolute power than from a desire for the power and aggrandizement of France and of its government. Among many proofs, I will adduce one which emanates from Louis XIV himself. In his Memoirs, under the year *1666*, if I remember right, we find a note nearly in these words:

"I have had, this morning, a conversation with Mr. Sidney, an English gentleman, who maintained to me the possibility of reanimating the republican party in England. Mr. Sidney demanded from me, for that purpose, 400,000 livres. I told him that I could give no more than 200,000. He induced me to summon from Switzerland another English gentleman, named Ludlow, and to converse with him of the same design."

And, accordingly, we find among the Memoirs of Ludlow, about the same date, a paragraph to this effect:

"I have received from the French government an invitation to go to Paris, in order to speak of the affairs of my country; but I am distrustful of that government."

And Ludlow remained in Switzerland.

You see that the diminution of the royal power in England was, at this time, the aim of Louis XIV. He fomented internal dissensions, and laboured to resuscitate the republican party, to prevent Charles II from becoming too powerful in his country. During the embassy of Barillon in England, the same fact constantly reappears. Whenever the authority of Charles seemed to obtain the advantage, and the national party seemed on the point of being crushed, the French ambassador directed his influence to this side, gave money to the chiefs of the opposition, and fought, in a word, against absolute power, when that became a means of weakening a rival power to France. Whenever you attentively consider the conduct of external relations under Louis XIV, it is with this fact that you will be the most struck.

You will also be struck with the capacity and skill of French diplomacy at this period. The names of M.M. de Torcy, d'Avaux, de Bonrepos, are known to all well-informed persons. When we compare the dispatches, the memoirs, the skill and conduct of these counsellors of Louis XIV with those of Spanish, Portuguese, and German negotiators, we must be struck with the superiority of the French ministers; not only as regards their earnest activity and their application to affairs, but also as regards their liberty of spirit. These courtiers of an absolute king judged of external events, of parties, of the requirements of liberty, and of popular revolutions, much better even than the majority of the English ministers themselves at this period. There was no diplomacy in Europe, in the seventeenth century, which appears equal to the French, except the Dutch. The ministers of

John de Witt and of William of Orange, those illustrious chiefs of the party of civil and religious liberty, were the only ministers who seemed in condition to wrestle with the servants of the great and absolute king.

You see, then, that whether we consider the wars of Louis XIV, or his diplomatical relations, we arrive at the same results. We can easily conceive that a government which conducted its wars and negotiations in this manner, should have assumed a high standing in Europe, and presented itself therein, not only as formidable, but as skilful and imposing.

Let us now consider the interior of France, the administration and legislation of Louis XIV; we shall there discern new explanations of the power and splendour of his government.

It is difficult to determine with any degree of precision, what we ought to understand by *administration* in the government of a state. Nevertheless, when we endeavour to investigate this fact, we discover, I believe, that, under the most general point of view, administration consists in an aggregate of means destined to propel, as promptly and certainly as possible, the will of the central power through all parts of society, and to make the force of society, whether consisting of men or money, return again, under the same conditions, to the central power. This, if I mistake not, is the true aim, the predominant characteristic of administration. Accordingly we find that in times when it is above all things needful to establish unity and order in society, administration is the chief means of attaining this end, of bringing together, of cementing, and of uniting incoherent and scattered elements. Such, in fact, was the work of the administration of Louis XIV. Up to this time, there had been nothing so difficult, in France as in the rest of Europe, as to effect the penetration of the action of the central power into all parts of society, and to gather into the bosom of the central power the means of force existing in society. To this end Louis XIV laboured, and succeeded, up to a certain point; incomparably better, at least, than preceding governments had done. I cannot enter into details: just run over, in thought, all kinds of public services, taxes, roads, industry, military administration, all the establishments which belong to whatsoever branch of administration; there is scarcely one of which you do not find either the origin, development, or great amelioration under Louis XIV. It was as administrators that the greatest men of his time, Colbert and Louvois, displayed their genius and exercised their ministry. It was by the excellence of its administration that his government acquired a generality, decision, and consistency which were wanting to all the European governments around him.

Under the legislative point of view, this reign presents to you the same fact. I return to the comparison which I have already made use of, to the legislative activity of the consular government, to its prodigious work of revising and generally recasting the laws. A work of the same nature took place under Louis XIV. The great ordinances which he promulgated, the criminal ordinance, the ordinances of procedure, commerce, the marine, waters, and woods, are true codes, which were constructed in the same manner as our codes, discussed in the council of state, some of them under the presidency of Lamoignon. There are men whose glory consists in having taken part in this labour and this discussion, M. Pussort, for instance. If we were to consider it in itself, we should have much to say against the legislation of Louis XIV; it was full of vices, which now fully declare themselves, and which no one can deny; it was not conceived in the interest of true justice and of liberty, but in the interest of public order, and for giving more regularity and firmness to the laws. But even that was a great progress; and we cannot doubt but that the ordinances of Louis XIV, so very superior to anything preceding them, powerfully contributed to advance French society in the career of civilization.

You see that under whatever point of view we regard this government, we very soon discover the source of its power and influence. It was the first government that presented itself to the eyes of Europe as a power sure of its position, which had not to dispute its existence with internal enemies— tranquil as to its dominions and the people, and intent only on governing. Up to that time, all European governments had been unceasingly thrown into wars, which deprived them of security as well as leisure, or had been so beset with parties and internal enemies, that they were compelled to spend their time in fighting for their lives. The government of Louis XIV appeared as the first which applied itself solely to the conduct of affairs, as a power at once definitive and progressive; which was not afraid of innovating, because it could count upon the future. There have, in fact, existed very few governments of such an innovating spirit. Compare it with a government of the same nature, with the pure monarchy of Philip II in Spain;

it was more absolute than that of Louis XIV, and yet far less regular and less tranquil. But how did Philip II succeed in establishing absolute power in Spain? By stifling the activity of the country, by refusing to it every species of amelioration, by rendering the condition of Spain completely stationary. The government of Louis XIV, on the contrary, showed itself active in all kinds of innovations, favourable to the progress of letters, of arts, of riches, and, in a word, of civilization. These are the true causes of its preponderance in Europe; a preponderance such that it became upon the continent, during the whole of the seventeenth century, the type of government, not only for sovereigns, but even for nations.

And now we inquire—and it is impossible to help doing so—how it happened that a power, thus brilliant, and, judging from the facts which I have placed before you, thus well established, so rapidly fell into decline? how, after having played such a part in Europe, it became, in the next century, so inconsistent, weak, and inconsiderable? The fact is incontestable. In the seventeenth century the French government was at the head of European civilization; in the eighteenth century it disappeared; and it was French society, separated from its government, often even opposed to it, that now preceded and guided the European world in its progress.

It is here that we discover the incorrigible evil and the infallible effect of absolute power. I will not go into any detail concerning the faults of the government of Louis XIV; he committed many: I will speak neither of the war of the Spanish succession, nor of the revocation of the edict of Nantes, nor of excessive expenses, nor of many other of the fatal measures that compromised his fortunes. I will take the merits of the government as I have described them. I will agree that perhaps there has never existed an absolute power more fully recognized by its age and nation, nor one which has rendered more real services to the civilization of its country and of Europe in general. But, by the very fact that this government had no other principle than absolute power, and reposed upon no other base than this, its decline became sudden and well merited. What France, under Louis XIV, essentially wanted, was political institutions and forces, independent, subsisting of themselves, and, in a word, capable of spontaneous action and resistance. The ancient French institutions, if they merited that name, no longer existed: Louis XIV completed their ruin. He took no care to endeavour to replace them by new institutions; they would have cramped him, and he did not choose to be cramped. All that appeared conspicuous at that period was will, and the action of central power. The government of Louis XIV was a great fact, a fact powerful and splendid, but without roots. Free institutions are a guarantee, not only of the wisdom of governments, but also of their duration. No system can endure except by means of institutions. When absolute power has endured, it has been supported by true institutions, sometimes by the division of society into strongly distinct castes, sometimes by a system of religious institutions. Under the reign of Louis XIV institutions were wanting to power as well as to liberty.[3] In France, at this period, nothing guaranteed either the country against the illegitimate actions of the government, or the government itself against the inevitable action of time. Thus we see the government helping on its own decay. It was not Louis XIV alone who was becoming aged and weak at the end of his reign: it was the whole absolute power. Pure monarchy was as much worn out in 1712 as was the monarch himself: and the evil was so much the more grave, as Louis XIV had abolished political morals as well as political institutions. There are no political morals without independence. He alone who feels that he has a strength of his own is always capable either of serving or opposing power. Energetic characters disappear with independent situations, and dignity of soul alone gives birth to security of rights.

This, then, is the state in which Louis XIV left France and power: a society in full development of riches, power, and all kinds of intellectual activity; and, side by side with this progressive society, a government essentially stationary, having no means of renewing itself, of adapting itself to the movement of its people; devoted, after half a century of the greatest splendour, to immobility and weakness, and already, during the life of its founder, fallen into a decline which seemed like dissolution. Such was the condition of France at the conclusion of the seventeenth century, a condition which impressed the epoch that followed with a direction and a character so different.

3. In exploring the consequences of the growth of absolute power under Louis XIV, Guizot's argument that France, in effect, lacked any political constitution or guarantees built on a similar argument made by Madame de Staël in her book on the French Revolution.

I need hardly say that the onward impulse of the human mind, that free inquiry was the predominating feature, the essential fact of the eighteenth century. You have already heard much concerning this fact from this chair; already you have heard that powerful epoch characterized by a philosophical orator, and by that of an eloquent philosopher. I cannot pretend, in the short space of time which remains to me, to trace all the phases of the great moral revolution which then accomplished itself. I would, nevertheless, fain not leave you without calling your attention to some characteristics which have been too little remarked upon.

The first—one which strikes me most, and which I have already mentioned—is the, so to speak, almost complete disappearance of the government in the course of the eighteenth century, and the appearance of the human mind as the principal and almost the only actor.

Except in that which is connected with external relations under the ministry of the duc de Choiseul, and in certain great concessions made to the general tendency of opinion, for instance, in the American war; except, I say, in some events of this nature, perhaps there has scarcely ever been so inactive, apathetic, and inert a government as was the French government of this period. Instead of the energetic, ambitious government of Louis XIV, which appeared everywhere, and put itself at the head of everything, you have a government which laboured only to hide itself, to keep itself in the background, so weak and compromised did it feel itself to be. Activity and ambition had passed over wholly to the people. It was the nation, which, by its opinion and its intellectual movement, mingled itself with all things, interfered in all, and, in short, alone possessed moral authority, which is the only true authority.

A second characteristic which strikes me, in the condition of the human mind in the eighteenth century, is the universality of free inquiry. Up to that time, and particularly in the seventeenth century, free inquiry had been exercised within a limited and partial field; it had had for its object sometimes religious questions, sometimes religious and political questions together, but it did not extend its pretensions to all subjects. In the eighteenth century, on the contrary, the character of free inquiry is universality; religion, politics, pure philosophy, man and society, moral and material nature, all at the same time became the object of study, doubt, and system; ancient sciences were overturned, new sciences were called into existence. The movement extended itself in all directions, although it had emanated from one and the same impulse.

This movement, moreover, had a peculiar character; one which, perhaps, is not to be met elsewhere in the history of the world: it was purely speculative. Up to that time, in all great human revolutions, action had commingled itself with speculation. Thus, in the sixteenth century, the religious revolution began with ideas, with purely intellectual discussions, but it very soon terminated in events. The heads of intellectual parties soon became the heads of political parties; the realities of life were mixed with the labour of the understanding. Thus, too, it happened in the seventeenth century, in the English revolution. But in France, in the eighteenth century, you find the human spirit exercising itself upon all things, upon ideas which, connecting themselves with the real interests of life, seemed calculated to have the most prompt and powerful influence upon facts. Nevertheless, the leaders and actors of these great discussions remained strangers to all species of practical activity—mere spectators, who observed, judged, and spoke, without ever interfering in events. At no other time has the government of facts, of external realities, been so completely distinct from the government of minds. The separation of the spiritual and temporal orders was never completely real in Europe until the eighteenth century. For the first time, perhaps, the spiritual order developed itself wholly apart from the temporal order: an important fact, and one which exercised a prodigious influence upon the course of events. It gave to the ideas of the time a singular character of ambition and inexperience; never before had philosophy aspired so strongly to rule the world, never had philosophy been so little acquainted with the world. It became obvious that a day must arrive for coming to facts; for the intellectual movement to pass into external events; and as they had been totally separated, their meeting was the more difficult, the shock far more violent.[4]

---

4. Here Guizot shows how the lack of political liberty, and especially the destruction of local self-government, resulted in a kind of political idiocy in France—the reign of general ideas unconstrained by social facts, projects whose ambitions were so wide that they carried intimations of Revolutionary excesses to come.

How can we now be surprised with another character of the condition of the human mind at this epoch, I mean its prodigious boldness? Up to that time its greatest activity had always been confined by certain barriers; the mind of man had always existed amidst facts, whereof some inspired it with caution, and, to a certain extent, checked its movements. In the eighteenth century, I should be at a loss to say what external facts the human mind respected, or what external facts exercised any empire over it: it hated or despised the entire social state. It concluded, therefore, that it was called upon to reform all things; it came to consider itself a sort of creator; institutions, opinions, manners, society, and man himself, all seemed to require reform, and human reason charged itself with the enterprise. What audacity equal to this had ever before been imagined by it!

Such was the power which, in the course of the eighteenth century, confronted what still remained of the government of Louis XIV. You perceive that it was impossible to avoid the occurrence of a shock between two such unequal forces. The predominant fact of the English revolution, the struggle between free inquiry and pure monarchy, was now also to burst forth in France. No doubt the differences were great, and these necessarily perpetuated themselves in the results; but, at bottom, the general conditions were similar, and the definitive event had the same meaning.

I do not pretend to exhibit the infinite consequences of this struggle. The time for concluding this course of lectures has arrived; I must check myself. I merely desire, before leaving you, to call your attention to the most grave, and, in my opinion, the most instructive fact which was revealed to us by this great struggle. This is the danger, the evil, and the insurmountable vice of absolute power, whatever form, whatever name it may bear, and towards whatever aim it may direct itself. You have seen that the government of Louis XIV perished by almost this cause only. Well, the power which succeeded it, the human mind, the true sovereign of the eighteenth century, suffered the same fate; in its turn, it possessed an almost absolute power; it, in its turn, placed an excessive confidence in itself. Its onward impulse was beautiful, good, most useful; and were it necessary that I should express a definitive opinion, I should say that the eighteenth century appears to me to have been one of the greatest ages of history, that which, perhaps, has done the greatest services for humanity, that which has in the greatest degree aided its progress, and rendered that progress of the most general character: were I asked to pronounce upon it as a public administration, I should pronounce in its favour. But it is not the less true that, at this epoch, the human mind, possessed of absolute power, became corrupted and misled by it; holding established facts and former ideas in an illegitimate disdain and aversion; an aversion which carried it into error and tyranny. The share of error and tyranny, indeed, which mingled itself with the triumph of human reason, at the end of this century, a portion which we cannot conceal from ourselves, was very great, and which we must proclaim and not deny; this portion of error and tyranny was chiefly the result of the extravagance into which the mind of man had been thrown, at this period, by the extension of his power.

It is the duty, and, I believe, it will be the peculiar merit of our times, to know that all power, whether intellectual or temporal, whether belonging to governments or peoples, to philosophers or ministers, whether exercising itself in one cause or in another, bears within itself a natural vice, a principle of weakness and of abuse which ought to render it limited.[5] Now nothing but the general freedom of all rights, all interests, and all opinions, the free manifestation and legal co-existence of all these forces, can ever restrain each force and each power within its legitimate limits, prevent it from encroaching on the rest, and, in a word, cause the real and generally profitable existence of free inquiry. Herein consists for us the grand lesson of the struggle which occurred at the end of the eighteenth century, between absolute temporal power and absolute spiritual power.

I have now arrived at the term which I proposed to myself. You remember that my object, in commencing this course, was to present you with a general picture of the development of European civilization, from the fall of the Roman empire to our own days. I have traversed this career very rapidly, and without being able to inform you, far from it, of all that was important, or to bring proofs of all that I have said. I have been compelled to

5. Guizot returns at the end of the 1828 lectures to his dominant theme—the necessity for dispersing power, not only through the separation of powers in central government, but also by finding a balance between central power and local autonomy. It was to be the Doctrinaires' central political project, taken up and immortalized by Tocqueville in *Democracy in America*.

omit much, and often to request you to believe me upon my word. I hope, nevertheless, that I have attained my aim, which was to mark the grand crises in the development of modern society. Allow me yet one word more.

I endeavoured, in the beginning, to define civilization, and to describe the fact which bears this name. Civilization seemed to me to consist of two principal facts: the development of human society, and that of man himself; on the one hand, political and social development; on the other, internal and moral development. I have confined myself so far to the history of society. I have presented civilization only under the social point of view; and have said nothing of the development of man himself. I have not endeavoured to unfold to you the history of opinions, of the moral progress of humanity. I propose, when we meet again, to confine myself especially to France, to study with you the history of French civilization, to study it in detail, and under its various aspects. I shall endeavour to make you acquainted, not only with the history of society in France, but also with that of man; to be present with you at the progress of institutions, of opinions, and of intellectual works of all kinds; and to arrive thus at a complete understanding of the development of our glorious country, in its entirety. In the past as well as in the future, our country may well lay claim to our tenderest affections.

END OF THE HISTORY OF CIVILIZATION IN EUROPE

Index

Abailard, 129–30
administration, xxx, 263–64. *See also* centralized government
administrative despotism, xviii–xix, xxxviii, 37, 148n5
Agobard, archbishop of Lyons, 128
Albigenses, 191, 195–96, 212
ancient civilizations: contrast to European civilization, 32–34; Egyptian, 30, 31, 100; internal struggles of, 30–31; liberty in, 49; literature of, 31, 216; tyranny in, 31; unity and simplicity of, 30, 31–32; urban centers in, xxv, 35–37. *See also* Greek civilization; Roman Empire
anti-clericalism, xv, xix, 20n3, 64n3
Arabs: invasions of Europe, 61, 67, 68–69; in Spain, 68–69, 158, 159, 207. *See also* Islam
aristocracy: in antiquity, xxv, 76–77; destruction of, xvi, xvii; English, xvii, xxxiii, 100n3, 199, 208–9, 238, 253; feudal, xxx, 53, 157; in fifth century, 59; French, xi, xiv, xvi, xvii; in states-general, 198. *See also* feudal lords
Aristocracy and the Communes (Barante), xvii, xxxi–xxxii
Arles, 38–40
arts and literature, 31, 33, 88, 89, 216, 223, 237–38

assemblies: of Charlemagne, 67; French, 197–99, 206; members of, 197, 198, 200; moral effects of, 198; political activity of, 198, 199–200; religious, 242; states-general, xxix, 197–99. *See also* Parliament, English
atomization, xvii, xviii, xx, xxi, xxix, xxxii, 133n1, 154n1
Austria, 208, 221

Bacon, Francis, 121, 223
Barante, Prosper de, xiii, xv, xvii, xxxii, 155
barbarian monarchies, 176, 178–79
barbarians. *See* Germanic tribes
Basle, council of, 213–14
Beaumont, Gustave de, xxxii
Bembo, Pietro, 217
Benedict, St., 126
Bentham, Jeremy, xxxix, 120
Bernard, St., 129, 130
Bible, 77
Biran, Maine de, xi, xxiii, 19n2, 56n1, 59n2
bishops: barbarian groups and, 126; council of Toledo, 65–66; elections of, 112, 214; English, 237, 240, 241–43; in feudal societies, 109, 116, 128; French, 128; history of, 43; relations with Rome, 164; in towns, 44–45, 137, 138

273

This book is set in Adobe Arno Pro, designed by
Robert Slimbach and inspired by early humanist typefaces of the
15th and 16th centuries. Arno is a meticulously-crafted face in the
tradition of early Venetian and Aldine book typefaces.

This book is printed on paper that is acid-free and meets the requirements
of the American National Standard for Permanence of Paper for
Printed Library Materials, z39.48–1992. ♾

Book design by Louise OFarrell
Gainesville, Florida
Typography by Apex CoVantage
Madison, Wisconsin
Printed and bound by Edwards Brothers Malloy
Ann Arbor, Michigan